Chasing The Horizon

One Man's Account Of The 2008 Round Britain Powerboat Race

Derek Wynans

ISBN 978-0-9563938-0-7

Cover image Copyright Chris Davies

Printed by Lightning Source Ltd.

www.chasingthehorizon.co.uk

Derek Wynans was born in Holland, raised in Scotland, and at 37 he still says things like: "*When I grow up I want to be...*" He shares his isolated croft in Argyll, Scotland with his beloved wife, two cats, and an assortment of curious wildlife. He has held a bewildering number of jobs, including mechanic, barman, shark fisherman and gravel crusher. This is his first book.

Praise for *Chasing The Horizon*:

Acknowledgements.

Buy the Ticket, Take the Ride.
(Hunter S Thompson.)

This is all Hugo Andreae's fault. As Editor of *MotorBoat & Yachting* magazine I hold him entirely responsible for every bruise, sprain and blister I sustained during the ten days of the Round Britain Power-boat Race. Every missed meal, sleepless night and anxious moment are as a direct result of his evil and sadistic suggestion that I cover the race on the magazine's behalf, and there's only one thing I can say to that: Thanks Hugo.

Rob Peake, Hugo's right hand man, deserves a mention too— hell, he deserves some sort of literary award for taking my gibbered phone calls and turning them into coherent daily reports.

Of course I owe a huge debt of gratitude to the people who let me race with them: *Silverline, Ocean Pirate, 747, Lionhead* and *Buro.* Special thanks to Drew and Jan for their incredible generosity and patience, and Jonathan Napier for his continuing support (and for making me an honourable member of *Team 747*).

Annie, Gill and Mary at Race Control put up with my constant boat-swapping, and Guy, Gary and Rob were ridiculously patient with me at every Scrutineering session. Thank you.

I'd also like to thank the hugely talented Chris Davies for agreeing to contribute some of his stunning pictures. This book really doesn't do him any justice at all; I strongly recommend that you go to his website to get a true sense of just how good he is: www.powerboatpix.co.uk.

Yoks, old buddy old pal, the cheque's in the post. Cheers Bubba.

And finally my Beloved. Thank you for everything.

D

Contents.

Prologue.

There comes a point in every man's life when he is forced to realise that his assumptions on certain matters are perhaps, well, a little skewed. At around 2 am on the morning of June 22nd, 2008, I was slowly coming to the realisation that offshore powerboat racing wasn't all about scantily-clad models and handsome, square-jawed men of great daring. In fact I was strongly starting to believe that, far from exciting life-or-death duels on the high seas, the 2008 Round Britain Powerboat Race was destined to feature the most miserable, monotonous and soul-destroying 10 days of my life.

At two o'clock that morning I was on board an aging 40 foot motorboat that was slowly starting to disintegrate under the onslaught of a Force 6 storm in Lyme Bay, on the English south coast. Every time the bow slammed down with an exceptionally hard crash the ship's bell, mounted behind the wheelhouse at the open helm, would give off a muted *clang*! We had all cheered the first couple of times it happened, but after four hours of increasingly frequent *clangs*!, the novelty had worn off, and the noise no longer registered on our exhausted minds.

The wheelhouse was equipped with two skylights, both of which leaked a constant dribble of icy water onto us poor bastards beneath, the dribble occasionally becoming a torrent whenever we smashed into a particularly large wave. It was of course impossible to predict when such a wave would slam into the boat's bows, because beyond the ineffectual windscreen wipers we could make out nothing at all in the impenetrable black night. The carpet in the aft cabin was becoming sodden with sea water that was finding its way up past the rudder stocks, and in the forward cabin a jumble of bags, coats and other personal belongings lay scattered over the wildly-lurching floor.

Directly beneath our feet were two mighty Cummins 380 engines, which were our only source of warmth. This eased my suffering somewhat, with the heat soaking into the soles of my feet through the floor, but sadly it wasn't enough to keep the chill off the rest of my battered body. Their incessant roar made conversation impossible, but that was probably a good thing: after five god-awful hours of this misery I was in no mood for diplomatic chit-chat or any false bonhomie.

As the conditions worsened that night we dropped our speed from 28 knots to 25, then 22, before finally crawling our way through the darkness at a lowly 12 knots— hardly an awe-inspiring speed for a powerboat race, I sneered to myself. But I thought it prudent to say nothing since I was merely a guest on board *Ocean Pirate*, and considering we were still 40-odd miles from our destination it looked like

I would be spending what was left of the night sleeping on board, as opposed to the warm, welcoming guesthouse bed that I had booked many weeks earlier.

Finally the aging crew of *Ocean Pirate* decided that the going was getting too tough for them, and so instead of rounding Start Point and following the coast westwards towards Plymouth, our intended destination and the first of eight finishing lines, we tucked our tired, waterlogged tails between our legs and slinked into a cold and uninviting Brixham marina to wait out the weather. Since the start flag had gone up in Portsmouth seventeen hours earlier, we had damaged one propeller, been hoisted out and then back into the water, and had covered a miserable 90 nautical miles. We were already 40 miles behind the rest of the fleet, with another 1,250 miles to go. Things, to put it mildly, were not going at all well.

1.
Driver's Briefing.

At 90 miles per hour the Italian countryside was a picturesque blur of red tiles, faded yellow farm buildings and rolling green fields. Between gaps in the trees I could just make out the Adriatic, glinting green-blue in the warm spring sunshine. But I had no time to enjoy the picture-postcard scenery; Drew's Fiat Punto was fast becoming a distant dot further up the motorway, merging with a handful of similar cars as he blasted southwards down the Autostrada.

My rented Panda was struggling to keep up, despite frantic lane-switching and liberal use of high beams and horn. My right foot was starting to cramp from the effort of keeping the throttle mashed into the carpet, and I was getting seriously concerned about losing Drew and the two mechanics as they weaved in and out of the unperturbed traffic. My own two passengers, however, showed no such concerns. Either they had an instinctive faith in my ability to keep up, or they were under the mistaken impression that I actually knew where I was going.

Nothing could have been further from the truth. This was only my second ever experience of driving on European motorways, and up until two weeks ago I had never even heard of San Benedetto Del Tronto, our intended destination. If I lost sight of the anonymous blue Punto I would be completely screwed. What's more, the crack navigator for the Team *Silverline* Powerboat P1 team would be lost with me, jeopardizing the team's chances of competing the next morning.

When Drew Langdon, *Silverline* team owner and throttle man, had screeched out of the Avis carpark an hour earlier, I had still been messing about with adjusting mirrors and twiddling with the car's radio in search of some decent music, lulled into a false sense of security. After all, Drew's passengers consisted of Rob Jenkins and Steve Causley, the mechanics responsible for looking after the boat that Drew would be racing the next day. I, on the other hand, would be chauffeuring Jan Falkowski, Drew's navigator. I felt that there was no need to rush; after all, who better to guide me to our destination?

"Sorry Derek, I haven't got a clue." Jan's grin was mischievous. "Never been here before in my life. Probably best if you just follow Drew." Oh fuck...

It was Bethan Ancell, Jan's fiancé, who spotted the Punto's brake lights flashing on before it swerved off the road at a sickening speed. I followed suit, silently praying that I wasn't following Drew into a horrific accident, but when we slid to a halt and I finally opened my eyes I realised that it was just a pit stop— we'd pulled up outside a motorway café, and as we clambered out of the two cars we were all rolling our shoulders and working the kinks out of our legs.

Over freshly-made rolls and perfect cappuccinos the others gossiped idly about other teams competing in the season's first P1 powerboat race. I, on the other hand, was still trying to come to terms with the fact that I was taking a short break from chasing one of Britain's top powerboat racers down Italy's east coast.

My reasons for being here were dubious, to say the least. In a nut-shell, I had just travelled 1200 miles so that Drew and Jan could see if I was going to squeal like a little girl or throw up my salami and sun-dried tomato ciabatta when riding in the back of their 85 mph powerboat. No wonder my editor wasn't prepared to stump up for my expenses. Of course there was a fundamental reason for this sun-filled excursion— if I passed the test and kept my breakfast down, I would be permitted to join the *Silverline* team on their quest for glory as they attempted to win the most demanding, gruelling endurance event ever staged: the 2008 Round Britain Powerboat Race. But only if I promised not to cry...

I spent much of 2007 trying to supplement my income from my job with the NHS by writing short articles for *MotorBoat & Yachting*, one of the UK's top boat magazines. I wasn't particularly knowledgeable about these things, but the editor seemed to like my style, and it suited him to have someone who was willing to tackle some of the more unusual aspects of boating life. Whilst this was a pleasant hobby that brought me some extra cash in my spare time, I never considered it as a "proper" job, and as a result my dealings with Hugo Andreae were often laced with my own particular brand of dark and weird humour.

Which is why, when he emailed me to ask if I'd like to join one of the top teams taking part in the much-hyped Round Britain Power-boat Race scheduled for the following year, my reply was unprofessional to say the least:

Where do I sign?! This sounds like just the kind of masochistic, potentially lethal occasion I love so much! And besides, my fillings were due for replacement anyway...Who's it with? I'm hoping it's one of the larger boats, you know, nicely-kitted out with galley, mini-bar and a Laser sailing dinghy strapped to the foredeck...

It was blatantly apparent to Hugo that I had absolutely no idea what a powerboat race entailed, so with his sensible head tightly strapped on he advised me to do some internet research. And that was when I discovered the perils of YouTube.

My god! I thought. *What kind of living hell is this?* Hidden amongst innocuous clips of speedboats messing about on mirror-smooth Caribbean waters were graphic videos showing catastrophic accidents; crew members being thrown clear and smashing into the concrete-like surface of the sea at over eighty miles per hour; boats flipping and disintegrating as they lost control in monstrous seas... and this carnage was to be repeated, day in and day out, for 1400 miles?

My own experience with boats was based more in the commercial end of the spectrum— fishing boats and tugs mostly, with the occasional blast in a RIB for relatively short distances. Still, it promised to be an adventure, not to mention a nice paycheque, so I decided to concentrate on my "Ignorance is Bliss" mantra and resolutely stuck to my guns.

The next step was to meet up with Drew Langdon, owner and throttle man of *Buzzi Bullet II*, which he raced in the Powerboat P1 championship. Together with his navigator Jan Falkowski they made up Team *Silverline*, a combination highly regarded by people who know about these things. Clearly I was not one of those people, so I hit Google with a vengeance to find out a little more about these two obviously deranged nutcases.

Drew and Jan make a formidable double-act when it comes to powerboat racing; in spite of my almost total ignorance of the various Classes even I could see that *Silverline* was going to be one of the leading contenders for a podium finish in the Round Britain. Drew had started racing speedboats while he was still in short trousers, working his way up to ever-quicker boats. His father had been a driver with the Johnson factory team back in the seventies, and this had fired Drew's own ambitions. During the week Drew is a shrewd and successful property developer, but on the weekends he swaps his suit for fireproof overalls and a Grabner lifejacket to take to the water in a variety of race-prepared boats, as well as competing regularly in the SuperSport Class of the Powerboat P1 world championship.

Along the way he has befriended Jan Falkowski, another man who knows a thing or two about blatting about in boats, and who's Monday-to-Friday is just as much at odds with his racing career as Drew's. He's a highly respected London-based psychiatrist, but he's also broken world records for his exploits in RIBs, setting new times for prestigious events like London to Monte Carlo and, usefully, circumnavigating the British isles— something that would come in handy during the race, as it turned out...

Over the next couple of months Drew and I struggled to find a mutually acceptable date to meet up, so when the Race Organisers announced a Driver's Briefing for March it seemed to be the perfect time to finally chat face to face. The briefing, to be held at Driver's Wharf, Southampton, would officially confirm the race route and elaborate on the myriad of details that go into holding such an epic event.

It stands to reason that the briefing would take place in Southampton; this part of the south coast is arguably the UK's spiritual home of powerboat racing and the city has a nautical background reaching back many hundreds of years. As well as its deepwater estuary where two major rivers converge— the Itchen and the Test— it's also sheltered from the south by the Isle of Wight which protects the natural harbour's entrance. The Isle of Wight's presence also has an unusual benefit— its mass produces a double high tide, which ensures its higher reaches are navigable for longer which makes it ideal for marine trade.

This natural port has been the starting point for many of history's most important and famous ship journeys— in 1912 for example the *Titanic* set off from Southampton on a collision course with infamy. Three hundred years earlier the *Mayflower* had undertaken a similar voyage, no doubt carrying 102 loud, ignorant overweight bullies with poor dress sense— just think how different the world would be today if she had met the *Titanic's* fate. The Cunard line that operated that infamous liner also made Southampton the homeport for its other great ships— the *Queen Mary*, *Queen Elizabeth* and the *Queen Elizabeth II* all called Southampton home— a decision that still rankles today with some of the neighbours just a few miles down the coast in Portsmouth.

Southampton's link with powerboat racing in the 21st century can be traced back to the early 1920's, when a Southampton entrepreneur by the name of Hubert Scott-Paine decided to take on the Yanks at powerboat racing at a time when they were winning every important race in the world.

Having previously won the Schneider Trophy with his Supermarine seaplane in 1922 he set his heart on the most prestigious award in powerboating circles, the Harmsworth Trophy. He was so determined to win it that he bought the Hythe shipyard on the western shore of Southampton estuary, renamed it the British Powerboat Company and invested a fortune to place it at the cutting edge of modern boat design and building methods. Soon it was one of the most advanced boat-building yards in the world, churning out hulls that won him countless awards across Europe and, in 1928, finally secured the elusive Harmsworth Trophy with *Miss England*. To say that this was a bit of a big deal would be an understatement— so important was this victory that *Miss England's* owner and driver, Henry Seagrave, was actually knighted for thrashing his opponent, the legendary American racer Gar Wood.

Scott-Paine's gift for building outrageously quick boats saw Southampton establish itself as the epicentre of powerboating, and to this day there is a wealth of experts whose skill, knowledge and experience make it such a Mecca for serious powerboat racers and builders. Driver's Wharf was reputed to be the epicentre for this technical expertise, and I was looking forward to immersing myself in the world of ultimate marine performance..

So when my taxi pulled up outside a grim-looking boatyard on a wet Saturday morning, I was slightly confused. Surely, I asked the driver, this wasn't the Driver's Wharf, where the top British teams come to prepare their craft for combat on the open seas? But he just shrugged and told me he'd dropped off some boat-racer guy from Jersey here earlier, so I discarded my preconceptions and stepped out into the drizzle.

From the gate I could see the usual boatyard inhabitants— anonymous cabin cruisers and sailing yachts propped up with lengths of wood or sitting in bespoke cradles, each showing various degrees of their owners' dedication. Some had been freshly polished and anti-fouled, whilst others bore sagging tarpaulins and the scars of countless poorly-timed encounters with piers and pontoons. But it wasn't all run-of-the-mill stuff; secreted in amongst the day boats and dinghies were glimpses of razor-sharp prows and flashes of garish paint-jobs. It was like finding tiny slivers of emeralds and sapphires in amongst the drab gravel chips of a concrete pavement.

As I walked deeper into the deserted yard I came across my first actual powerboat— a stunning-looking Hustler 388 in red and silver livery. Sitting on a stainless steel 4-wheeled trailer, the boat was a fluid mass of sharp, aggressive angles and edges. As I made my way around it to take it in from every angle I took care not to brush against the hull, subconsciously worried that I'd cut open an arm on the knife-like chines. The hull had several "steps"; inverted ridges that ran transversely across the keel. The first started just past half-way down the length of the boat, and there was a foot or so between it and the next one.

I had read about this design feature: the stepped-hull design was as revolutionary to powerboats as spoilers were to Formula 1 cars— they dramatically improved performance by creating a thin cushion of air between the hull and the water, but whilst this gave a higher top speed and faster acceleration, it also came with a downside: the boat's grip in the water was compromised, making it harder to control in tight turns.

As it turned out, a powerboat was pretty much what I would call a speedboat: a sleek, pointy-looking machine with little in the way of creature comforts but masses of pose-ability. It was lacking in the kind of practicalities I was used to seeing; the cleats looked flimsy and way too small, there wasn't an anchor on the bow, and as far as rubber fending strakes were concerned— forget it. Clearly this boat would be totally impractical for any kind of commercial work, and therefore nothing more than an expensive toy, a £100,000 plaything. And I loved it.

I was just hopping up and down to try and get a look at the boat's interior when a door opened in a steel shed behind me. After the emerging man confirmed that I was indeed in the right place I slipped inside to hide from the chilling rain, keen to warm up and dry off. The interior was just as resplendent and glamorous as the outside: basically, it was a shed. Admittedly some efforts had been made to sex the place up a bit, with the occasional banner pinned to the grey steel walls, but that didn't stop it being a cold, unheated garage in the middle of a cold, deserted boatyard.

There were around 50 empty plastic chairs set up in orderly rows, facing towards the front of the room where a large white projector screen contributed generously to the lighting arrangements. Just inside the door to my left a couple of folding tables held two big stainless urns of gently boiling water, a regimented army of polystyrene cups and Tupperware tubs with teabags and coffee. I made myself a cup of plastic Nescafe and set out to introduce myself. Not that it took long; there were only three or four others in the room, each of them looking just as bewildered as I felt.

Over the next hour or so the room slowly started filling and I tried to mingle, feeling just as uncomfortable and awkward amongst these experienced racers as I would at a stranger's wedding. Many people knew each other from previous encounters on the water, and the world of powerboat racing is a very small one. The only time I felt on equal footing with someone was when I stepped out into the relentless drizzle for another cigarette.

I've discovered that the UK's Draconian smoking laws have created an entirely new tribe of people. This emerging society doesn't distinguish between Classes or individual wealth; it is united in the humiliating ceremony of huddling under overhangs or in doorways, collars turned up to protect against the elements as they suck mournfully on cigarettes. This subculture of society's outcasts is the 21st century's version of the lepers that walked the streets in the Middle Ages, but instead of a bell warning others of our hideous afflictions we now carry packets emblazoned with Benson & Hedges or Marlboro, complete with disposable lighters that send out sparks to warn the healthy to keep clear— Unclean! Unclean!

And it was amongst this tribe of smoking pariahs that I felt most at home. With our backs to the wind and our hands cupped round glowing embers to protect them against the driving drizzle I chatted nonchalantly with men who regularly race boats worth over a quarter of a million pounds, men who have ripped across the unpredictable surface of the sea faster than I have driven along smooth, tarmac-clad motorways, without fear of being exposed as a bewildered civilian, uneducated in the ways of water-borne speed.

Eventually we were called to order by a very stern-looking woman in her late forties. By now the shed had filled dramatically, and after the usual jostling and chair-scraping and everybody had finally settled down I was surprised to see that virtually every seat was taken, with at least another twenty or thirty people standing at the back.

I had spent much of my time trying to find the two men who had agreed to take me on this unique journey, Drew Langdon and Jan

Falkowski. Nobody had seen them, and from time to time I would check the register to see if they had signed in. But just as I was hunting round for a seat I noticed someone who resembled the pictures of Jan I had found on the Web. I fought my way over and introduced myself, and he graciously offered me the seat next to his. Just as the room was settling down he whispered to me: "So, are you here to cover the briefing?"

I was slightly taken aback. "Erm, actually I'm supposed to be racing with you in June."

He was genuinely surprised. "Are you? That's fantastic! It'll be great to have you along. Are you coming on all the legs with us?"

I suddenly became aware of the stern woman staring intently at us, so I nodded dumbly and faced front, my mind racing. *How the hell could he not know I was joining him and Drew? Was he even racing with Drew, or had he joined another team? And where was Drew anyway?*

As if reading my mind, Jan leant across and whispered that Drew was running late, but he'd be here soon. I nodded and politely told the man about to occupy the seat next to me that it was reserved for someone else, earning me another glare from the woman who resembled the headmistress of some strict Jesuit boarding school.

Suddenly there was the whine of feedback over the PA system and a slightly overweight man in his early sixties stepped in front of the screen displaying the Round Britain logo, clutching a microphone in one hand. "Good afternoon gentlemen, it's absolutely wonderful to see so many of you here today. For those of you that don't know me, my name's Mike Lloyd and it's my privilege to be organising, along with many others, the 2008 Round Britain Powerboat Race!"

Over the next two hours Mike went on to explain every facet of each race leg. The course had been finalised; we would leave from Gunwharf Quays in Portsmouth on the 21st of June and race 130 nautical miles to Plymouth. The next day we'd leave Plymouth for Milford Haven, rounding Land's End. From Milford Haven we'd cross the Irish Sea and run north-west for 200 nm into Bangor, in Northern Ireland. Then on to Oban, on Scotland's west coast, a mere 115 nm away and my home town. Wednesday the 26th would see the fleet travelling to Inverness either by road or through the Caledonian canal, with Thursday being designated a lay day. This would give everybody a chance to relax and carry out any major repairs, before setting off to Edinburgh on a 210 nm slog. The Edinburgh to Newcastle leg the following day was a shorter one, covering only 115 nm, before another 210 nm down the east coast to Lowestoft. The final stretch from Lowestoft back to Portsmouth would be almost 190 nautical miles, and would see us crossing the finishing line sometime on Monday the 30th of June.

Mike then covered in detail the finish and start lines at each venue, as well as berthing, fuelling and craning facilities. There was no mention of accommodation or meals; this was because there wasn't going to be any— or not from the Race Organisers anyway. Their sole contribution to the feeding and watering of the hungry masses was a barbecue, due to be held at Inverness on the lay day. My heart sank. Having a barbie in Scotland is like picking a fight with a Grizzly bear— there's a slim chance you'll be able to pull it off, but the odds are very much against it.

Mike made no bones about it— this was definitely not going to be a glamorous, all-inclusive jaunt round some of Britain's prettiest harbours. This event was being run on a shoe-string, with absolutely no frills whatsoever. At the time I found that easy to believe; after all we were sitting in rented plastic chairs in a damp, cold shed in some godforsaken boatyard. But during the course of the next few months his words of warning slipped from my mind, especially after witnessing the spectacle of P1 in Italy...

But that wouldn't be for some time in the future; for now I had no problem accepting what he said to be Truth, and I felt oddly comfortable with the prospect of a no-nonsense race. Like standing out on the stoop smoking a cigarette in the rain, I felt that a stripped-back event like this would make for a great equaliser. In that respect, at least, I was to be proved right.

Mike also introduced some of the race officials who would be watching over us. The first person he pointed out to us was the intimidating head-mistress, Annie Beakhust. Along with Gill Purnell and Mary Downey she would run Race Control, our source of all Knowledge, where papers would be checked, crew lists confirmed and where teams would have to sign in and out every day. These three women would get to know me well, to the extent that they would physically try to hide whenever they saw me coming.

Annie's husband, Rob Beakhust, was in charge of a team of four other Scrutineers who would check both boats and crews prior to every leg to ensure that we were safe to race that day. These five men had the power to stop a boat leaving the pits or to prevent a crewmember from taking his place on board, and during the course of the race I was destined to have dealings with them on numerous occasions.

More names were mentioned: some people were present, others weren't. It was clear that organising and running such a massive event took a small army of unpaid volunteers, some of whom wouldn't even step a foot on board any of the boats during the entire event, let alone experience the phenomenal adrenaline rush of chasing, then overtaking, the Start Boat, jostling for clear water amongst almost fifty other boats as they accelerate to speeds in excess of ninety miles an hour.

So why do it? Why give up two weeks of valuable holiday time to deal with the stress and frustrations of trying to shepherd nearly over 150 racing crew who had to be coaxed and bullied into carrying out the simplest of tasks, 150 men with the attention spans of reluctant school children on the last day of term before the summer holidays.

Guy Childs, one of the Scrutineers, explained it to me some time later. "It was, quite simply, a once in a lifetime opportunity to be part of such a prestigious event. Plus, since I couldn't afford to actually race myself, this seemed like the next-best thing." He certainly wasn't there for the money. The race officials were given a small daily stipend to cover food and drink, and that was it. For them, there would be no glory; just an endless procession of very early starts and very late nights.

I must confess that I forgot the names of most of the people mentioned that day; not because their roles seemed superfluous but because I found the whole thing a little bewildering and intimidating. There were people whose jobs I had never even heard of: pit marshals, fuel marshals, Officers Of the Day, RYA commissioners...

Halfway through the meeting a small figure sneaked in, his entrance given away by a blast of cold damp air when he opened the door. He quietly made his way through the standing crowd and grabbed the seat next to mine. Jan leaned over and whispered a brief hello, and I ventured a curt "Hi, I'm Derek."

A quick handshake and: "Derek, good to finally meet you. I'm Drew," before we turned our attention back to the front of the room.

The rest of the meeting was fairly unremarkable, with Mike using aerial photographs and illustrations on the projector to explain the layout of each port, where boats could refuel or be lifted out, and where the start and finishing lines would be every day. I found it all pretty basic and slightly tedious until it came to questions. There was a real mix of racing experience here, something I hadn't expected. I was under the illusion that I was in the midst of Europe's finest racers, but it soon became apparent that there were plenty of racing virgins in the room as well. Some poor fool left himself open to ridicule when he dared to ask what the starting procedure was. The question was answered with an abrupt: "Read your RYA racing rulebooks. Next?"

Someone else wanted to know if there would be any time allowances for a team that stopped to help another boat in distress. At this point Jan and I turned to each other and simultaneously waved a cheery goodbye. Without saying a word we had reached the same conclusion; there would be no stopping to help some poor bastard unlucky enough to get rope wrapped round his prop. *Silverline* was a race boat, not a salvage tug. (In fact that attitude was purely light-hearted bravado. When it came to the crunch nobody would ignore another boat in trouble, something that would be demonstrated time and time again during the race.)

In reality, if a team had to stop to help a fellow competitor their lost time would be taken into account at the end of each day. This lost time would be established thanks to the MarineTrack device that every boat was obliged to fit. MarineTrack relies on a GPS (Global Positioning System) transmitter and receiver fitted to the boat. This unit sends the boat's position, heading and speed back to a satellite, which then relays the information to the web. During the race this information would be visible to anybody with access to the internet— the Race Organisers, shore teams, family members and even anyone who wanted to keep up with the race could sit down in front of a computer and follow events live.

Following on the heels of that question came another. What would happen to a team that had to put a crew member ashore for any reason? someone wanted to know.

The answer was fairly obvious. It was perfectly acceptable to put an injured crew member ashore, provided that Race Control was notified by VHF or satellite phone as soon as possible. No one was to be abandoned or jettisoned. This caused a ripple of laughter, and I turned questioningly to Jan, who stopped making notes long enough to explain.

It turned out that during an offshore race back in the 1990's one team's mechanic was injured in the rough conditions. Unwilling to surrender their lead in the race, the driver instead chose to make a beeline for a passing yacht, and instructed the navigator to throw the injured team-mate over the side, relying on the yacht's crew to fish him out again and tend to his injuries. When the navigator objected, the driver reputedly told him "It's OK. Relax. This is endurance racing."

Jesus! I thought to myself. *These people are animals! Best not to show any fear: no doubt they can smell weakness on a man at twenty paces.* So I smiled and whispered back to Jan not to get any ideas. It would make for some pretty lousy PR, I told him.

When the meeting finally wound down I introduced myself formally to Drew and Jan. Drew Langdon measured around five foot six, and somehow reminded me of a mouse or a shrew, both in appearance and in his quiet, unassuming manner. He certainly didn't resemble my preconceptions of a hugely experienced powerboat racer, but then almost all my preconceptions were going to be proved badly wrong in this race. By contrast Jan is a good four inches taller, and is one of those self-confident types that ends up chatting up your woman within two minutes of entering a room, but you don't really mind because he's such a nice guy.

For half an hour or so after the meeting was adjourned there was much jostling, back-slapping and catching up going on as people from all over Europe greeted friends and acquaintances. Fortunately Jan had brought his fiancé Bethan Ancell along, so the two of us chatted about this and that whilst Jan and Drew did the rounds.

Most of the people there were men ranging from their late thirties to their mid fifties, although I had noticed several who looked to be in their sixties— quite an advanced age, I thought, for such a physically

-demanding undertaking. They were all dressed casually, snug in their Henri Lloyd windbreakers and Saint James fleeces, and while some of them spoke with regional accents, there were also a lot of the "Hooray Henry" brigade about. Sprinkled amongst the chatter of voices I could also make out the harsh twangs of German and Scandinavian accents, and what they lacked in numbers they made up for in volume, with much hearty laughter and joking.

Eventually Drew suggested we found a quiet pub so that we could chat in comfort, so five minutes later we were propping up the bar at a pub round the corner, and I was desperately trying to act the part of Seasoned Journalist. In retrospect I should have followed Mark Twain's advice: *It is better to remain silent and be thought a fool than to speak out and remove all doubt.*

I was relieved to discover that Drew and Jan are two of the nicest guys around, and that evening they showed huge levels of patience as I tried to get my head around the upcoming race and powerboat racing in general. My biggest worry was the physical pounding my feeble body would receive, and the two men did little to ease my mind. They talked of shattered kneecaps and splintered ribs with a twisted glee I found disturbing, and Drew impressed on me the importance of being fit enough to endure the punishment. Naturally I reassured him that I had begun running, and whilst it was technically the truth, I neglected to tell him that I could jog only a couple of hundred yards before collapsing by the side of the road and reaching for a cigarette to stop the world from spinning crazily about its axis. Still, at least I was making the effort.

One thing I wasn't clear on was what defined a powerboat. As it turns out, there are no hard and fast rules to provide a definitive answer. The engines can be inboards or outboards, diesel or petrol. You can have a single hull, or a catamaran. The boat can be open, or there can be a cabin, or it can even be fully enclosed. As long as it can go at a decent lick, pretty much everything goes. For the Round Britain Race, the Organisers had decided that boats must be monohulls only, capable of <u>at least</u> 30 knots. For Drew and Jan, that wouldn't be a problem: in P1 they are limited to an astounding 85mph, which equates to 78 knots.

To get these kinds of speeds into some sort of perspective, let me try to explain. The first thing I should clear up is the knots/miles per hour thing: 1 knot is equal to one nautical mile per hour, or 1.1 landmiles per hour. The term "knots" goes back to the good old days, when sailors used to drop a piece of weighted rope off the stern of a moving boat. At set intervals there would be a knot tied into the rope, and they would count how many knots had passed through their hands in a predetermined length of time to give them their speed.

Of course in this day and age technology has taken care of that for us, either by mechanical instruments or, more commonly, by GPS.

Short for Global Positioning System, GPS utilises satellite information to determine a boat's position, and from that the speed can be determined, usually to within a very fine tolerance.

So, if we take the minimum speed required to be able to enter the Round Britain, 30 knots, that equates to 33 mph. To the layman, that sounds pretty unimpressive. Driving at 33 miles per hour down the A1 is tractor territory; even the woeful electric-powered G-Wiz can (somehow) manage an astounding 50 mph. the problem lies with efficiencies— it's just a lot tougher to get a boat moving efficiently through the water than it is to propel a car with the same engine power along a road.

And speaking of roads: doing 33 mph down the smooth tarmac surface of the A1 is a gentle, soothing experience. Try driving across a freshly-ploughed field at the same speed, and you'll be spitting teeth and pissing blood within minutes. And that's with rubber tyres and all -round suspension. The open sea is seldom mirror-smooth, and the only shock-absorbers you're likely to find on a boat are your knees (or, if you're very lucky, a springy seat).

I asked Drew if it would be fair to compare the boats in P1 to a Formula 1 car.

"No, not really," he replied. "A better comparison would be a World Rally Championship car, like a race-prepared Subaru Impreza or Mitsubishi Lancer Evo. These boats have to be incredibly tough to take the continuous pounding they get."

The two men were, and still are, incredibly modest and self-effacing about their achievements, which is why I was so lucky that Bethan had come along. Her background in PR makes her Jan's perfect foil; whenever he hides his accomplishments under a bushel she'll gently coax and coerce him into revealing the truth.

For instance, we were talking about the advantages of RIBs versus "hard" boats in rough weather when Bethan mentioned that Jan had been one of the crew on board the RIB *Spirit Of Portsmouth,* a 7.5 meter open RIB. With nothing to protect them from the elements, Jan and four others had crossed the Atlantic ocean from Portsmouth, USA to Portsmouth, England via Greenland and Iceland— the first ever RIB to do so. This jaw-dropping achievement had to be teased out of Jan, whereas I would have it emblazoned on a bright yellow t-shirt for the world to see. The problem is, Jan would need a t-shirt the size of a Boy Scout's tent to advertise all his similar feats.

At one point I asked the two men a question I was going to ask a lot of people over the course of the race. "Are you racing to win, or are you there for the adventure?"

Given that Drew was primarily a racer whereas Jan seemed to specialise in Herculean odysseys (and if that isn't a clumsy mix of Greek legends, I don't know what is), I naively assumed that their answers would match their preferences. Naturally, I was wrong. They were both entering the race with only one goal in mind— winning. Their answer was unequivocal, but they also confessed that the lure of adventure added a great deal spice to the mix— after all, the bigger the challenge, the greater the feeling of accomplishment, and this was promising to be one hell of a challenge.

By now I was beginning to get a real taste for the Guinness, which was definitely a Bad Thing since I hadn't eaten a thing since the frustrating debacle of breakfast at my hotel that morning. When a person can't tell the difference, either visually or taste-wise, between the fried bread and the bacon, then surely that person would have sufficient grounds for complaint? It seemed that the waitress (a surly Eastern European who had become bitterly disillusioned with the dream of British life) thought otherwise, and the result was what my wife would call "a scene". The only reason it didn't develop into a full-blown "drama" was because of the timely arrival of my taxi, which ferried me away just as conditions were becoming fraught.

It's no surprise to me that Drew took advantage of the fact that my normally razor-sharp mind was temporarily dulled by beer and hunger: after all, these men have an uncanny animalistic ability to sniff out weaknesses in others, and he chose that moment to drop a vicious bombshell on me. "It would be great to have you along on all the legs with us," he started, "but unfortunately there won't be a seat for you on the boat for a couple of the longer stints. Of course you're more than welcome to ride on the support truck."

And there it was. It seemed like a minor setback at the time, a tiny crack in the foundations of the Story, but as time went on this tiny flaw would grow into a massive fissure that would jeopardise the entire project.

Drew papered over this discrepancy with logical, clear-cut reasoning. "You see, although the boat has four places, there will usually be at least three of us on board— myself, Jan, and Miles-"

"Miles? Who's Miles? You never mentioned any Miles," I spluttered numbly.

"Miles Jennings. Didn't I tell you about him?" he answered innocuously. "He'll be driving, I'll be on the throttles, and Jan will be in the back, navigating." Had Drew told me about him already? I couldn't remember.

When they're racing in P1, it's just the two of them— Drew on throttles, and Jan doing the steering. This works fine for the one-hour races they have in P1, where they thunder round a marked-out course only a couple of hundred yards from the beach, but in the Round Britain each leg could take anywhere from 2 to 6 hours. What's more, there's a floating maze of lobster pots, plastic bags, ropes, hunks of wood and other flotsam and jetsam bobbing around the British coast to catch a speeding boat unawares, and the more eyes watching the sea, the better.

But that still left a fourth seat— *my* seat, damnit! Drew went on: "The problem is, on some of the longer stretches, when we're miles away from any harbours, we'll want to take a mechanic along— just in case. But he'll only be with us on a few of the legs— Plymouth to Milford Haven, Milford Haven to Bangor, and Newcastle to Lowestoft. It's just a precaution", he added reassuringly.

My mind was numb. How could I salvage this? "I suppose," I mused aloud, "that this could work in my favour. It might add a bit of flavour to the piece— show the 'behind the scenes' aspect of the race."

Naturally Drew jumped on the suggestion. "Sure! Let the readers know about all the hard work that the shore team put into it, that kind of thing. Besides, you'll probably be grateful of the rest by then."

"But it's just for those three legs?"

"Absolutely. Those are the three stages where it would be almost impossible to get any help from the shore team should anything go wrong. It's vital that we have our mechanic with us. Over the rest of the course the truck will be shadowing us along the coast. Another Guinness?"

By this time my mind was a ruined mess. I'd spent the last ten hours trying to get my head round a sport that was completely foreign to me, and the combination of alcohol and prawn cocktail crisps wasn't helping. I needed sleep: sleep and a handful of powerful painkillers to drown the murderous headache that had settled around my skull. Feeling like the lightweight pussy that I was I said my farewells and stepped out into the perpetual rain to find a taxi to take me back to my hotel.

Of course, the moment my head hit the wafer-thin pillow, my mind started to wake up, and in the orange glow of a streetlight considerately located directly outside my window I tried to sift all the new information into some sort of order. It was several hours before sleep finally overcame me, and my last cohesive thought wasn't that of fifty boats racing towards a hazy horizon, but whether hotel kitchen extractor fans were specifically designed to keep weary travellers awake on purpose, or if it was just some sadistic co-incidence.

2.
Italy.

Glasgow airport is usually a two-hour drive from my house outside Oban, but at three in the morning a brave man with little regard for his own well-being and a supernatural faith in the reflexes of errant red deer can cover the distance in one hour thirty. By the time I boarded the plane my body was torn between sheer exhaustion and massive residues of adrenaline, a paradox compounded by a coffee and a quick nap on the one-hour hop to Stansted.

It was now May, two months after my introduction to the Round Britain Powerboat Race (or RB08 to give it its abbreviated name), and since meeting Drew and Jan at the Driver's Briefing we had remained in close touch. Drew had been anxious to take me out for a run in the boat prior to the RB08 so that we both knew what we'd be letting ourselves in for. From past experience I was pretty sure I wouldn't be sick, but I couldn't make any promises about not shrieking like a frightened girl, so we made several unsuccessful attempts to set up a suitable meeting. Finally Drew told me that we were out of time; the P1 race season was about to get underway, and for the next couple of months *Buzzi Bullet* would be travelling all over Europe from one race venue to the next. There was, however, a chance to go for a quick blast between races in Italy. Perhaps I could meet him there?

Excited at the opportunity to visit a foreign country at someone else's expense I got in touch with Hugo, my editor at *MotorBoat & Yachting*. Who promptly shot me down in flames. "The magazine can't afford to send you swanning around all over Europe" he told me, "but if it helps I'll agree to reimburse you for your other expenses." This news came as a bit of a blow to me; after all, what's the point in being able to eat all the linguini and cannelloni Italy's finest chefs can prepare when I couldn't afford to get there? Fortunately financial aid came from Darrell Morris, the director of *Silverline* UK who sponsor *Buzzi Bullet*. Darrell quickly realised that having pictures of the boat (emblazoned with the *Silverline* logo) splashed over four pages of one of Britain's biggest boating magazines would be an advertising coup, and he generously agreed to spring for the flights and a couple of nights in a cheap hotel.

Air travel has compounded the concept of "culture shock" to a level we won't reach again until they finally get round to perfecting teleportation, and when that miserable day finally rolls around expect to see Arrival lounges swarming with specially-trained psychiatrists working around the clock to deal with the sudden rise in mental breakdowns, nervous collapses and random psychotic outbursts that will be a natural by-product of such a heathenish contraption.

Within the space of an hour I had left behind the soft-spoken brogue of the Scottish dialect, so soothingly familiar to my ears, and had been transported into a surreal world where everyone, it seemed, was auditioning as an extra on an EastEnders episode. Cockney accents always set my teeth on edge, and for the first couple of minutes as I stood in line for a coffee I could hardly make sense of what they were saying, their conversations as incomprehensible to me as that of the Polish staff serving behind the counter.

Finally my brain adjusted to the babbling of Estuary English, and with a pounding headache I made my way to the Departure lounge to join my flight for the next leg of my journey. Standing in the queue for the Ancona flight I spotted Bethan, Jan and Drew up ahead so I subtly nudged and elbowed my way forward to say hi. We chatted for a while, but as soon as we boarded I slumped into my seat and promptly fell into a deep, impenetrable sleep, courtesy of my early start and lousy travelling ability.

I woke to the sound of the Boeing's engines in full reverse thrust, and after wiping the drool from my chest and composing myself I stepped out with the rest of the passengers into the bright brilliance of an Italian afternoon. With just a small holdall as my only baggage I side-stepped the rest of the rabble waiting impatiently for the heavy rubber conveyor belt to grind into life and walked out into the immaculately clean Arrivals hall of Ancona airport.

I have always held a deep disdain for public transport, and so I stepped to the Avis desk and picked up the keys for my hire car— not the sexy stylised lines of the new Fiat Punto, but a deeply un-cool boxy Panda. Still, all I had to do was make sure nobody I knew saw me in it, and my self-respect would remain intact.

Just as I turned to leave with the hateful keys buried deep in my jeans pocket I saw Drew, Jan and Bethan piling up an impressive heap of bags in the middle of the floor. Drew asked if I was also going to San Benedetto del Tronto by train. When I told him I'd hired a car instead, he turned pensive. "That's not such a bad idea. Why don't we do that guys?"

The others agreed, and Drew stepped up to the desk to try and hire a car for his group. By this time the pile of luggage had grown as two more men appeared from the luggage hall. I was introduced to Rob Jenkins, a big, friendly bear of a man with an endearing baby-face and a West country accent so heavy it could crush cider-apples, and Steve Causley who was Rob's boss and co-owner of Race Marine, a Taunton-based workshop where they prepared and fettled racing powerboats. They, along with John Christensen of Cummins Mercruiser Diesel, would be the mechanics tending to the *Silverline* boat and several other teams.

Ten minutes later the six of us and the small mountain of bags were wandering round the rental car park, looking for our cars. I found mine first; the humiliation of driving a Fiat Panda was compounded by the colour, which was a pale, sickly blue and about as manly as a feather boa. Not a good look for a man in the country where the word machismo originated. Of course Drew had somehow bagged a sleek Punto, but was decent enough to keep his comments to himself. His smirk, however, spoke a thousand words. We divvied up bags and passengers and soon I was thrashing my puny Panda to within an inch of its life, desperately trying to keep up with Drew before his car became just another anonymous dot on the horizon.

As we ate lunch in a clean, efficient diner by the side of the Autostrada I tried to shake off the absurdity of flying 1200 miles just to test my masculinity and instead focussed on trying to digest the reams of information Jan and Bethan had been feeding me in the drive down. They had once again done their best to educate me in the mysterious ways of the powerboat-racing world, but I have never been quick to grasp matters second-hand. I've always found that if I'm to understand something, I need to get my hands on it, experience it for myself, regardless of how well someone's trying to explain things to me.

Take the concept of "stuffing" for example. This refers to what happens when a boat buries its bows into a large wave at speed instead of climbing up and over the crest. Stuffing a boat can result in tonnes of water flooding the boat, stopping the engines and even sweeping crew over the side. Clearly, this is not a good thing. But no matter how eloquent, how descriptive the narrator is in explaining this occurrence, I feel I'll never really understand the sensation unless I experience it first-hand. So, despite Bethan and Jan's best efforts, I was still struggling to come to terms with what powerboat racing actually involved.

Lunch break over, we piled back into the cars and continued our headlong dash southwards, the occasional tunnel breaking the monotony and giving brief respite from the sun that burned down from a perfect blue sky. As we got closer to San Benedetto del Tronto I closed the gap between Drew's car and my own, determined not to lose him so close to our destination.

The next ten minutes turned into something out of the Italian Job, mixed with the comedic hysterics of Smokey And The Bandit. Drew weaved in and out of the heavy traffic, indicators flashing in polar contradiction to his actual intentions. He would head down off-ramps with gleeful self-assurance, only to change his mind at the last possible moment, with mere inches between him and the barriers, the car rocking on its suspension as he flicked it back onto the Autostrada. Naturally I would follow suit, narrowly avoiding major catastrophes as I screeched back onto the main road, cutting in front of other traffic with the howl of horns in my ears. *At least nobody was going to confuse us for tourists,* I thought grimly to myself.

After what felt like a lifetime of naked fear, hysterical giggling and crashing up and down the gears we finally arrived in a sandy car park, the far end ostensibly closed off to the public by temporary railings beneath a grand arch festooned with Powerboat P1 logos. I clambered out of the car and wiped my sweaty palms on my jeans. Drew seemed mildly surprised that I'd managed to keep up with him, and I think I passed some sort of test that day. Perhaps it wasn't a significant test, or even one that Drew himself had consciously set me, but I had passed all the same, and I'm convinced it went some way to establishing my worth in the upcoming Round Britain race.

We stretched the kinks out of our backs and legs, then shouldered our bags and set off towards the dry pits which were located— typically— at the other end of the marina. There was no security at the first barrier, and people were wandering in and out unhindered. Once through we walked along the quayside, and I took the opportunity to ask Drew about his P1 record. He and Jan had come second in their SuperSport Class not once, not twice but three times, and in the boating media were regularly described as "always the bridesmaid, never the bride." I asked him if it bothered him at all, to which he replied that it didn't, but there was a flash of anger in his eyes when I mentioned the "bridesmaid" line, and I decided not to push the subject.

We soon came to another huge arch that proclaimed that we had reached the dry pits. Here the security gate was manned, but the others merely mentioned that they were Team *Silverline* and were ushered through. I muttered something about being a journalist and "here for an exclusive" at the security guard, but he just nodded and let me past. The guard's appearance had given me a bit of a jolt; his splendid military-style uniform boasted a Glock automatic, a baton, handcuffs, a can of Mace and a vicious Bowie knife. His eyes were unreadable behind standard-issue mirrored Aviators, and I felt mildly uncomfortable and naked without any form of legitimate ID.

As soon as we passed through into the dry pits I voiced my concerns to the rest of the group. We had just rounded a corner and Jan pointed to a row of white marquees that boasted various signs: Race Control, Doctor, Race Officials and Media. "They'll look after you," Jan told me. Then he pointed past the row of tents. "The truck should be down there somewhere; come and find us when you get sorted."

I ducked into the Media tent to see about a press pass. Inside stood six folding tables and chairs, occupied by a couple of people lethargically punching away at computer keyboards. At the back of the room sat three or four others, looking official in their P1 polo shirts. I wandered over and introduced myself, where I was asked to fill in some form or another. I scribbled barely-legible answers and asked about my pass. I was told that it wouldn't be ready until the next morning, and in the meantime I was to simply tell the security guards that I was with the media, and they would let me pass unmolested. I wasn't convinced, but decided a little show of faith would be the diplomatic thing to do and stepped back out into the warm sunshine.

The row of white plastic tents lined a short, broad access road, and on the other side, behind a high fence, was a boatyard where men were repairing, welding and painting a variety of craft. I stopped for a moment to watch someone grind the anodes off the hull of a 120 foot steel motorboat, then lit another cigarette and wandered down towards where Jan told me the *Silverline* lorry should be. My way was blocked by another temporary gate, and another security guard sporting mirrored sunglasses. Like a fool I tried to explain I was a journalist again, but he merely grinned and let me through. I felt like a moron as I realised that I was leaving the pits, not trying to get in. Christ, any freak could get out; getting back in was always going to be the tricky part.

I crossed the road and in the car park in front of me I finally laid eyes on the *Silverline* boat in the flesh for the first time. Unfortunately all I could do was look, since my way was once again blocked by yet another metal barrier. I swung it open and stepped through, and as I closed it behind me I noticed the guard watching me. I hit him with one of my most trustworthy smiles and gave him a big cheesy thumbs-up. It seemed to do the trick and he smiled back, the sun glinting off a gold front tooth.

Buzzi Bullet sat on the back of the lorry looking like a child's idea of a ballistic missile. Her hull and topsides were ice-white, with the sponsor's name *Silverline* outlined in blue letters running down her length. The tip of her bow was painted bright orange, as were the two small wings that sprouted there like a rocket's stabiliser fins. She looked sleek and sharp, and sitting on the back of the lorry looked considerably longer than 42 feet. At only nine feet wide she managed to continue the illusion of being missile-like, especially when I remembered that her two 5.9 litre turbo-charged Cummins diesels produced almost 1,000 horsepower.

Steve and Rob had already begun to check the boat over, and had propped a ladder up against the hull so that they could get the engine covers open. I was starting to feel like a lemon, so I was glad to help when Bethan produced a small marquee. Setting it up was to prove the hardest of the day's tasks, but we eventually mastered the mass of aluminium poles and assorted bits of string.

Next came the ritual of Sponsorship. I was handed a *Silverline* t-shirt and cap, which made me a little uncomfortable. Don't get me wrong; I love free stuff. Anything that costs me precisely nothing will be cherished and guarded as if it was the most precious gift I have ever received. My dilemma was this: here was I, trying to be a proper grown-up journalist, determined to write an honest and unbiased article about the *Silverline* team during the opening race of the P1 championship. How then could I possibly walk around in clothing emblazoned with the team's name? I would be a walking hypocrite, nothing more than a poorly-paid PR man. On the other hand, I could feel my scalp start to smoulder under the Italian sun, so I decided to compromise and wear the cap but not the shirt. I wouldn't get head-cancer and the boys would get their team's name on a wandering writer. Win-win all round then.

I was dying to get out on the water, desperate to experience the sheer power of the boat for myself to see if I could handle it. To my massive disappointment, however, I was told that the boat wouldn't get launched until the next day. It turned out that they had spent many weeks testing and fine-tuning the boat prior to Italy, and so there really wasn't any point in risking anything by having her craned into the water before the day of the race. I nodded like a sensible adult, but the little boy inside me sulked and brooded the rest of the day.

A day which was spent wandering all over the marina. While the rest of the guys caught up with friends, discussed developments and filled out paperwork I decided to go exploring amongst the millions of pounds' worth of powerboats that had been steadily arriving at the dry pits.

Teams seemed to demonstrate their wealth by inundating the pits with vehicles. For the more modest teams like *Silverline* there was just one lorry, but as the budgets grew bigger so too did the fleet of toys. There was a clear winner in this game— Team *Skater*. This Italian Evolution-Class team were eager to show the rest of the world that money was no object to them, and during the course of the weekend their collection of vehicles grew and grew, until by Sunday morning I was tripping over Dodge Vipers, stretched limos, a Dodge Ram pick-up, countless mopeds and even a large luxury yacht— all finished in jet-black paint and sporting the team's number 53. Whenever I mentioned this to anybody not connected with the team I was either rewarded with a sad shake of the head or a more honest "flash wankers."

Despite their distinctly unremarkable debut the previous year, Team *Skater* were at the pinnacle of glamour in what is undoubtedly a very glamorous sport. The Powerboat P1 championship is made up of two different Classes— Evolution and SuperSport. The Evolution Class is made up of about a dozen boats, each one a prototype. They are ridiculously powerful, their twin engines easily powering them to speeds in excess of 100 mph, and the inherent dangers in racing at such speeds are reflected in the fact that all Evolution boats need to be fitted with a jet-fighter-style canopy to protect their crews should the worst happen.

The SuperSport Class is a little more sedate— but not much. These boats are limited to 85 mph, and are based on production hulls, so in theory you could watch them racing on a Sunday and nip down to your local marine broker on Monday and order one for yourself. In both Classes the boats have to be a monohull design, so no twin-hulled catamarans that dominate Class 1, the pinnacle of powerboat racing. Also, both Classes are governed by a power-to-weight rule that ensures that there is no outright advantage between teams, placing the onus on the drivers and throttlemen to race their socks off. It also evens the field, making the racing a much more competitive prospect for spectators and participants alike.

Eventually I tired of watching stunning, sparkling speed machines arriving on the back of custom-built low-loaders and made the long slog back to the car. By some divine fluke I found my hotel just 300 yards along the Viale Trieste, and within minutes of checking in at the Hotel Arlecchino I was lying face-down on the bed, drooling into the cool crisp sheets.

The next day I woke up hungry and confused. Instead of the usual morning sounds I was accustomed to in Scotland (rain on the slate roof tiles, wind whistling round the eaves etc) I instead woke to the generic soundtrack of virtually every Mediterranean town getting ready for work. There was the clattering of bins, twittering of birds, and somewhere down the hall a couple were embroiled in a monumental shouting match that was certain to end in either a gruesome murder or a marathon session of sweaty morning-sex. All this was set against a background of the ubiquitous whine of a hundred two-stroke moped engines as Vespas and Lambrettas shuttled people to work, school and the shops.

After showering and trying to blot out the sounds of noisy lovemaking from the couple three rooms down I made my way downstairs where I was told there was to be no breakfast that morning. Since this information was relayed to me via unintelligible Italian and manic arm-waving by the elderly woman behind the reception desk, I might have been mistaken, but I think it was because the chef and the waitress were having some sort of a domestic. I briefly considered telling the receptionist that I had reason to believe that the situation was being resolved in a room on the second floor, but the mental image of trying to relay that information via sign language didn't appeal, so I smiled and sauntered out into the gentle morning sunlight instead.

Rather than endure the humiliation of being spotted in a powder-blue Panda I chose to walk down the palm tree-lined road towards the marina. In fact, pretty much every road, avenue and promenade in town has a palm tree or ten bordering it; they are so prevalent that the town is also known as "Riviera delle Palme".

San Benedetto del Tronto is a bit of a schizophrenic town, with dual incomes from the fishing industry and a thriving tourism trade. It's shoreline— around 5 miles of immaculate sandy beach— is dissected by the marina, its long concrete breakwater jutting out into the Adriatic. At the northern end of the marina the fleet of fishing boats provide the, er, *rustic* aroma you'd expect from a working port, whilst the southern half is dedicated to the usual mix of masts and motors that represent the leisure-boating community. The town climbs the gentle foothills at its back, peaked by the Torrione, a 32 meter high tower that overlooks the entire old town.

In early May the streets were devoid of tourists. Which was nice for the locals, as it meant they didn't have to open their cafes and restaurants until a month or so later, but a bit of a bugger for an aspiring writer who hadn't eaten anything since the previous afternoon.

Luckily for me the P1 Organisers had laid on breakfast for the teams back in the dry pit, so after blagging my way past the stony-faced security guard again I nonchalantly slipped inside the giant marquee and gorged on muesli, fresh rolls and a smorgasbord of meat. After my fifth espresso doppio the staff manning the coffee machine cut me off, so I quick-stepped outside and sparked up a cigarette with jittery hands.

It wasn't just the massive influx of caffeine making my nerves zing and sparkle; today I was going for a blast in *Buzzi Bullet*. I was magically transformed from a 35-year old man with a job, wife and responsibilities into an excited little schoolboy who could barely stop grinning at the prospect of blasting across the water at potentially lethal speeds.

Of course when I spotted Drew a little later I was cool, calm and collected, just like any cynical journalist should be. "Drew! Hey! Over here! How's the boat? Are we going soon? Are we? Because you promised I could go out in the boat. Remember? Drew? Well? When are we going? When?" Yep, cool and detached, just like a pro...

Fortunately Drew and Jan were genuine professionals in their field, and they weren't about to rush into anything. Everything on the boat had to be double-checked: electrics, navigational equipment and intercoms were all given the once-over by Rob, while John Christensen checked over the engines and gearboxes.

John was the official engineer for Cummins-Mercruiser Diesels, or CMD, and he was the filthy thieving bastard who would prevent me from taking my rightful place on board the *Silverline* boat for the full eight legs. Apparently Drew would rather have some mechanical genius on board for the more exposed sections, instead of me... to be fair, I could see his point, but the pill wasn't made any sweeter by the fact that John was such an immensely likeable guy. I was all ready to hate him, but his laid-back Kiwi nature combined with a staggering depth of knowledge made it difficult (even for me) to maintain any kind of a grudge.

After half an hour of conscientious checking and tweaking the two men had finished prepping the boat for launching. They had even remembered to bolt the two props on; a crucial detail I hadn't even considered.

Each 5-bladed "cleaver" propeller is a masterpiece, a magnificent object of modern art fashioned out of high-grade stainless steel. They can measure over 16 inches across, and weigh in at over 10 kilos each. Starting with a wax mould, each one is cast in stainless steel and machined before finally being finished off by hand— a process that can take up to three weeks. Each one can cost up to £8,000, and as such they are stored in a well-secured locker until the boat is ready to be launched. They are often referred to as surface-piercing props, as they're designed to run with only the bottom half under water. This means that there's only half the resistance, which lets the engines rev quicker and higher than with conventional props and shafts. They are also one of the few components on a boat that can be changed to suit the conditions. Where a car or motorbike can be fitted with tyres for wet or dry racetracks, so a powerboat can utilise a variety of props, depending on the sea state.

Finally, after a short ice-age, we were ready to go. Except that I wasn't. Jeans and a Hunter S Thompson t-shirt might be acceptable apparel to a shore-bound onlooker, but if I was to fool the P1 authorities into thinking I was the third crewman of Team *Silverline* for the day then clearly I would have to dress accordingly.

A lengthy rummage through the cab of the truck revealed that the spare racing overalls had been left behind, and so Drew had to go on a scrounging mission round the rest of the pits to find me a fireproof race suit. Ten minutes later he returned victorious, brandishing black Sparco overalls. My joy soon turned to concern however, when it became blatantly obvious both to me and to the small crowd of onlookers I had somehow attracted that the suit was designed for someone a foot shorter than me.

I was sweating profusely as I found new and agonising ways to twist and bend my limbs in a desperate effort to force my 6 foot frame into the five foot suit. When Jan suggested I remove my jeans I popped another pint of sweat. "Ah, yes, well, I would, only I, er, prefer to go commando," I stammered in a whisper.

"Commando?" bellowed Jan. "What does that mean? Are you wearing camouflage boxers or something?"

"Actually, no. That's just it— I'm not wearing anything," I hissed back.

"Ah. I see. In that case, maybe you'd better keep your jeans on then," he replied. And with that he turned on his heel and made a dignified exit. I wished I could do the same but I wouldn't have looked quite so classy, staggering around a crowded car park with a pair of overalls wrapped round my knees, so I grimly ignored the sniggers coming from the sizeable crowd that had now gathered and resolutely got on with trying to heave them the rest of the way up.

Fifteen minutes later I was doing an admirable impression of John Wayne's walk down the pontoon. This wasn't due to any horse-riding experience, but simply because this was the only way I could move without castrating myself. As if the heat wasn't bad enough, I was then handed yet another item of apparel: my life jacket. Instead of the lightweight Crewsaver-type of inflatable vests, my Grabner life vest was a big, bulky thing with laces down each side and numerous chunky buckles for connecting a myriad of straps: three buckles across my chest, and another two looped round each thigh to ensure it wouldn't come adrift if I hit the water hard.

Once I was fully kitted up I was hot, uncomfortable and about as nimble as the Michelin man after an 8-course meal. My discomfort was quickly forgotten by the time I stood alongside *Buzzi Bullet* however— finally I could clearly see where I would be sitting for my induction into the world of powerboat racing. Except there weren't any seats.

Bullet is strictly Standing Room Only, capacity: 4. The driver and navigator stand side by side in their own padded compartments, with two more behind them for idiots like me. I was invited to slide down into my spot, and found it oddly comfortable.

My back and sides were hugged by vinyl-upholstered foam reaching from about nipple-height down to my hips, and my feet stood on rubber matting an inch thick. Directly in front of me was a bright orange grab-bar, which I was pleased to discover was very solidly secured. And that was it. There are no restraints of any sort permitted in open -topped race boats, for the simple reason that if anything were to go wrong a seatbelt could well stop a crewmember from getting out. This rule applies to all the SuperSport Class boats, regardless of whether they're standing or sitting which is why Drew prefers to stand. At least that way you can wedge yourself in; when you're seated it's a lot harder to stop yourself being flung around.

Drew's explanation didn't exactly fill me with confidence, and when he started telling me that it was much better to be thrown clear of a cart-wheeling boat rather than be trapped and dragged to the icy depths I quickly changed the subject.

"So where do you stand then?" I asked, mentally trying to destroy the image of a handsome writer in a too-small race suit being alternatively hurled through the air and trapped in a sinking boat.

"I'll be right in front of you, in the left-hand spot." Fixed to the dashboard in front of him was a chart plotter, and above it another orange grab bar. Just above *that* were two rubber-encased rocker switches, which Drew explained operated the trim tabs. Between him and Jan were the gear and throttle levers, that he would also be operating. This left Jan with nothing to do other than steer the boat. Simple really. Apart from a selection of straight-forward gauges showing crucial engine data, that was about it.

I couldn't help but wonder aloud about why there were so few dials; after all, some of the other cockpits I'd gawped at were festooned with dozens of them, all looking like designer watches with their white faces and shiny chromed bezels. "That would just complicate things," he replied. "When you're in the middle of a race you don't have time to work your way through hundreds of gauges; you need to be able to check them in the blink of an eye to make sure the boat's running right." Fair point, I thought.

As I looked at the simple display of instruments on the dash I couldn't help but notice that they were a tad, well, scruffy. The boat itself was also, on closer inspection, showing the odd scuff here and there, and the orange paint on the bow had faded somewhat. Don't get me wrong, I'm not saying that *Bullet* was held together with Duck tape and spit or anything, it's just that when I compared it to the other boats in the pits and tied up further along the pontoon, it was clear that Team *Silverline* wasn't the biggest player at the table.

Having said that, just competing in P1 is expensive, never mind racing consistently enough to be on the podium, like Drew & Jan. In 2008 to enter P1 for one season of 7 races (the eighth, scheduled in Bahrain, was dropped) cost 17,500 Euros. Then, of course, you'll need a boat. Scouring the classifieds might turn up a suitable second -hand boat from around 125,000 Euros, which would do for the SuperSport Class. Clearly, since Evolution is for prototypes, it would probably be wise to leave that category to the professional builders. So you've got a boat and your laminated license takes pride of place in your wallet. That doesn't mean you're done. You'll still need to transport your boat to the various venues (in 2008 they included Italy, Spain, Malta, France, Portugal and Tunisia), and you'll also need to take along someone a bit handy with the spanners in case something falls off. Then there's the pile of spare parts (including a spare engine), fuel for the transport lorry and the boat, flights, food and accommodation to consider. All told, expect to shell out around 300,000 Euros for seven weekends of glamour, sunshine and fourteen races.

I mentally shrugged off *Bullet*'s shortcomings and set about trying to wrap the kill cord round my calf instead. The kill cord is a coily length of elastic; it's wrapped around the lower leg and clipped back onto itself so it's got you in a noose. The other end is connected to a kill switch. Thanks to the elastic properties of the cord, the wearer can move his leg a good foot or so; any more than that and the cord will pull on the switch and kill the engines stone dead. This way, if anyone is thrown overboard there's no danger of the boat carrying on its merry way.

This little device frightened and reassured me in equal measure.

On the one hand, it was comforting to know that if I were somehow ejected from the boat, at least the sudden death of the engines would alert Drew and Jan that they were one writer short. Unfortunately this only added extra detail to my vision of hurtling through the sky and smacking into the ocean. But my real concern came with the thought that I might inadvertently tug on the cord a little bit too hard, bringing the boat to a sudden standstill— undoubtedly at a crucial point in the proceedings.

27

Drew and Jan took their places in front of me, and once they got the engines fired up Rob the mechanic dropped the engine hatch and locked it down. Drew squirmed round in his seat and handed me a bright orange full-faced helmet with a cord dangling from it. Over the gentle burble of the exhausts he pointed out where the jack plugged in, and I slipped the helmet over my head. Drew did likewise, and suddenly my head was filled with a deafening roar that gave me such a start I almost leaped straight up into the air.

Drew frantically fiddled with the volume knob and the bellow turned into Drew's calm voice. "Sorry about that, I had the sound up a bit high there."

"Jesus Drew," I replied. "You scared the crap out of me! I think I'd better get this race suit cleaned before you give it back!"

Drew turned to face forward again, but slightly disconcertingly I could still hear his voice in my ear. "OK Derek, you ready to go?" Like a moron I nodded and gave the thumbs-up to the back of his head. When he asked me again I had the sense to use actual words instead of visual signals, and Jan threw a thumbs-up to Rob and Bethan on the pontoon. They untied us, and Rob fended us clear with a couple of well-placed shoves from his foot.

In order for a boat to travel as fast as possible, it's important that only the bare essentials are dragging along beneath the hull. To keep the drag down to an absolute minimum, *Bullet*'s single rudder is ridiculously small— so small, in fact, that at speeds below 8 or 10 knots, it might as well be a Kleenex for all the good it does. So instead of Jan wasting his time twirling the small racing wheel this way and that, Drew manoeuvred us out towards the harbour mouth entirely by using the engines, dropping them from forward to astern depending on which way he wanted the boat to turn. It was beautifully done, but slightly disconcerting to see Jan fiddling about with his helmet, lifejacket and whatnot whilst the boat weaved its way in and out of pontoons and other boats.

As we gently motored past the wet pits I saw another race boat being lowered by one of two massive mobile cranes. The race course was now open for free practice, and other teams were starting to mobilise their lorries to form an orderly queue behind the cranes.

Over the intercom I heard Drew get clearance to leave the harbour, and finally we cleared the long breakwater and turned south, our course running parallel to the sandy beach, about quarter of a mile offshore. Slowly Drew opened the throttles, and behind me the two Cummins diesels changed their sedate grumble to a slightly louder moan. As the speed increased so did the angle of the bow, leaving us totally unsighted for what seemed like an age, but after we passed the 12-knot mark she started levelling off, and I breathed a quiet sigh of relief.

As well as the GPS chart plotter mounted directly in front of Drew, both the men also had a laminated chart of the course. I say "chart";

in reality it was just a very basic outline of the course lay-out. It showed the shore, the seven markers they'd have to race around, the distances between each marker and the compass heading they'd have to follow to reach the next one— and that was it. It had been kept as simple as possible for the same reason the dashboard wasn't festooned with dozens of glitzy dials— both men could, with the very briefest of glances, read everything they needed to know from the chart without any unnecessary distractions.

As we got closer to the course I could hear the two men discussing optimum racing lines and best angles of attack. I didn't really pay much attention; I was too busy feeling my way round my first ever powerboat ride. We were skipping across the Adriatic at a nifty 30 knots or so, and the gentle waves were posing no problems at all. I was following the advice from a friend of mine who regularly ran RIBs in all conditions back home— legs slightly apart, knees unlocked, and keep your body relaxed but ready. Piece of piss. Then, over the inter-com, Drew asked if I was ready. "Yep, bring it on," I cockily replied.

Drew firmly opened the throttles, the moan behind me rose to a thunderous howl and I was literally pushed back into the padding as the boat hurtled towards the first yellow marker at an outrageous speed. Honestly, the amount of *oomph* produced by those two turbo-charged diesels was frightening. To propel four and a half tons of boat through the water takes a fair amount of power; to seemingly *hurl* four and a half tons at the horizon like that is simply astounding.

Throughout the acceleration there wasn't even the tiniest hint of the bow pointing skywards, which went against all my expectations. In-stead, as we were catapulted towards the magic 85 miles per hour, perfectly flat and level, there was only a faint click click click in my ear. I hardly noticed it, however, because now those gentle, inoffen-sive waves from a few moments ago had somehow turned into con-crete sleepers. We were hurtling across the water, hitting these ap-parent sleeping policemen with relentless force. I had to force my knees to unlock, but it felt like I would be driven into the deck of the boat by each jarring blow. I was gripping the orange bar in front of me with such force that I was sure I could feel the stainless steel bending and twisting beneath my claw-like fingers; it was only a matter of mere seconds before I would crush it like an ice-cream cone.

Meanwhile, I could make out Drew and Jan chatting amiably about the course. "Nice layout, don't you think Jan?" "Yes, and it's not too far from the shore. Should make for a decent show tomorrow." "Yes. Now, see the church tower over there? You can use that to line up on the next marker. See it?" "Oh yes. It looks lovely in the sunlight, doesn't it?" "Mm. It's really pretty round here, don't you think? OK Derek, we're going to turn now, so you might want to hang on."

Huh? Hang on? I thought I was hanging on. What the fu-

With a deft flick of the wrist Jan gave the wheel a sharp twist to

29

starboard and suddenly we were pointing inland. A bright yellow blur literally brushed past the boat, I found myself crushed against the protective padding, there was some more clicking in my ear and that was it. We had just made a 90 degree turn at almost 80 miles per hour, and were now thundering towards a second yellow marker buoy. I barely had time to crap myself again when we screamed round that one as well, and now we were pointing north as we made the run up the back straight of the course, back in the direction of the marina.

The course was laid out roughly in the shape of the letter "R", and as we skimmed up the straight towards the top of the course (and the top of the letter) Drew decided that this would be an opportune time to tell me about trim tabs. "Do you hear the clicking?" he asked me as he twisted round to talk to me. "Every time I adjust the trim tabs, you'll hear the click over the intercom. The tabs are really important— they keep the boat riding nice and level through the water." He held up a hand to demonstrate, and I couldn't help but notice how there wasn't the slightest sign of a tremor. I doubted that my hand would be so steady— provided I could ever detach it from the grab bar, that was.

"When we go into a turn, I use the tabs to get us round as efficiently as possible. Depending on how tight the turn is, I can either get the back end to slide round, like this-" he demonstrated with his hand "-or I can also get the stern to really dig in, like this. Of course, I have to be very careful. If we dig in too much, there's a real danger we could suddenly hook and then we'd flip, like this:" he dropped the leading edge of his hand, then suddenly flicked his palm upward, mimicking a 42-foot boat somersaulting into the air. I could clearly see a tiny little man in a too-tight race suit being hurled out of the hand-boat and smashing lifelessly into the sea...

"Uh-huh, yeah, OK, I get it." I had just spotted the next marker, and it was getting closer and closer by the second. "Ah, Drew? You want to turn around for a second?" I'd like to think I managed to hide the fear in my voice, but deep down I'd just be lying to myself.

Drew looked over his shoulder, shrugged nonchalantly and turned round to face the oncoming marker buoy. He'd barely made it round before Jan once again gave the wheel a quarter turn, and once again we changed direction with the kind of speed and accuracy not seen since the motorbike chase in that otherwise god-awful 1980's movie Tron.

We were now following the full course at race speed, and after another half a lap I was starting to relax a little. I could begin to see the benefits of standing as opposed to sitting; I was firmly plugged into a padded hole, with the bulwarks almost at the same height as my shoulders and the foam padding gripping me nicely. The rubber mat under my feet was surprisingly effective at cushioning the ride, and I soon realised that, thanks to the bulk of the lifejacket, the chances of me being driven to the deck were pretty slim. I was virtually stuck, and instead of feeling claustrophobic I actually felt reassured and oddly comfortable.

Before long though, we had covered about seven or eight laps, and the boys were happy with the way the boat was handling. They had figured out the best lines to take the markers, and had made mental notes of useful landmarks on shore. I was feeling quite proud of myself: I hadn't squealed like a stuck pig, and the inside of my helmet was delightfully vomit-free. Imagine my disappointment then, when Jan said over the intercom: "It's a real shame it was so calm out there today; it would have been nice if you could have experienced it with a bit more of a sea running."

I made pathetic little noises supposed to reflect my sadness, but I don't think anyone bought it. However, I managed to be a little more honest when we dropped off the plane to enter the harbour. Drew asked me what I thought of my little experience. "Drew," I replied, "I have *got* to get me one of these! That was the most incredible ride of my life! Seriously, I don't care how much this fucker costs, I just *have* to have one in my life. What a fucking rush!" This time they seemed to believe my sincerity.

Back on dry land I struggled to coax my limbs out of the life vest and race suit. I was bathed in sweat, my trembling fingers were cramping up and I had a nasty friction burn on my inner forearm and yet I was grinning like the village idiot who's just been given a bucket of radishes. It was one of the most exhilarating rides of my life, and I couldn't wait for my next opportunity to scream across the surface of the sea at such astonishing speed. I seemed to have passed muster with the guys, which was a relief in itself. They told me that their top speed was only down by about one knot; a handicap they could live with during the RB08. Since I hadn't made a total arse of myself it looked like I'd be joining them in June.

I was however slightly concerned about my fitness levels. We'd only been out for half an hour in pitifully gentle seas, and yet I could feel my thigh and calf muscles beginning to ache slightly. Nothing drastic, you understand, I wasn't anxiously looking round for a stretcher or a wheelchair, but if that was how I felt after thirty minutes, how the hell was I going to cope with 6-hour long stages across notorious stretches of water like the Irish sea? This was a serious reality check, and I resolved to take training more seriously as soon as I got back home.

I spent the rest of the day in a happy glow, wandering the length and breadth of the marina several times to immerse myself in the hubbub of a real-life powerboat race. Everywhere I went there were signs of the glamorous lifestyle that went hand-in-hand with racing: beautiful women in skin-tight Lycra smiled enticingly at all and sundry, the air reverberated to the sounds of high-performance engines being fired up and revved, racers sauntered around with their race suits unzipped to the waist, beautiful women in Lycra, P1 officials in their identical uniforms scurried here and there... did I mention the women in Lycra? Whilst I couldn't quite imagine Inverness bathed in the same dazzling sunshine, I felt sure that the spectacle of the powerboat racing paraphernalia would easily translate to Britain's shores...

Saturday morning was an acoustic repeat of the previous day, but this time without the raging argument down the hall. Perhaps they had found an empty sound-proof suite on the top floor, I mused as I strolled towards the first barrier at the marina. Today was race day, however, and this morning it was manned by another intimidating security guard. And I still didn't have a press pass. I gulped and started jabbering, but before I got a chance to totally confuse the stoic guard one of the P1 staff recognised me and waved me through. I thanked him and set off towards the media tent, this time determined to get my hands on the little plastic card that would let me come and go unhindered, but first I would have to negotiate the guard at the entrance to the dry pits. Fortunately this guard had seen me wandering around so often in the last two days that he knew me by sight, and he waved me through with a big grin. I paused to light a smoke and offered him one, which he cheerfully accepted. We stood for a minute or two, trying to make small-talk about the boats and the people, but his English was almost as poor as my attempts at Italian so we both decided to stick to thumbs-up and smiles instead.

Roy Mantle, head of P1's media relations, finally came up with the goods, and with the magic laminated card dangling round my neck I went off in search of food, coffee and the *Silverline* team.

The atmosphere in the dry pits was now noticeably tenser than the previous day. Today was the first of two race days, with the endurance race for the SuperSport Class due to start at 11:30, and testing permitted from nine to 10:30. Not wanting to distract the boys, I said an unobtrusive hello and went off for another wander.

My wife claims she loves me dearly (and who am I to argue?) but I'm painfully aware that I have one serious character flaw that I know drives her nuts: I just can't keep still. Whilst she's happy to sit at a pavement café for hours on end, simply watching the world pass her by, I find myself knocking back my coffee and itching to get going. I've never used that hackneyed old phrase "I'm like a shark, me," but I can certainly relate to the simile. I hate to be stationary, soaking up atmosphere and enjoying the view. I'm convinced that the atmosphere and the view over *there* is bound to be better, and even if it is, I'll still want to go round the corner to see what's going on there.

This is a horrible compulsion I just can't seem to break, and it explains why so many of the fearsome security guards were starting to recognise my bow-legged gait from quite some distance. This morning, however, I had somewhere new to explore— the VIP area at the southern end of the marina. Because today was race day, and there was suddenly a massive influx of local celebrities, team guests, hangers-on and general lookie-lou's swarming around the marina. To cater for the lucky invitees, a row of marquees had been set up offering drinks, snacks, and somewhere to sit and gossip.

My first beer hit my parched throat just before ten, and by god it tasted sweet. The second beer was almost as good, and as well as quenching my thirst it managed to chill me out just enough to help me attain that highest of Buddhist goals— inner tranquillity.

From my vantage-point sitting at a table outside one of the beer-tents I could see the length of the harbour side running away to my left. Directly in front of me was the walkway leading on to the pontoon where the race boats would tie up, and across the marina I could watch the two cranes as they prepared to lower the SuperSport boats into the glassy water.

People-watching is such a popular past-time (especially in my house) that I'm surprised it hasn't been suggested as a new Olympic sport. When they do finally see sense and include it amongst the more boring activities of running and swimming I think that Italy would make the ideal training ground. Every tier of the Italian class structure is obsessively preoccupied, either subconsciously or otherwise, with the art of posing. It doesn't matter whether you're fabulously wealthy or piss-poor, stunningly beautiful or overwhelmingly fugly— just as long as you project an air of aloof coolness. I watched as an elderly fellow, clearly down-at-heel, blagged a cigarette from a stranger. The stranger lit it for him and the old man strode off in a haze of blue smoke and with the same arrogant superiority as the guy in the Armani suit who tried to pay for his espresso with a 500 Euro note. All of Italian life was represented here, and it all paraded past my little table like models on a Paris catwalk.

I managed to sit quietly and study the local wildlife for a good thirty minutes before my travelling genes started clamouring for a change of scenery, so after another stroll along the marina to wish Drew and Jan good luck I headed back towards the marina entrance.

Running along the back of the VIP area was the concrete-and-boulder finger that made up the harbour's breakwater. Again, this area was fenced off and manned by more sunglass-wearing security, this time representing the local Navy cadets. A flash of my shiny new pass got me through the gate, and I found myself a nice flat rock to perch on. From here I could see the yellow buoys that made up the northern end of the circuit; the far end was hidden from view in a light haze that blurred the line between sea and sky. For a moment I thought that the course had been extended: during my run in the boat the day before it seemed like the course was no bigger than a football field. But as I watched one of the safety boats roar round the cans on a last-minute check I realised that it was merely my sense of perception letting me down.

Suddenly the PA crackled into life, and an over-excited male voice started babbling incoherently in an unrecognizable language that may have been the Queen's English or Italian in a Sicilian accent for all I knew. Because of the myriad of speakers dotted round the marina, the time-delay from one speaker to the next and the echo as the sound bounced off harbour walls and buildings the entire running commentary was nothing but an indistinguishable babbling that only served to drive a cold steel spike deep into my frontal lobes. Sadly there wasn't going to be much chance of following the race by eye; as the fleet of nine SuperSport boats lined up for a rolling start behind the Start Boat it was virtually impossible to tell who was who.

The Start Boat raised the green flag and a moment later the sound of nine race-trimmed boats putting the hammer down roared across the sea. Their massive rooster tails of spray soon disappeared towards the southern horizon, only to grow again a minute later as they thundered up the straight towards the start/finish gate, made up of two chequered buoys. Luckily for the spectators the gate was located only a few hundred yards off the shore, and we got a good look at the boats as they screamed past us and turned back out to sea to round their next mark.

To be honest though, for most of the time there was little to see. A Robinson R22 buzzed through the air, the little helicopter carrying a camera man and a photographer, and it was often the only way of figuring out where the leader was; the small craft clung on to the leader like a pilot fish following a shark. After a couple of laps I started getting bored, and not even Tiff Needell's cheery presence a few rocks over could keep me from once again setting off for a stroll.

Back inside the marina's gates I bumped into Bethan, who was playing hostess to two very excited-looking Englishmen. They were introduced to me as James and Jamie, but my memory is so ridiculously poor that I immediately managed to forget their names, and spent the rest of the time simply calling them "mate" and "pal". They were here to do a little research, both on P1 and Jan, as they were planning to produce a TV film based on Jan's torment at the hands of a stalker a few years previously. At the time the case made all the headlines because of the irresistible lure of a top Harley Street psychiatrist/powerboat racer, a deranged woman, and several bizarre twists and turns. Now it appeared that ITV were ready to turn Jan's experience into a movie.

After an hour of racing, the SuperSport boats headed back into harbour. The inaugural race of the season was won by *Conam Yachts*, who had won the SuperSport championship last year. Second place went to the Hustler boat, the exact-same one I first laid eyes on at Driver's Wharf on that miserable spring morning a couple of months before. Jan and Drew finished in third, and it was hard to tell if they were happy with that or not. I didn't feel like pressing the issue; they had the sprint race to concentrate on the next day, and they would have to find a bit more performance by then.

By that point I felt that my job was done. I had spent some time with the team, I had been out for a burn in the boat, and I had started to get some sense of what was involved in a powerboat race. I was ready to move on, but my flight didn't leave until the next day. I managed to blag an invite to an exclusive bash in one of the town's trendy bars, but by ten o'clock I had had enough of the glamorous posing, and instead I wolfed an over-priced steak at the beach-front restaurant next door and staggered back to my hotel.

At noon the next day I was once again sitting on my sandstone rock watching rooster tails in the hazy distance, but I only managed to grab a couple of laps of the Sprint race before it was time for me to head back up the Autostrada to Ancona airport.

I abandoned my nasty little Fiat in the Avis carpark, returned the keys and was just settling down with my last perfect cappuccino when I spotted the two ITV guys in the café queue. We passed the time with some idle chitchat, and had somehow gotten into a deep discussion of how to apply for the post of astronaut on the next space Shuttle mission when we were interrupted by the boarding announcement. I was only too glad to retreat to the anonymity of my seat & doze my way back to Stansted, and then Glasgow. The weekend had been mentally exhausting, not just physically (my feet would still ache from all the walking three days later) but especially mentally. My brain was burning with new information, and it would take a while to adjust to the notion of bouncing across the North sea at terrifying speed for hour after unstoppable hour. There was still so much to do: book flights, hotels and B&B's, get protective clothing organised, find another boat to take me for the three legs I wouldn't be with the *Silverline* team, and get into some semblance of physical shape— and it all had to be done within five frighteningly short weeks...

Top– *Buzzi Bullet*

Below– Jan Falkowski, Derek Wynans, Drew Langdon.

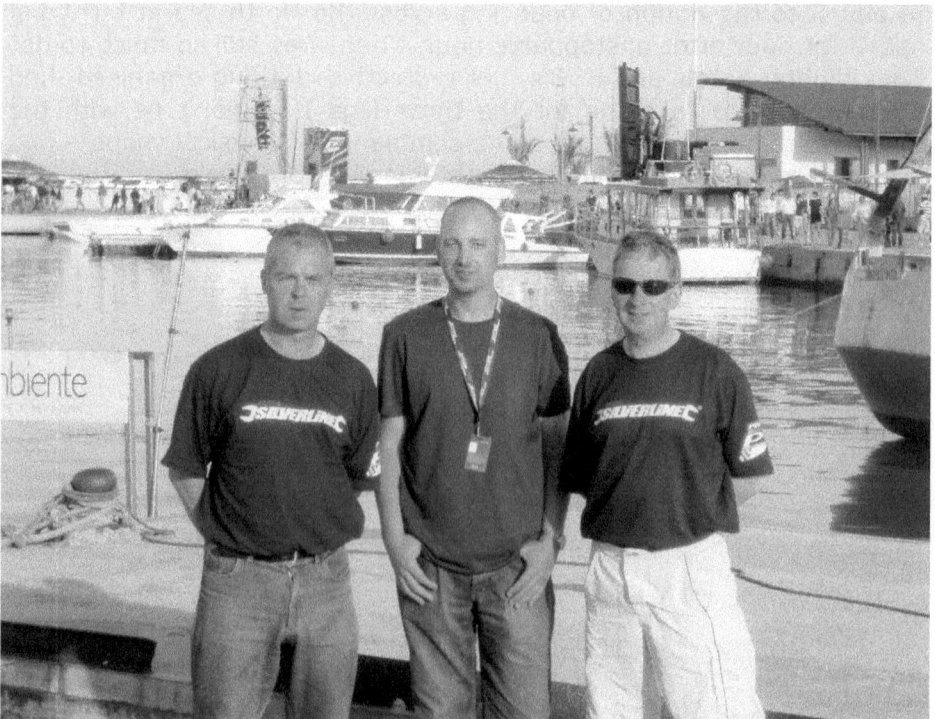

3.
Scrutineering.

Thursday 19th June.

After another manic race to the airport, followed by another spirit-crushing flight and a truly miserable train ride I found myself in the heart of Portsmouth, the starting and finishing point for "the Everest of offshore powerboat races" as it had been labelled. Sadly it soon became apparent that not everybody was as excited about the event as I was. In fact, almost nobody had even heard about it.

Any half-bright traveller will tell you that whenever you find yourself in a new city, the best way to find out what's going on is to ask a taxi driver. They spend their entire working lives ferrying people to and from all sorts of interesting places, and soon find out— either through conversation or plain old eavesdropping— more priceless information than any "What's on" guide. Any nuggets of wisdom they extract from their fares are quickly spread round the rest of the drivers at the next taxi rank. Think of them, if you will, like busy little honey bees, zooming around hither and yon, gathering the pollen of Knowledge before occasionally returning to their hive to spread the news to their comrades (but probably without performing the funky little dance).

So I was more than a little surprised to hear from my cabbie that he had heard absolutely nothing at all about the race. Initially I assumed that the man was some sort of a hermit— after all, my head had been filled with nothing but racing for the last four weeks— however he was adamant that there had been no publicity at all, and proved it by calling his mates on the radio and asking if they knew anything about "some boat race".

When half a dozen drivers replied that they had seen or heard nothing, I became a little concerned. It was now June 19th, and in two days time 47 of Europe's finest racers would be roaring westwards en masse in a thundering cloud of spray and smoke. Mike Lloyd, the Race Organiser, had not seemed the quiet, retiring type when I first met him at the Driver's Briefing a few months ago. So what had happened to all the publicity?

Whilst they had found several smaller backers, the Organisers had failed to secure the vital main sponsor. Without a Big Name pushing for all the publicity it could get, the best the Organisers could hope for was plenty of interest from the local media. And in a city like Portsmouth, where there is some sort of waterborne event virtually every week during the summer, Mike and his team would struggle to make their event stand out amongst the blizzard of other races, regattas and rallies.

The very first Round Britain Powerboat Race was held in 1969, and the joint sponsors, the Daily Telegraph and BP, undoubtedly did well out of the gig. The next one, held in 1984, was backed by Everest, the double-glazing firm. The balance of benefit v. cost was not so apparent this time, as the race failed to muster much interest, either with the public in general or the country's boating fraternity. Where 50 teams had entered the first race, only 29 made the start line for the second.

Investing in a race like this is fraught with financial dangers: one moment your name is linked to exotic ideals like Glamour and high-speed Heroism, and the next you find yourself humiliated and thousands of pounds out of pocket when one or more legs are cancelled due to bad weather. Or, worse case scenario, one of the boats sinks, taking its crew down with it. The media would be all over that story like a rash, and the papers and TV news reports will all show pictures of the doomed boat; a boat plastered with stickers of your business's logo. The Six O'clock News will mention your company, and in the same sentence they will use words like "drowned" and "tragedy" and "disaster". Those are not words the Marketing Department like to deal with, but it's a very real possibility in an event such as this.

So, without a heavyweight corporation willing to lend its name and its PR Department to the race, I took it upon myself to fill the driver in on all the details as we weaved our way through the drab grey streets of Portsmouth. I dropped my bag off at my guesthouse then jumped back into the cab and made for Solent Marina, where Scrutineering was already underway.

At the entrance gates to the marina there were still no signs mentioning the race, so finding the dry pits was a matter of luck and perseverance. But finally, as my sceptical cabbie nosed the taxi towards the very far end of the impressive marina complex, I spotted the *Silverline* boat sitting on the back of its truck, and I knew we had finally found it.

The dry pits were, to be honest, more than a little disappointing. I was expecting a P1-style ring of security, with armed guards and gaggles of curious onlookers. Instead I found myself in a gravel car park surrounded by a loose fence of waist-high barriers, each placed a couple of feet apart. Inside this lowest of low-security fencing were no more than four or five boats, sitting on their trailers, each one with two or three pick-up trucks or vans in attendance. There wasn't an armed security guard or paparazzi in sight.

To be fair, it was only around two-ish on Thursday afternoon, and the rest of the teams had until around five the next day to complete Scrutineering. Also, the fleet was split in half because there were two different locations where Scrutineering was to be carried out: here, at Solent Marina, and four miles further down the coast, at Gunwharf

Quays. It was at the latter that the entire fleet would finally assemble on Friday night, in preparation for the race start on Saturday morning.

I wandered over into the shadow of *Buzzi Bullet* for a chat with Drew, Jan and John Christensen, the Cummins engineer I had met at the P1 race in Italy. They were in fine fettle and, true to form, quietly confident. Although the boat was fundamentally ready to go, there was still the small matter of stowing all the safety equipment.

Safety was paramount to the Race Organisers, and the list of rules and regulations ran to seven sheets of A4. Since several legs would see the fleet many miles from land, it was imperative that each boat was fully loaded with all sorts of safety gear: towing lines, fenders, an assortment of flares, VHF radio, EPIRB, First Aid kit, thermal blankets, life raft, a sea anchor and a regular anchor with at least 50 metres of line, a powerful searchlight, a retirement flag and a fog horn.

Jan had laid all this out on the ground for the Scrutineers to check over, and as my eye casually scanned the mountain of gear I came across a blackened canister. Jan saw me staring at the charred artefact and picked it up with a smile. "What's the matter?" he asked me. "Haven't you ever seen a fog horn before?"

"Well, yes," I replied, "but never one in such a crappy condition. What happened?"

"Oh, nothing really. This was lying next to a pack of flares that suddenly decided to ignite. We were in the middle of a race at the time; we lost first place because we had to stop to put the fire out. There was orange smoke everywhere!" He thumbed the molten plastic blob that used to be the trigger, and the fog horn gave out a healthy PAAARRRPP!!! that freaked out half a dozen mechanics and made me leap a good five feet in the air. "See?" he laughed. "Still works a treat!"

Just the mandatory equipment by itself was quite a lot of gear to try to stow into a race boat; it was a challenge akin to loading your weekly shopping into a Formula 1 car. But it didn't stop there. They had chosen to add some more stuff to the growing pile on the ground. There was a toolbox, a couple of boxes of energy bars for emergency rations, a dozen bottles of water, a second First Aid box complete with suturing equipment (which I hoped never to see used in anger), and, oddly, a diver's mask and snorkel. I had to ask.

"If we get a rope round a propeller," explained Jan, "there's no way in hell we'll ever get it off from in the boat. So I'll have to jump in and untangle it." A dangerous thing to do, since he would be floating in the icy sea hanging off the props, their five blades razor-sharp and undoubtedly rocking violently as the boat lay dead in the water. In rough seas the stern of the boat would be rising and falling six or eight feet, and on the downward movement the weight of the engines would force the stern down like a pile-hammer. Hopefully not on top of Jan's head. But it got worse.

Lying next to the mask and snorkel, sparkling in the weak afternoon sun like a pair of madman's blender blades, were two spare propellers. Why, I asked naively, were they carrying two of these heavy buggers?

On performance boats with twin engines, it's standard practice to have the propellers turning in opposite directions, Jan explained. Therefore, each prop is "handed"; a prop that turns clockwise on an anti-clockwise shaft is even less use than tits on a boar, and so they had to carry a spare for each.

The biggest headache, however, was not the idea of trying to safely store fifty pounds of razor-edged props within the narrow confines of *Buzzi Bullet*'s hull, but the prospect of having to change one of those heavy buggers out at sea. If clearing a rope in rough seas was dangerous, then changing a five-bladed propeller in the same conditions would be bordering on the suicidal.

To make matters worse, the spares were pitched differently to the main props. The set that were fitted to the boat were perfect for mild to moderate seas, and the spares were pitched to suit much rougher weather. And whilst it was nice to be able to match the props to the anticipated weather conditions, it also had a serious drawback— the boat would handle like a dog if it was fitted with one of each. This meant that if, for example, one of the "smooth water" props was damaged, Jan would have to change it *and* the other one so that the boat would once again have matching props. This would double Jan's workload, and double the possibility of having his skull crushed by the wildly-bucking sterngear. Changing the props was a potentially life-threatening job, and they would only decide to do it if it was absolutely essential— but Jan was prepared to go over the side if necessary.

Built into the sides of the lorry's flatbed were an assortment of lockers holding tools, ropes, and other bits of equipment. Every now and again a muffled voice from deep within the bowels of the boat would shout down for something, and Drew or Jan would fish the requested bit of kit out of one of the lockers and climb the ladder leaning up against the boat's hull to hand it to the unseen shouter.

At one point I found myself closest to the ladder, and after another yell for a spanner Drew asked me to climb up and deliver it. "Introduce yourself to Ian," he told me. "He's fitting some straps that should work as seats. Could you see if he needs a hand?"

I said Sure and clambered up the ladder onto the deck of the boat. From the dark depths of the cockpit came muffled swearing, vicious expletives in a West Country accent. I stuck my head down and asked if that was Ian. A bald head, red from exertion, popped up into the watery sunlight. I handed him the spanner he'd shouted for and introduced myself, and he struggled to extricate one arm in order to shake my hand.

He was rigging up rudimentary seats consisting of 2" webbing straps. I tried out one "seat" he'd just rigged, and found it surprisingly comfortable. The idea, he told me, was that it would offer support, but it wasn't intended to take a person's full weight. That was just as well; travelling across rough water at over 80 mph sitting in some sort of swinging sling was never going to be a good idea. The chance to take the weight off tortured legs from time to time was the best anyone could hope for, and would be a welcome reprieve from the constant pounding the crew could expect.

I helped him to mount the last sling-seat, and we scrabbled back down the ladder to let the blood flow back to Ian's legs. Just then a fresh-faced youngster in his late teens wandered over. Ian introduced me to Josh, his son. Josh would be joining his dad on their own gruelling race, driving the lorry with all the spares and tools from port to port.

The public face of any motorsport is always the driver, either spraying champagne from the top spot on the podium or crawling painfully out of the wreckage of his last mistake. Either way, these are the guys who get all the kudos, respect and admiration for doing their thing. Rarely, however, does the public eye linger on the faces of those who have worked countless hours, days or even weeks before a race to make sure that the hero's ride is performing to its absolute best. Often, while the driver is tucked up in a warm, comfortable bed (or out on the town, wining and dining) the crews are still up to their elbows in oil and bolts, living off cold chips and coffee the consistency of mud.

Conditions are tough enough for the crews during a single race, but with the Round Britain they faced an almost impossible task. Every single race day they would have to make sure that the boat performed perfectly prior to the start. Then they would have to hang around for half an hour or so once the race was underway, in case the boat had to return to port for any reason. Once it looked like everything was going well, they would have to pack up their stuff and sprint for the next destination, hopefully beating the boat there so that everything was ready and waiting for them when they crossed the line. And whilst the racing crew were getting showered and changed, had a nice meal and a couple of drinks with the rest of the heroes in the hotel bar, the shore team would be swarming all over the boat: servicing engines, checking props and shafts, adjusting belts, and generally going over every inch of their charge to make sure it was ready to race the next morning, when they would have to do it all over again. They could expect to live off three hours sleep a night for the next 10 days, their waking hours spent under immense pressure, secure in the knowledge that at the end of it all, if all their hard work had finally been proved worthwhile and theirs was announced as the winning boat, they still wouldn't get their pictures in the paper.

Wandering around the dry pits, I cast my unskilled eye over some of the other competitors. Cowering in the shadow of the *Silverline* boat was the white Ocke-Mannerfelt B28 "bat-boat" of Team *Jersey*, resembling some sort of futuristic child's toy, complete with two 200 horsepower jet-black Mercury XR2 outboards strapped to the stern. At 28 foot long, the B28 was just over half the length of the *Silverline* boat, and where there was space for four in the bigger boat, in the smaller the driver and navigator had to sit one behind the other, in tandem-fashion.

There were two or three RIBs also there, sitting on their bespoke trailers, but it wasn't the boats that caught my eye. Clustered around them were cars and vans, all loaded to the roof with tools, spare parts, foul-weather clothing and overstuffed hold-alls— the entire assortment of paraphernalia needed to keep boats and crewmembers going for the next 1400 miles. I was lucky— I had only packed enough gear to get me to Oban, where I would swing by my house and dump all my dirty clothes on the floor and fill up my hold-all with fresh stuff. For the teams, however, most would have to pack everything they might possibly need for the next ten days or so.

As I shouldered my way through non-existent crowds of onlookers and TV film crews, I realised I hadn't yet signed in with Race Control. They had commandeered a small office down by the pontoons, so I set off to announce myself and go through the relentless paperwork.

I was met by two women seated behind a desk, one in her late thirties with hair dyed an unnatural shade of orange-red, the other slightly older, with a kindly librarian look about her. I introduced myself and dropped my laminated RYA license on the desk with a flourish while the red-head flipped through a stack of folders. Eventually she pulled the one marked "*Silverline*/471". She made a note of my license number in the folder then asked if I'd submitted a Next of Kin form. I told her I had, and that I'd posted it several weeks previously. This resulted in burrowing through another fat folder marked "Next of Kin", her lips silently moving as she searched for my surname.

She whipped a sheet out with a flourish and studied it for a moment before uttering a jubilant "Aha! I thought I recognised your name; you're the one with the odd sense of humour!" She turned to her colleague and smiled. "Watch this one Mary. He's going to be trouble."

I was a little dumbfounded by this unwarranted comment until I turned my attention to my form. Where it asked for details of my next of kin, I had written "my Beloved wife". (To be honest, I had initially put simply "my Beloved", but I was worried they might not understand to whom I was referring so I had grudgingly added "wife".) I shrugged— there wasn't much else I *could* do— and signed my name at the bottom. I then signed a disclaimer of some sort, stating that I was fully aware that powerboat racing was a potentially life-threatening undertaking and handed the papers back to the sniggering red/orange-haired woman.

She asked me to hold out my arm, and for a moment I thought I was going to have to undertake some sort of random blood test, no doubt to screen me for performance-enhancing drugs of some sort. My mind raced— was I clean? How long did TCH stay in the system? A day? A week? But instead of drawing blood she merely attached a plastic bracelet round my wrist. It was of the sort that adorned patients in hospitals, and it displayed my name and the number 471— Team *Silverline*'s number. This, she told me with an innocent smile, would help to identify me when I washed up on some secluded beach.

"Ah. Right. Erm, the thing is, I won't be racing with *Silverline* on every leg. I'm also joining *Ocean Pirate* for a couple of stages. Is that a problem?" I asked.

The two women exchanged looks, as if to say "I told you he'd be trouble." "OK," said the red-head. "Who are you racing with on the first leg?" I told her it would be *Silverline*. "In that case, don't worry. You have to sign in every morning before each day's race anyway, so let us know who you'll be with on that morning, and we'll issue you with a new bracelet. All right?"

Relieved, I nodded and thanked them for their help.

As I reached the door I turned round. "I almost forgot. Have you got a Press pass for me?"

The two women looked at each other and laughed. "Don't you worry about that Derek. I'm pretty sure we'll remember you!" I'm still not sure if that was meant as an insult or a simple statement of fact.

That was to be the first of many encounters with Gill Purcell and Mary Downey, and over the next couple of weeks barely a day would go by without me causing them some sort of headache...

...but so far things were going well. Although I wasn't going to be able to join Drew for every stage, I *had* managed to find a spot for the rest of the legs on board *Ocean Pirate*, a 40 foot cabin cruiser in the Historical Class with a fine pedigree. She would make a fine subject for the "Contrast & Compare" piece I planned to write for the magazine, I thought. The clichés and metaphors were all to hand— tortoise and the hare, chalk and cheese, David and Goliath... with the added benefit that *Ocean Pirate* had all the luxuries of home— bunks, galley, a head, not to mention the blissful luxury of a fully enclosed wheelhouse. I was looking forward to spending a couple of legs sitting at the table with a nice hot mug of tea, writing up my notes as *Ocean Pirate* transported me effortlessly across the finishing line...

After Drew had told me he would be forsaking me for John Christensen the Cummins mechanic on some of the more exposed legs Hugo, my Editor at MB&Y, had been frantically chasing round to find me another seat. With only a week or so to go before the race he had put me in touch with Mike Barlow, owner of *Ocean Pirate*.

Mike assured me he would be happy for me to join his crew, but he warned that it would be unlikely that they would be in the vanguard. Instead, this would be a gentle stroll down Memory Lane for *Ocean Pirate*; a chance for her to retrace the route she had taken way back in 1969, during the inaugural Round Britain Powerboat Race. Built the previous year, this aluminium-hulled cruiser was given odds by those who know about these things of 7-1, and she did well, finishing in seventh place overall. But that was then and this is now, as they say, and even with a pair of new Cummins QSB 380s and a total refit she was still barely capable of breaking the 30 knot minimum required to enter the race.

I made my way back to the dry pits, collar up against the cold wind that whistled round the buildings and rattled the halyards of yachts tied up to the pontoons. When I got there I was called over by Drew, who introduced me to the man who would be at the helm of *Buzzi Bullet*.

Miles Jennings gets a lot of stick, both in the media and from his contemporaries in the racing world, for his looks and lifestyle. He often gets tagged with the term "playboy", thanks to his long hair which may or may not be bleached and his preference for ostentatious Italian supercars. Maybe that's an unfair assessment; I'm not qualified to be the judge of that, I barely know the man. But it struck me as slightly odd to single one person out in a world that, at first glance, is teeming with wealthy individuals who partake in a very expensive hobby that is both glamorous and dangerous. On closer inspection, however, this sport is made up primarily of middle-aged businessmen with wives and children. They are, for the most part, sensible adults who have their heads screwed on very firmly indeed, and since they spend much of their working lives wearing fine Saville Row suits the idea of cultivating shoulder-length hair and roaring around in impractical Lamborghinis seems, well, rock star-esque.

Miles didn't appear stoned, nor did he offer me a line of coke— instead he shook my hand with a friendly smile and politely asked how I was. So much for the alleged playboy antics, I thought. Pity. Mind you, I don't suppose people who show up for work off their tits and grinding their teeth until their gums bleed are likely to win many P1 World Championships. Nor are they the type of person to make their fortune selling tiles, both of which Miles has achieved, despite being only ten or so years older than me. Perhaps if I had taken the other road, I too might now be zipping around in my private helicopter, trying to decide which house to use next weekend. But no! Such self-analysis never leads to anywhere good. It's always better to blame one's shortcomings on Karma and Fate, rather than have to face the possibility that maybe, just maybe, we are all responsible for our own destinies.

Our friendly chat was rudely interrupted by a caravan of trucks and vans that suddenly rolled into the dry pits. At its head was a flatbed truck bearing a massive boat in red. Behind it, a second lorry bore an immaculate blue powerboat. The Buzzi circus had just rolled into town.

Of the 47 boats entered, no less than six of them were designed and built by the illustrious Fabio Buzzi. And the red monster that now dominated this quiet little corner of the car park was none other than the former *Cesa 1882*, possibly his most famous creation. Now renamed *Red FPT* in honour of her newest sponsors, Fiat Powertrain Technologies, this machine was to powerboat racing what the Audi Quattro was to rallying or Red Rum to horse racing. Even with her new name and her distinctive massive "wing" missing (it was strapped to the deck during transportation; once mounted in its proper place above the cockpit it would jut out over a foot past the gunwales) she was instantly recognisable.

This boat was legendary, but her birth was a difficult one. Designed and built in 1985 by Fabio Buzzi, a god in the powerboating community, she initially failed to live up to expectations for being too heavy and underpowered. After several rebuilds, numerous engine and gearbox transplants, a respray and no less than three name changes she finally delivered: in 1988 she cleaned up, winning more trophies than any other boat on the planet— seventeen consecutive podiums, fourteen of which were Firsts. She was the Italian, European and World Champion, as well as beating the Americans in their "own back yard" as they say, winning the historic Miami-Nassau-Miami offshore race that year.

However, just as in any other motorsport, powerboats are continually evolving, and unless an owner is willing to constantly improve and update his boat he will soon find himself at the back of the pack. This is exactly what happened to *Cesa*, and she sadly slipped out of the limelight and into disrepair. She might have joined the fate of dozens of other once-legendary powerboats and disappeared forever, if it wasn't for a certain Drew Langdon.

Drew was in the States, looking for a suitable project when he came across a very neglected *Cesa* in the corner of a boat yard in Florida. Excited at his find, he bought her and had her shipped back to the UK, but it soon became apparent that he had bitten off more than he could chew. He dropped Fabio a line to see if he would be interested in taking *Cesa* on, and soon a deal had been struck.

Fabio shipped his beloved *Cesa* back to his Italian factory and set about lavishing the care and attention on this once-great boat that she deserved. She had to be strengthened in order to support her new engines— not two but *four* FPT engines producing an astronomical 2,400 horsepower through two gearboxes. It was reckoned that even with one engine out of commission she was still capable of around 80 knots, and an overall top speed of over 100 knots, helped by that massive aerofoil that was designed to physically lift the hull out of the water. A respray and a smattering of stickers finished the rebuild, and *Red FPT* was born.

I really should explain who this Buzzi fellow is. Fabio Buzzi is unarguably one of the giants of offshore powerboat racing. Born in Italy in 1943, he first started racing in 1960. In 1978 he won the Italian and European Class 3 offshore championships, and a year later he set a new world record for diesel-engined boats, clocking an impressive 119 miles per hour. His faith in diesel over petrol power saw him become one of the designers of the Seatek engine, a marine power plant much vaunted for its reliability and performance.

In 1971 he established FB Design, a company at the forefront of designing and building high performance power boats— much like a modern-day version of Southampton's Scott-Paine. But where Scott-Paine set up shop on the shores of the Solent, Fabio elected to locate his factory just outside Lecco in northern Italy. Lecco might be over 120 miles from the sea, but right on its doorstep is Lake Como, one of the most stunning test tracks in the world.

Fabio's creations have won the hugely prestigious Harmsworth Trophy four times, won fifty-two World Championships in various Classes, and set an astounding fifty-six World speed records. Fabio himself is no slouch behind the wheel, and currently has ten World Championships to his name. And now, at the venerable age of 65, he was going to take the helm of his most famous creation to race in the Round Britain.

The second boat that rolled into the pits was named *Blue FPT*, so named because— well, she was blue, and was the second of the Fiat Powertrain Technologies boats entered. Another Buzzi design, *Blue FPT* was very much an unknown quantity. Little was known about the boat, apart from her three engines that put out a combined 1,440 horsepower. Her crew consisted of three anonymous Greeks and one Englishman— Dag Pike. At 75, Dag was the oldest competitor in the race. But he was also one of the most experienced navigators, and had been one of Buzzi's crew when he won the last Round Britain race in 1984.

I didn't get much time to admire either of the two boats, however, as Bethan suddenly reminded us that we had to attend the Driver's Briefing across town. There was much scurrying and fretting about cars when we were approached by an elderly gentleman with a thick Italian accent. He had plenty of spare seats in his van, he told us, but he didn't know how to find his way to the Royal Naval Club and Royal Albert Yacht Club, where the briefing was due to take place. Perhaps if one of us would drive...?

Drew thanked Fabio and hopped into the driver's seat, whilst Jan and I joined Antonio Binda, Fabio's co-driver, in the back. Fabio himself naturally rode up front with Drew, and the two men chatted idly about this and that as we weaved our way through the rush-hour traffic. Between Binda's feet stood a dark wooden box, about a foot square. Trying to make polite conversation with the Italian I tapped it with my foot. "What's in there?" I asked. "Someone's ashes?"

Binda just looked at me like I was some sort of babbling ape, but Fabio had overheard and he turned in his seat to address me. "You'll find out soon my friend. Just be patient..." And with an enigmatic smile he faced forward again.

As a Professional I should, of course, have taken the opportunity to grill the great man while we were trapped in a van in the middle of Portsmouth, but to be perfectly honest I wasn't sure how to go about it. For a start, he and Drew were talking amongst themselves and I was loathe to interrupt— especially since I was very much a stranger and a guest. And secondly, I was quite unprepared for this unusual turn of events. It was like being offered a lift by Formula 1 legend Jackie Stewart, and I was very much taken aback.

Half an hour later we reached the imposing Royal Naval and Royal Albert Yacht Club on Pembroke Road. Across the Governor's Green stood the Royal Garrison church, looking oddly isolated in the large expanse of well-manicured grass, and behind it the Solent, shimmering in the late afternoon sun. The wind had dropped, and it was pleasantly warm there on the quiet street lined with imposing Georgian buildings. But there was no time to enjoy it; the Briefing was due to begin any minute so we hustled our way through the large double doors.

I would have loved to have lingered in the lobby a while as well, as the walls were covered in beautiful photos and paintings of all manner of boats, past and present. But I was anxious not to lose Drew and the others in the busy swirl of bodies that were slowly funnelling down a corridor, so I made another one of my mental shrugs and fought not to lose sight of my compadres.

We found ourselves in a large, elegant room filled with rows of padded chairs. Most of them were taken, but we spotted a row that was yet to be filled and we jostled our way over and took our seats.

Once again Mike Lloyd took centre stage, armed with his trusty microphone and overhead projector. As he urged the crowd to settle down I craned my neck around to cast my eye over the room. Once again it was standing room only, with well over 100 people filling the room to capacity.

After the usual welcome speech, Mike began by telling us exactly what we would be racing for. There would be no cash prizes on offer; teams would be racing for something much more permanent— their names on historic trophies.

For the overall winning team, there would be not one but two prestigious trophies to be had— the Beaverbrook Trophy and the Round Britain Trophy. The Beaverbrook Trophy is awarded to winners of various races, including the classic Cowes-Torquay-Cowes race amongst others, and is hugely coveted.

The Round Britain Trophy was established for (unsurprisingly) the winner of the first ever Round Britain race in 1969, when it was won by Timo Makinen, the famous Finnish rally driver. When Fabio took to the stage with his mysterious wooden box tucked under his arm, I slowly began to see the significance. The second time the race was held, back in 1984, it was Fabio who took the trophy home to Lake Como, and now, twenty-four years later, he faced the possibility of losing it to one of 46 challengers. He reverently opened the box to show the room the trophy they might be going home with in less than two weeks' time— then pointed out that he had become quite attached to it, and wasn't about to let it go without a fight.

Fabio was also on hand to announce another award to aim for. Fiat Powertrain Technologies were offering a trophy and a special edition Fiat 500 for the boat that showed the best improvement between the four legs running up the west coast and the four eastern legs. This, he told us, was to encourage developments in design for the future, but personally I struggled to see how much development could take place in the space of just a few days.

There was also the Duke of York International Trophy up for grabs. Another historical bit of tin, this would be awarded to the first British team home. Of the 47 teams taking part, thirty were eligible, and many fancied their chances, eagerly imagining their names engraved alongside other powerboating greats like Seebold, Spalding and the notorious "Joe" Carstairs.

Mike then got on to the serious business of the briefing proper, outlining the agenda for the next two days. Tomorrow (Friday), would be more Scrutineering, launching and checking paperwork with all the boats rounding up the day by assembling at Gunwharf Quays, in the shadow of the impressive Spinnaker Tower. Then, in the evening, a select few would be invited to a little evening soiree in the presence of Royalty— Princess Anne, the President of the Royal Yachting Association. My invite obviously got mislaid by a careless Post Office employee... At 8am on Saturday there would be yet another Driver's Briefing, and then we would all head out to the muster area, prior to the off.

But to be honest, I wasn't really paying attention. I was tired, hungry, and more than a little worried about how long this meeting was going to take. I had arranged to pick up some foul-weather clobber from a shop half a mile from here, but he shut at seven, and it would be tight. Fortunately the briefing wound down by about half past six, and I hurriedly excused myself to keep my appointment.

My experience with boats had always involved getting cold, wet and dirty, and so my garb of choice was usually a floatation suit— basically a waterproof well-padded boiler suit, stolen from a film set on an island in the Outer Hebrides (a long story). For this event, however, I had been advised by Jan that nothing less than a pukka dry-suit would be in order, and so my handlers at *MotorBoat & Yachting* magazine had got in touch with the people at Crewsaver to blag one of theirs under the guise of "an in-depth test". Despite endless promises, however, the promised package never made arrived, so the day before I flew down I had taken matters into my own hands and phoned the manager of the Gul shop at Gunwharf Quays. He promised that he would put a drysuit to one side for me, but I would have to pay for it. The magazine agreed to reimburse me, so all was right in the world. Except I suspected that this Plan B would also go tits-up, which is why I wanted to keep the next day free— I felt sure that even this simple arrangement go sideways on me...

I made it to the Gul store just fifteen minutes before it was due to shut. The manager, a laid-back and friendly sort by the name of Luke Davison, went into the storeroom to pick up my drysuit whilst I hit the shelves, grabbing gloves, sunglasses and a thermal base layer. Five minutes later he came out, shaking his head. The drysuit was gone. After swearing continually for five minutes without repeating myself (and emptying his shop of customers in record time) I took off my coat and rolled up my sleeves. The two of us waded through his storeroom, pulling out every single drysuit and double-checking the sizes. By the time we were done the storeroom was completely empty, and the shop floor was buried under fifty-odd drysuits, wet-suits and other miscellaneous clothing— but nothing was going to fit. Unless...

Luke fidgeted awkwardly. There was one other option, he said, avoiding my angry stare. He did have a drysuit in large, except, well, it was a woman's drysuit. By this time I was in no mood for standing on gender protocols, so I told him to find it. When he finally recovered it from one of the mounds on the floor, I was pleasantly surprised. Apart from having the word "Gul" picked out in pink and a little pink piping on the arms, it looked perfectly masculine. I tried it on, and while it wasn't the roomiest drysuit I'd ever worn, at least I could bend my arms and legs in it. It was a result.

We then spent another ten minutes looking for a waterproof drybag to keep my shore clothes in, and then another five haggling over the final price. As I walked out of the shop I heard Luke lock the door behind me. It was half past seven, half an hour after his closing time, plus he still had to tidy the gargantuan mess I left behind. The place looked like it had been ransacked by rabid baboons, and I'd knocked him down by 25% to boot. I felt guilty right up to my first beer of the day, three minutes later.

Friday 20th June.

By ten the next morning I was back at Port Solent marina, now badly impatient to get going. The dry pits had filled with more boats, trailers and vans, and it soon became apparent that the lack of security was causing a major problem— it appeared that those bloody Vikings were up to their old shenanigans again, and they had invaded the area en masse. Now calling themselves Norwegians, they had caught up with the 21st Century with a vengeance and had forsaken their traditional wooden longships. This time they came armed with RIBs; three of them in fact. Goldfish produce outstandingly quick and well-built boats, ranging from 22 to 36 feet in length. They had decided to enter a pair of identical 36-foot RIBs in the race as a chance to test their latest developments; essentially, they were treating the event as a massive test drive. They were joined by a private entry in a 29-foot Goldfish, who would be strongly supported by the factory team— after all, it would look bad for the company if they left one of their customers in the lurch.

There wasn't much for me to do, so I wandered around, feeling out of place and a little lost. Around midday I had a visitor— Rob Peake, the news editor at the magazine. We'd never actually met, and it was good to shake the hand of the man who I'd be dealing with over the next ten days (Hugo had passed the mess that was me over to Rob several weeks earlier).

At the end of each leg, I was to call Rob with an account of what had happened that day. He would then try to make sense of my gib-berish and post it onto the magazine's web site as a daily blog. This made me deeply uncomfortable. When it comes to speaking, I have never been particularly sharp. Those that know me will confirm that I'm prone to almost Tourette-esque swearing, with some obscenity or another invariably finding its way into even the most harmless of conversations. (During one particular rant, my wife quietly calculated that one word in four was some profanity or other, to which I natu-rally replied: "Christ! That's fucking disgraceful!" without a hint of irony.)

I was sitting at an outside table at one of the marina pubs when Drew finally found me. I was onto my twentieth cup of coffee and be-ginning to feel a little jittery, so when he told me they were ready for a last-minute test drive and would I like to join him, I nearly hit the ceiling.

By now my feet were really starting to hurt. My choice of footwear— a brand new pair of Converse All-Stars— was obviously a wrong one, but my hike back to the dry pits was surprisingly painless, the adrenaline and caffeine in my system working like a state-of-the-art painkiller. I wrestled my ladies' drysuit out of my dry-bag, quietly smug that no-one had picked up on the subtle pink highlights, but just to make sure I covered it up with the Grabner racing life-vest loaned to me by Ian Brown.

We slowly motored through the marina lock and down the naviga-tional channel towards open water, Miles at the wheel. Drew was on the throttles, and in the other back seat was Jan, still punching way-points into the chart plotter in front of him. Drew had installed a plot-ter for both of us, so that should one pack in they would still be able to call upon the back-up. Since I didn't know a damn thing about plotters I chose to leave mine well enough alone, and hoped that they would never have to call on me to navigate the boat.

We slowly cruised past the Portsmouth Naval base, dodging countless ferries returning from or departing for Cherbourg and Bilbao. Spinnaker Tower gleamed and sparkled in the sun, but we couldn't see into Gunwharf Quays due to the high walls. A little further on, at the narrowest point of the harbour entrance, stood the Round Tower. Opposite it on the western shore stood a messy jumble of red-bricked buildings that made up the Fort Blockhouse, built nearly six hundred years ago to protect the strategically important port from invasion. Over the years the fort has gone under numerous changes, and until ten years ago was known as HMS Dolphin, home of the UK's submarine service. It wasn't pretty, but to us it marked the end of the excruciatingly slow 10 knots speed restriction and the start of open water.

Miles opened *Bullet* up to twenty knots or so and pointed her roughly south-west in the general direction of Gilkicker Point while Jan finished plotting some waypoints to refer to during this practice run. I fussed with my lifejacket straps and made sure my helmet was comfortable before Jan gave the go-ahead over the intercom.

Miles opened the throttles and we leapt forward, the speed building relentlessly like some supercharged tsunami. That rush of fear and awe that I had first experienced in Italy a few months earlier came rushing back to me, and every cell in my body buzzed with adrenaline and pure, undiluted joy. It was blowing about a force four, and a choppy sea had developed as the wind was funnelled towards us down the Solent. *Buzzi Bullet* skipped across the tops of the waves as we roared past unsuspecting sailing yachts, our cheery waves returned with astonished stares as we powered past at over 80 miles per hour.

Buzzi Bullet was originally fitted with a bow tank, but the Powerboat P1 rules don't allow them to be used so it had been de-activated years before. But its use was allowed for the Round Britain, so everything had been reconnected and Drew set about reacquainting himself with how to use it effectively.

A bow tank is— well, it's pretty self-explanatory really; it's a large tank fitted in the bow of the boat. By pulling on one lever, Drew opened a valve which let seawater flood into the tank, and another lever would purge it. By effectively adding or removing weight from the bow, Drew could alter the boat's trim, tweaking it to keep her running as smooth and flat as possible.

We spent a good twenty minutes or so thrashing up and down the Solent, taking to the air several times as we flew off several particularly large waves, courtesy of the Cowes ferry. It seemed that the potential drawbacks of carrying so much weight were actually working in the boat's favour. A heavier boat will generally make smaller work of lumpy seas. This, coupled to the performance tweaks John Christensen had carried out, took the boat to a whole new level. Satisfied that everything was working perfectly, we turned back to Portsmouth.

Before tying up at Gunwharf Quays we nipped across the harbour to Halsar Marina to top up the fuel tanks. While we waited for someone to take the lock off the diesel pump I chatted with Miles about how he felt the boat was running.

"Oh, she's fantastic. Really smooth," he told me. "I'm not sure about the driving position though. I'm used to sitting down; this standing lark is pretty heavy going!"

"Didn't the straps Ian fitted help?" I personally had found them comfortable for quick rests, but they wouldn't be ideal for more than ten minutes at a time. Miles shook his head.

"So why didn't you fit a proper seat?" I asked.

"Because I didn't know I'd be standing. This is the first time I've ever driven the boat."

He said it very casually, but I was stunned. "Eh? This was your first time of driving this boat, with the start-" I checked my watch "— only eighteen hours away?"

"Yep. I'd never even set foot on board until this afternoon. It'll be fine though," he continued, "she's a great boat. Too bad about the lack of seats, but I'm sure I'll manage." And with a smile he wandered off, leaving me slightly incredulous.

A quick chat with Drew confirmed that Miles wasn't winding me up, so I dropped it and instead asked about how he felt the boat was handling.

"I'm really happy with her. Even with four bodies and all the extra gear on board she'll still go well. In the smooth I reckon she'll be good for ninety miles per hour or so." The last statement was followed with the ubiquitous "Of course, I hope it won't be smooth— we run much faster in rough seas."

Now, I've noticed that it doesn't matter who you talk to, or what kind of boat they have: they all claim to prefer rough water. They'll all tell you that when the going gets tough, theirs is the boat that gets going. It's invariably because their hull is better suited to tumultuous seas, or because the crew underwent some punishing training regime to "toughen them up", but it always comes back to that one slightly puzzling claim. Over the coming days I would lose count of how many teams would utter this mantra, which was used as an excuse for a poor result on a leg— "Yeah, if only it was a little rougher we would have won that stage"— but when the conditions *did* worsen they would use the confused sea state as an excuse: "We couldn't really open the taps fully because we were taking such a beating out there."

When we finally made it across to Gunwharf Quays we tied up alongside *Going Lean*, the 38 foot Sunseeker of Dean Gibbs. Dean was a bit of an oddity for the Round Britain. Eighteen months previously he had heard about the race, and being a keen motorsport fan (but having never raced a boat in his life) he decided to support the event by becoming a member. However a few weeks later he was stunned to receive a race number in the post— due to a clerical cock-up he had become an entrant! While any sane, rational human being would get on the phone sharpish to rectify the error, Dean decided instead to take up the challenge. It was a brave decision, but with the help of Neil Holmes, a nationally-renowned powerboat instructor and Shelley Jory, one of the very few women to take part in power-boat racing, he would have just as much chance of winning as any-one else.

I had just managed to extricate myself from my sweaty drysuit and was eagerly eyeing up the numerous bars that overlooked the quay when Drew decided to hit me with another one of his patented sur-prise announcements.

"Ah, Derek. Could I have a word?" My heart sank. I had learnt the hard way to fear his little "words". "Did you say you had managed to get a seat with another team for the legs we can't take you?" I told him Yes, *Ocean Pirate* had offered me a spot. "That's good. I'd hate to see you stuck." He faltered for a moment, then went on. "The thing is, well, since it's our first leg tomorrow I think I'd feel happier having John Christensen along, just in case. Do you think the boys on *Ocean Pirate* might let you join them on tomorrow's leg as well?"

Jesus Christ! I thought, stunned. Twelve hours before the start and he's kicking me off the fucking boat?!

"Jesus Drew! I don't know. I'll need to call him. It's cutting it a bit fine though mate!"

Drew squirmed, clearly unhappy about dropping me in the crap. "Well look, if it's a problem I'm sure you can ride on the truck with Ian and Josh," he offered. "It'll be a bit of a squeeze, but I'm sure the boys won't mind. At least you'll get to Plymouth. I don't want to see you stuck, but..." he trailed off, his palms raised upwards.

"OK, well, let me call Mike Barlow and see what he says. If he says no I'll have to take you up on the lift in the lorry."

Drew stumbled his apologies and walked off, leaving me to my rac-ing thoughts.

Although *Ocean Pirate* was tied up at Gunwharf Quay, there didn't seem to be any sign of life on board so I dragged my gear up the pontoon steps and appropriated an outside table at one of the pubs. After several Morgan's Spiced and Coke (purely for the shock) I gave Mike a call.

After explaining what had happened I was hugely relieved to hear him say I was more than welcome to join him and his crew. "But there is a price of course", he added ominously. I told him to name it, and it would be his. "I'll need a bottle of fine malt whiskey and a bot-tle of Sapphire Gin. It's vital to keep the crew's morale up you know!"

I knew the price was cheap, and agreed immediately. After arrang-ing to meet up at the Driver's Briefing the next morning I hung up, left a message on Rob's phone letting him know the change of plan, and threw back the rest of my drink.

On my way to the taxi rank I spotted a little shop selling all sorts of practical oddities. I was relieved to see they sold black stick-on numbers and letters, and I bought two threes and a two. Then, with my feet starting to burn, I clambered into a taxi and directed him to my digs. Once safely ensconced in my room I carefully stuck the numbers 323 (*Ocean Pirate*'s race number) to the top of my lid. The rules insisted that each crewmember wore a bright orange helmet with their team numbers clearly visible from above. This was to make it easier for the Search & Rescue helicopters to spot us, should we wind up in the drink instead of safe and secure on the boat.

With this done, I decided that I hadn't yet seen the full visual effect of £600's worth of full racing gear draped on a 6-foot idiot's frame. Unfortunately the helmet seriously impaired my hearing, and I failed to notice my landlady's entrance until it was too late— she had already managed to sprint to the phone and dial two 9's before I managed to explain myself.

Below- Annie Beakhust, Richard Salaman (holding a MarineTrack unit) and Mike Lloyd

4.
Runners and Riders.

The fleet that assembled at Portsmouth was forty-seven strong, divided into eight different Classes: **RB1**, **RB2**, **RB3**, **RB4**, **MC1**, **MC2**, **Historic** and, due to Fabio Buzzi's controversial entry, **Classic**. The Classes were based on the boat's length and engine size, with the exception of the Historic and Classic Classes, which I'll explain a little later.

The **RB1** Class represented the big hitters: the boats had to measure between 40 and 50 feet, weigh at least four and a half tons (five for diesel-powered craft), with engines no bigger than a total of 23 litres. As it happened, there were only two teams that qualified, and both of them were Buzzi-designed RIBs— *Venturer*, a 40 foot RIB driven by Andy Macateer, and Wettpunkt.com, a monstrous creation in green and white, run by an Austrian millionaire by the name of Hannes Bohinc and navigated by Ed Williams-Hawkes, a well-known character easily recognised by his eye patch.

The **RB2** Class included the likes of Team *Silverline*, Team *Bandit* (with one of the ugliest yet menacing RIBs I'd ever seen) and *Round Britain Challenger*, Team *Blastoff*'s entry— an American-built Fountain running a pair of V8 petrols that sounded truly awe-inspiring. *Garmin Racing* was supposed to offer a sprinkling of public-friendly celebrities in the form of Nick Knowles and James May (of Top Gear fame), which would hopefully raise the event's profile. Boats had to measure at least 33 feet, with total engine capacity no more than 17 litres if they were diesel, or 13½ litres for petrol engines.

RB3 was one of the most popular Classes with twelve teams entered. Again, the minimum size dropped, this time to 27 feet, and permitted engine sizes was limited to 6,560cc for 2-stroke outboards or 9,000cc for 4-strokes, and for inboard engines the limits were 13 litres for petrol lumps or 11 litres for diesels. Noteworthy entrants in this Class included *Lionhead* and *Guttaboyz*, the two prototype RIBs entered by Goldfish, a Norwegian boat builder who wanted to use the race as a testing ground for their latest products and Dean Gibbs with *Going Lean*, a boat he entered because Race Organisers had sent him an entry number by mistake. Other RB3 entrants worth keeping an eye on were *Vilda*, a Swedish entry who had driven the boat across the North Sea and passed Scrutineering without a hitch, and *Hot Lemon*, crewed by father and son team Mike and Dave Deacon who regularly break Endurance records before breakfast.

RB4 boats dropped a little more in length and engine size, and was another one of the best-represented Classes. The B28 bat-boat I had admired at Port Solent marina fell into this category, racing under the name of Team *Jersey*. The only other hard boat in the RB4 Class was *swipewipes.co.uk*, a Phantom fresh out of the mould. Nick Gilley and Jon Fuller had barely managed to get the boat ready in time, literally launching her just hours before the race start. Other noteworthy competitors in this category included *Mud, Swell & Beers*, a 28 ft Picton RIB driven by Tom Summerton and Joe Leckie, who were both only 19 years old at the time. Tom's father, Roger, would be joining them as a mere passenger. Team *Pulsar* had entered two boats— *Vampire* and *Wolf*— with the former the smallest boat entered in the race at only 25 feet. But they would all have to keep a close eye on *Sealbay*, the Goldfish RIB entered as an independent by Frederik Selvaag and the affable Eirik Jaer.

The production motor cruisers fell into two Classes— MC1 and MC2. MC1 boats had to measure between 30 and 45 feet, while MC2 boats had to be within 24 and 30 feet long. The **MC1** Class held possibly the most eclectic group of boats in the fleet, including the stunning, but unknown, *Blue FPT*, otherwise known as "the other Buzzi boat". Powered by three Fiat Powertrain Technology diesel engines putting out a Goliath 1440 horsepower, she would be in direct competition with *Buro*, one of the unlikeliest entrants. *Buro* was a 42 foot Botnia Targa, a workmanlike cabin boat with sound sea-keeping abilities but of dubious relevance to a powerboat race. Another odd-looking craft in the MC1 Class was *Braveheart III*, widely considered to be "pissugly" and sneered at by the racing pros prior to the start. This was because it was a RIB built for the Mediterranean crewed by a bunch of Scottish trawlermen— hardly a winning combination.

The **MC2** crowd looked altogether more race-like by comparison, and featured Tom and Charlie Williams-Hawkes, the sons of Ed Williams-Hawkes, the eye patch-wearing navigator for *Wettpunkt.com* in *TFO*, their bargain-basement Revenger once owned by the renowned Countess of Arran back in the day.

For the older boats running for nostalgia's sake, there was the **Historic** Class. They could be anywhere from 27 to 50 feet in length, with no restrictions on engine size. To qualify, however, their hull design had to be at least twenty years old, and they had to be capable of at least thirty knots in order to stay competitive. This category was made up mostly of Faireys, an English boat manufacturer that had produced, in its day, the British equivalent of Riva that celebrities regularly placed at the top of their "must have" list. Perhaps the finest example of these was *Miss Daisy*, a restored Fairey Spearfish entered by a group of commercial pilots who called themselves Team *747*. Other entrants included *Ocean Pirate*, a 40 foot aluminium cabin cruiser that was forty years old and was to be my ride for the first leg, and her nemesis, *GEE*. This was the boat all the Historics wanted to beat. She was the same age and size as *Ocean Pirate*, and had a fine pedigree, winning the legendary Cowes-Torquay-Cowes race sev-

eral times in her halcyon years. Amongst the list of historically important boats and manufacturers, one boat stood out like a straight man
at a lesbian wedding— *Blue Marlin*. She was a 36 foot Supermarine
Swordfish, owned by a German by the name of Marcus Hendricks.
This wasn't particularly odd, but the boat was— she was almost
brand new. It turned out that although the boat was fresh from the
factory, her hull design was over twenty years old, so she was eligible for the Historic Class.

Some of the teams in the Historic Class had been up in arms a
month or so earlier when they discovered they would be racing
alongside on the most famous powerboats of all time— Cesa 1882,
now *Red FPT*. Due to her age, she was initially entered in the Historic
Class. Which seemed logical enough to me, until I compared her
specifications to the other old-timers. Until *Red FPT* joined the fray,
Blue Marlin was the most powerful boat in her Class— a respectable
880 horsepower. (By contrast, *Xanthus*— a 26-year old Fairey Huntsman— managed only 450 horsepower.) But nobody in this group of
veterans could possibly stand a chance against the simply awe-
inspiring 2,400 horsepower that *Red FPT*'s four engines were producing.

The Race Organisers clearly had a potential nightmare on their
hands with Buzzi's red monster wanting to come and play. The other
Historic teams were outraged, and yet *Red FPT* had nowhere else to
go. Her four engines totalled 26.8 litres, well above the 23 litre limit
set for the RB1 Class. Changing that Class's rules would undoubtedly
stir up more bad feelings amongst other competitors, but on the
other hand Fabio was not only bringing two major boats to the party,
he was also supplying two trophies, a car as a prize, and, most im-
portantly of all, kudos and publicity by the shed-load. Fabio was a
man the Organisers couldn't afford to lose, so in a moment of sheer
desperation (admittedly laced with a touch of genius) they came up
with the **Classic** Class, population: one— *Red FPT*.

List of Entrants.

RB1

Team/Number	Boat	Crew
Venturer/111	FB Design RIB, 40ft, 1500 hp	Andy Macateer, Nick Wilner, Andy Sutcliffe, Mark Wildey
Wettpunkt.com/81	FB Design RIB, 42ft, 1640 hp	Hannes Bohinc, Max Holzfeind, Ed Williams-Hawkes

RB2

Team/Number	Boat	Crew
Team Bandit/69	Hunton RIB, 38ft, 850 hp	Barry Deakin, Robin Reade, Graeme Youngs, Carl Hamp
Blastoff/100	Fountain, 38ft, 1000 hp	Dorian Griffith, Richard Griffith
Cinzano/558	CUV, 30ft, 1290 hp	Tim Grimshaw, Nik Keyser, Eric Smillie
Silverline/471	FB Design, 37ft, 946 hp	Drew Langdon, Jan Falkowski, Miles Jennings, John Christensen
Garmin Racing/72	Hunton, 39ft, 900 hp	Iain May, Jeff Hunton, Nick Knowles, Tony Hamilton

RB3

Team/Number	Boat	Crew
Carbon Neutral/343	Revenger RIB, 32ft, 600 hp	John Caulcutt, David Allenby
Going Lean/7	Sunseeker, 38ft, 740 hp	Dean Gibbs, Neil Holmes, Shelley Jory
Guttaboyz/33	Goldfish RIB, 36ft, 760 hp	Nick Tollefsen, Ivar Tollefsen
Hardleys/4	Revenger, 32ft, 630 hp	Tony Jenvey, Neil McGrigor
Ikon/18	Technohull RIB, 33ft, 600 hp	Konstantinos Konstantinou, Adam Younger
Hot Lemon/2	Scorpion RIB, 30ft, 630 hp	Dave Deacon, Graham Firmin, Mike Deacon
Lionhead/22	Goldfish RIB, 36ft, 760 hp	Pål Sollie, Henrik Sollie, James Sydenham
No Worries/11	Pascoe RIB, 33ft, 450 hp	Kevin Baskott, Simon Baker, David Young, Mathew Smith
Relentless/47	Revenger RIB, 29ft, 600 hp	Darren Hook, Kevin Marshall, Andy Brown
Seafarer/110	Scorpion RIB, 33ft, 600 hp	Grigoris Oikonomou, Antonis Dritsis, George Filtsos
Tequila/88	Scorpion RIB, 28ft, 450 hp	Jeremy Bennett, Tim Kary
Vilda/9	Ocke Mannerfelt RIB, 35ft, 870 hp	Mikko Oikari, Henrik Dahl, Michael Backhuvud, Titti Schultz

RB4

Team/Number	Boat	Crew
Black Gold/10	Scorpion RIB, 26ft, 300 hp	Gavin Howe, Roger Tushingham
Team Jersey/45	Ocke Mannerfelt, 28ft, 350 hp	Toby Clayson, Roy Smith, Neil Jackson
Mr Mako/96	Pascoe RIB, 29ft, 400 hp	Jamie Edwards, John Lindsay
Mud, Swell & Beers/14	Picton RIB, 28ft, 300 hp	Tom Summerton, Joe Leckie, Roger Summerton
My Pleasure II/3	Self-built RIB, 28ft, 315 hp	Gordon Compton, Brian Peedel, Dave Simpkins
Team Pulsar-Vampire/102	Ribcraft RIB, 25ft, 300 hp	Major Greg Marsden, Alex Rhodes, Captain Nigel Spencer MBE, Major David Hemming
Team Pulsar-Wolf/101	Humber RIB, 28ft, 300 hp	Justin McInerney, Derek Stanley, Paul Lewis, Guy Hayward
RIB International/144	Arctic Blue RIB, 29ft, 520 hp	Paul Lemmer, Tom Montgomery-Swan
Sealbay/77	Goldfish RIB, 29ft, 380 hp	Frederik Selvaag, Eirik Jaer
swipewipes.co.uk/43	Phantom, 31ft, 500 hp	Nick Gilley, Jon Fuller

MC1

Team/Number	Boat	Crew
Birretta/12	FB Design RIB, 33ft, 880 hp	Thomas Vandamme, Jean Pierre-Neels
Blue FPT/333	FB Design, 43ft, 1440 hp	Vassilis Pateras, Panos Tsikopoulos, Dag Pike, Lefteris Vasilou
Braveheart III/55	Scanner RIB, 33ft, 1050 hp	Bobby Cowe, Hamish Slater
Buro/15	Botnia Targa, 42ft, 700 hp	Peter Vanhauter, Louis Massant, Lieven Van Hoecke, Frank Willemkens
Mystic Dragon/6	Scorpion RIB, 30ft, 630 hp	John Puddifoot, Bob Nurse
Team Scorpion Dubois/16	Scorpion RIB, 30ft, 630 hp	Sarah Fraser, Miranda Knowles
Seahound V/80	Scorpion RIB, 30ft, 630 hp	Chris Strickland, Jim Fry, Phil Boarer

MC2

Team/Number	Boat	Crew
Fugitive/130	Shakespeare 29ft, 630 hp	Stuart Whitley, Francis Whitley
Northern Spirit/5	Flipper 29ft, 600 hp	Steve Hutchinson, Chris Adams, Terry Newton
Power Products Marine/8	Phantom 28ft, 500 hp	Martin McLaughlin, Gary Todd, Rod Hawkins
TFO/17	Revenger 25ft, 315 hp	Tom Williams-Hawkes, Charlie Williams-Hawkes

HC1

Team/Number	Boat	Crew
Blue Marlin/99	Supermarine, 38ft, 880 hp	Markus Hendricks, Nigel Davies, Jens Dietz, Mark Watkinson
GEE/185	Jim Wynn, 46ft, 760 hp	John Guille, Chris Clayton, Michael J Clark, Mark Clayton
Ocean Pirate/323	Brooke Marine, 40ft 760 hp	Mike Barlow, Bob Pennington, Tom Brissenden, Paul Carter
Swordsman/68	Fairey, 33ft, 480hp	Jonathan Townsend, Mike Neumann, Kurt Stechman
Xanthus/1	Fairey, 31ft, 450 hp	John Skuse, Kevin Martin, Chris Holmes
Team 747/747	Fairey, 30ft, 760 hp	Jonathan Napier, Andy Fielding, Mark Jealous, Cormac Lundy

CC1

Team/Number	Boat	Crew
Red FPT/177	FB Design, 44ft, 2400 hp	Fabio Buzzi, Antonio Binda, Simon Powell

Top– Gary Payne somehow manages to focus on Scrutineering duties

Below– The race fleet squeezed into Gunwharf Quays

5.
Portsmouth To Plymouth.

Saturday 21st June.

This was it. This was actually going to happen. Finally! I had only managed two hours of sleep the night before, and as I crept out of my B&B the butterflies in my stomach kicked it up a notch. My taxi dropped me off at Gunwharf Quays, and at the entrance to the Tiger Tiger bar where we would attend yet another Driver's Briefing I bumped into a very cool and calm Drew. We filed our way upstairs, where many other teams were anxiously milling around. The tension was terrific, with many nervous smiles and lots of too-loud bursts of laughter. Finally we were called to order.

Mike Lloyd again took centre stage, beginning the briefing on an ominous note. "OK people, first things first. As you know, it is a mandatory requirement that you all have a MarineTrack unit fitted to your boats." (This would enable the Organisers and general public to follow each boat in real time on the internet using GPS technology.) "Now, although MarineTrack have very kindly agreed to loan you these units, there is still a refundable deposit to be paid. I have been informed that some of you still haven't paid up, so unless their representative gets a cheque from you this morning he will be removing the units. And, since they're mandatory, if you don't have one fitted, you won't be allowed to race. It's that simple."

He paused, and the room was silent for a moment as the threat sunk in. I raised an eyebrow at Drew and he gave me a nod. "We're OK," he whispered.

One strong voice rang from across the room. "I don't think it's fair to expect people to pay even more money to run in this race." People craned their necks to see who this protester was. I caught a glimpse of an eye-patch; it was Ed Williams-Hawkes, navigator on *Wettpunkt.com*. "We were told that these MarineTrack units were to be supplied free of charge, and now you want a deposit? Come on Mike!"

There were grumblings across the room. Some people agreed with Ed, whilst others wanted to get going. I wasn't sure which camp I sided with. On the one hand, Ed was right— at the Southampton Briefing back in March Mike *had* assured the teams that the tracker units would be supplied free of charge, and if anybody wanted to keep them after the race they would be able to buy them. If not, they could just hand them back. So this did seem a little underhand.

However, this was never going to be an event for penny-pinchers.

Without a major sponsor picking up a sizeable chunk of the bill, the entrance fee was incredibly hefty: the (non-refundable) deposit was £500, followed by a payment of £10 for every horsepower up to 1,000 hp. Anything over that was charged at £5/horsepower. So for one of the smaller boats running 300 hp, they had to pay £3,500 just to enter. At the other end of the scale, Fabio's entry fee for *Red FPT* was an incredible £17,500— a truly astounding figure. With those kinds of numbers, it seemed slightly churlish to argue over the cost of a refundable deposit, which amounted to £900 or so.

It soon became apparent that Ed wasn't objecting for himself, but on behalf of several other teams, notably his two sons. Their boat, *TFO*, was fitted out on a shoestring, and their budget was stretched to the limit. Still, it was becoming apparent that neither Ed nor Mike were prepared to back down on this, and the stalemate was eating into our time. Suddenly one man spoke up. "Mike, this is getting us nowhere. How many teams have still to pay the deposit?"

Mike conferred with the MarineTrack representative and answered with: "Nine. Why?"

"Because I'm getting tired of this. Just tell me how much you want, and I'll write you a personal cheque right here. Now let's move on, OK?"

We were all stunned by this dramatic intervention, and a spontaneous swell of applause swept the room. Ed made one last feeble protest, but he was shouted down by a dozen others and Mike moved on with his talk.

(The MarineTrack units would continue to be a bone of contention throughout the event. The Race Officials would use MarineTrack data to accuse several teams of cutting through exclusion zones established to protect environmentally-sensitive areas from the buzz of a hundred madly-spinning props, but the system proved itself to be unreliable at times, showing some boats to be travelling at speeds well in excess of what they were physically capable of. Team *747* were at one point shown to be travelling at 80 knots!)

That morning there would be two separate starts. The first group to go would consist of the MC1, MC2, RB4 and Historic boats. These would— in theory— be the slower boats, and so they would be given a head start. Thirty minutes later the second fleet, consisting of the RB1, RB2 and RB3 boats would roar off. Oh, and they would of course be joined by the Classic Class— Fabio in his winged beast, *Red FPT*.

There were several reasons for splitting the fleet in two. Firstly, the Historic boats had pushed for a head start from the very beginning; since they would be at sea the longest in their slower boats, it made sense to let them go first. Secondly, it would make for a great spectacle for the hundreds of spectators who were lining Clarence Esplanade and elsewhere. It would also add a bit of spice to the competitors' day as well, with the slower boats feeling more involved in the racing as the quicker boats hauled them in. And finally, there was the logistical aspect to consider. Just twenty miles away the Solent narrowed to under one mile wide between Fort Albert on the Isle of Wight and Hurst Castle on the mainland. At 80 knots, the faster boats would reach this bottleneck in 15 minutes, and they would all be jostling for position this early on in the race. With other water users also navigating this narrow channel, the potential for catastrophe was obvious.

We would all leave Gunwharf Quays in an orderly fashion, sticking to the 10 knot speed limit and keeping out of the way of the myriad of ferries that continued to shuttle in and out of Portsmouth. Once off Southsea Castle we were to muster, circling in a tight anticlockwise formation until the Start Boat cut across the course with a yellow flag raised. The first fleet (including me on *Ocean Pirate*) would then crack open the taps and chase the Start Boat, which by then would be running down the course at around 35 knots. Once he raised the green flag the race to Plymouth would be on!

After the briefing I wished Jan and Drew good luck and elbowed my way through the gossiping teams to find Annie at Race Control. She had set up shop in the corner of the bar, and there was a large audience to witness my garbled explanation of why I would be swapping teams just hours before the start. I was treated to one of her infamous glowers, much to the delight of the bemused onlookers, but she finally relented and changed the paperwork and plastic wrist tag to show I would now be racing with *Ocean Pirate.* And so our daily ritual began; for the next nine days Annie and I would repeat this cumbersome process, and it never seemed to get any easier. Not for me at least...

Outside the fresh air helped to cool the sweat that had formed on my brow, and after three or four cigarettes I realised I wasn't going to get any calmer so I drew in a deep breath and made my way towards the security gate at the top of the pontoon steps. I was surprised at how many people had turned out to watch the fleet leave; several hundred curious bystanders had lined the railings to watch the fleet make its leisurely way out to the muster area off Southsea Castle and I had to literally elbow my way through clumps of bemused spectators.

Mike stepped out of the wheelhouse to welcome me, clearly as anxious as I was. He was in his mid-sixties, with a white goatee and bags under his eyes. Clearly just getting here had been an exhausting trial, and I hoped— rather condescendingly— that the next ten days wouldn't be too much of a strain for him. But he seemed all fired up for the off, and there was just enough time to be introduced to his crewmates before we slipped our lines and joined the long line of boats nosing our way into open waters.

Paul Carter had a friendly but no-nonsense way about him, and as a qualified RYA instructor with 23 years of RNLI experience under his belt it was clear that Mike hadn't asked him along just for the sake of his magnificent moustache. Bob Pennington reminded me of old-school Navy material, and I wasn't wrong. A trim, dapper fellow, he had served as Commander on Customs cutters, and so had an excellent knowledge of all of Britain's ports. The fourth member of the team was Tom Brissenden, who stuck out like a sore thumb thanks to his youth. He may have been lacking in age, but his role of Engineer at Brooms boatyard (where *Ocean Pirate* had been refitted) meant that he knew the boat inside out.

Ocean Pirate was laid out like many other cabin cruisers from that era; in the wheelhouse there were two bench seats, one for the helmsman to the left and another for the navigator to the right. Three steps amidships led me down below, where there was a comprehensive galley to port and a good-sized table to starboard with a padded bench running along the outboard side. Up forward I could just make out two single bunks in the bow, liberally festooned with bags, clothes and towels hanging up to dry. I dumped my gear underneath the table and headed back up into the wheelhouse, noting the head on the starboard side as I climbed up. It's always good to know where to find these things.

Back in the wheelhouse facing aft, there were two padded benches running along the back wall, with another set of steps leading down into a roomy aft cabin. Being the most spacious cabin, this was Mike's domain, with Bob taking the other bunk.

Pleasantries exchanged and snooping over I slipped into my borrowed lifejacket. As I tweaked the straps Mike handed me two sheets of A4. "Just give this a read, would you? I want to make sure everyone knows what to do at all times."

I sat down on the padded bench at the rear of the wheelhouse and, fighting to keep a straight face, I worked my way through the house rules. They included things like: "Lifejackets and helmets to be worn at all times", "No-one is to exit the wheelhouse whilst under sea" and "Smoking on board is strictly prohibited!" There were also protocols on the correct way to cast off and to come alongside, and other such mundane gibberish. I found the whole thing slightly surreal, and more than a little preoccupied with Health & Safety bullshit, but I was a guest on board, so I bit my tongue and decided to abide by Mike's rules.

The slow run from Gunwharf Quays to the muster area off Southsea Castle and the adjacent hovercraft port took ten minutes, and by quarter to ten we had become part of a massive pack of equally nervous race boats. But instead of circling anticlockwise like a shoal of beautifully-choreographed sardines, we were all over the place, with boats frantically trying to avoid colliding with other teams and dozens of curious spectators who had taken to the water to witness this spectacle.

As Bob struggled to keep us in a clear patch of water I did a quick bit of mental arithmetic. Plymouth was 130 nautical miles away to the west. *Ocean Pirate* could manage only 30 knots, tops. That meant that I would be spending the next four and a half hours on board. Minimum. Once we were clear of the Needles and the protection of the Isle of Wight, sea conditions would deteriorate, and I was worried we'd have to throttle back. If our new speed, then, was closer to 25 knots, it would add almost an hour to our time. It promised to be a slog, but at least I would be warm and dry.

There was a force three or four blowing from the west, and it was constantly nudging the fleet towards the eastern shore. Eagerly anticipating the start, many boats (us included) kept their bows pointed into the wind, and were so preoccupied with avoiding everyone else that they didn't notice how close they were drifting to the beach. Suddenly one of the locals buzzed by us in a small RIB. He was shouting something, but because we had all donned our mandatory orange helmets we couldn't make him out so Mike cracked one of the wheelhouse doors (in a direct defiance of his own rules).

"Sorry, what did you say?" he shouted.

"I said, 'Look out for the submarine barrier!' You're right on top of it!"

With a start we realised that we had drifted right across the submarine barrier, a chain of concrete blocks laid during the Second World War to prevent German subs from sneaking into Portsmouth harbour. Bob instinctively tapped the throttles to power us away from the barely-submerged blocks, and just as he did so one of the engines stalled. He turned the key and it started up again, but we feared the worst: one of the props had probably hit the barrier, causing the engine to stall.

The strain was painfully etched on everyone's face, but there was no time to think about the repercussions— the Start Boat had just crossed our bows, the yellow flag clearly visible.

"OK boys, this is it!" someone said, and Bob cracked open the throttles to chase down the Start Boat with the rest of the first fleet. But something was clearly wrong. With the GPS showing 10 knots there was a noticeable vibration running through the boat. Bob and Paul exchanged worried looks, but said nothing. By the time we hit 15 knots, however, it was impossible to ignore the obvious— *Ocean Pirate* was starting to shake herself to pieces, and Bob pulled back on the throttles.

As the bow dropped I could see the rest of the fleet streaming away to the west, an amazing spectacle to behold. But for us there would be no neck-and-neck racing with our contemporaries. We were out of the race, just thirty seconds after crossing the start line.

In muted tones the men discussed the options. It turned out that there weren't any; we would have to be lifted out of the water to assess the damage. It seemed obvious that one of the propellers had been damaged, but there could be much more going on. Perhaps the prop shaft had been bent, possibly damaging the gearbox or the seals. We wouldn't know until *Pirate* was out of the water.

Mike hailed Port Solent marina, where I had spent the last two days wandering aimlessly, and was told they would lift the boat out. During that long, slow cruise up Portsmouth Harbour the atmosphere in the wheelhouse was as black and despondent as a condemned man's cell. I quietly slipped down below to send Rob an anticlimactic text. "Hit barrier. Bad vibration at 15 knots. Heading to Port Solent marina for lift out. Fucking gutted."

He called me back straight away, something I hoped he wouldn't do, since it meant that I would have to describe every gory detail to him in front of Mike and his crew. After a hoarsely-whispered blow-by-blow account, he told me that Fabio Buzzi was also out of the running— he had done exactly the same thing as us! I relayed this bit of information on to my team-mates, but they seemed unimpressed. Clearly they were too engrossed in their own misfortunes to take any solace in Buzzi's.

As we tied up inside the lock to enter Port Solent marina we were hailed by Jonathan Hind, the marina's assistant manager. Mike filled him in on the details, and Jonathan assured him that the boat would be lifted out straight away. This was our first bit of good news, but clearly everyone was still mightily on edge. Once through the lock we motored over to where the massive blue hoist was waiting, its slings already lowered into the water. *Ocean Pirate* was carefully manoeuvred backward into place, and as soon as she was perfectly lined up the hoist slowly but surely lifted her clear of the water, then rolled back, keeping the boat suspended a few feet over the concrete. We all scurried round in search of stout wooden props, and once we had enough in place she was lowered down onto the hard.

Finally we were able to inspect the damage, and it was immediately clear to see what happened. One of the bronze blades on the port prop had its tip bent back 90 degrees, and another showed minor signs of damage. Anxiously we checked the prop shaft to see if it was out of alignment or bent, but it spun true and smooth. Thank Christ for small mercies.

The prop came off its shaft in a matter of seconds, and a few minutes later Mike's daughter showed up, ready to transport Mike and the damaged prop to Clement's Engineering in St. Neots, some 140 miles away. As Mike sped off, the rest of us were faced with the sudden realisation that if the prop was irreparable, *Ocean Pirate*'s race would be over. By now it was after noon, and soon the first of the fleet would be skimming past the Great Mew Stone and thundering up Plymouth Sound to cross the first finishing line while we were still in Southampton minus a prop.

But there was, for the time being, nothing more to be done, so I did what any smart, adaptable reporter would do— I headed for the nearest bar.

Except by now my feet were causing me so much discomfort that after a lightning-quick shot of Smirnoff Black for the pain I hobbled off to a chemist the barman told me was "just round the corner". Right. Except, after rounding several corners, there was still no sign of it. There was, however, a sodding great shop that sold all matter of sporting goods. I shuffled through the door and asked the bored-looking assistant if he sold blister plasters. He did— hurray!— but they were upstairs— bugger!— so off I limped to drag myself up a flight of stairs. After spending nearly fifty quid on a massive assortment of plasters, ointments and salves I forced myself back towards the nearest bar, where I could adorn my tortured feet in comfort. Fortunately there was almost nobody around, and it was a little eerie to see all the bars, shops and cafes open and lit up, but with hardly a customer to be seen. On the plus side, it meant that I had no trouble at all in finding a quiet little corner booth where I could tend to my feet in private.

Clearly my lovely new Converse high-tops needed a little more breaking in. My socks were literally sodden with blood. I gingerly dabbed the worst of the blood off my ragged feet and stuck plasters on all the rents and tears I could find. There were quiet a few; to any casual observer it would have looked like my feet had been caught up in a pair of whirling surface-piercing props. I then jammed my bare feet into my hateful trainers and hobbled into the bathroom, where I rinsed my socks and dried them under the asthmatic hand drier as best I could before dragging them back on. The squelching as I made my way back to my table was bearable, so I acted nonchalant and tried not to grimace.

While I was washing down handfuls of Nurofen with Morgan's spiced rum & Coke, the *Silverline* team were in Plymouth spraying champagne over each other. Despite some very rough conditions, the boys had covered the 130 nautical miles in an impressive two hours thirty-four minutes to take the chequered flag. They had beaten the prototype Goldfish RIB *Lionhead* into port by a mere 15 minutes, who in turn were only 16 minutes ahead of the third place boat *Blue FPT*. I was absolutely delighted for Drew and the rest of the *Silverline* team, but felt a little pissed off as well— after all, it was supposed to be me in that fourth seat, not John Christensen. But in my heart of hearts, I knew that Drew had made the right decision in taking the Cummins engineer along. He was, after all, a Professional, and as such he did whatever it took to get the job done.

It was a philosophy I could relate to, and with my own assignment hanging in the balance I started to consider my options. I could:
a) jump in a taxi and take the train to Plymouth
b) jump in a taxi and catch a plane from Southampton to either Plymouth or Exeter, 50 miles away.
With either of these options, I would still be stuck for a ride on the next leg to Milford Haven, since I was originally due to join *Ocean*

Pirate there. On the other hand, at least I would be where the action was. And there was always the fall-back option of squeezing into the *Silverline* truck with Ian and Josh.

Or there was c): take a gamble on Mike Barlow and *Ocean Pirate*. This meant praying that Clement's Engineering would be able to straighten out the bent blade, praying that Mike would make it back before the marina staff all went home, and praying that we could make it to Plymouth before the next morning.

After some frantic phone calls to Rob at the magazine I decided to pin my fortunes to *Ocean Pirate*'s, and took up Religion with the fervour of a condemned man.

With six hours to kill I decided to get comfortable in a welcoming bar and set about feeding and watering myself. Over a bland burger and an overpriced beer I turned my mental attentions to the man who had somehow managed to set up this entire race– Mike Lloyd.

To pull something like this off takes a huge amount of determination, and clearly Mike wasn't lacking in that regard. Building not one but two successful businesses from scratch and then selling them on, Mike knew a thing or two about organising and getting the best out of people. He caught the racing bug in 1980, going on to become National Class champion twice. He was also scheduled to race in the 1984 Round Britain Powerboat Race, but due to personal problems he had to pull out at the last minute. He finally hung up his life jacket in 1990, but the missed race continued to haunt him.

It wasn't until 2006 that he finally decided to resurrect the event, and when he put out a tentative suggestion the sheer scale of responses persuaded him to go ahead with his ambitious plans. Using the '69 and '84 races as rough templates he set about defining the course, but despite the evident popularity of the event, without a major sponsor to fill the coffers the whole thing would be unviable.

At an emotionally-charged meeting with the teams who had shown an early interest, Mike was forced to confess that the race was likely to be scrapped. After a fifteen minute recess the vast majority of the teams came back to tell Mike that they would be willing to double their entry fee from £5/horsepower to £10/horsepower, so negating the need for a big sponsor. It was a major milestone for the race, and one of Mike's most cherished memories.

Despite this massive vote of confidence, both in the race and in Mike himself, there were still many hurdles to overcome. Rumours abounded about financial jiggery-pokery, and the RYA— who's cooperation would be essential— were loathe at first to get involved. Even when they changed their minds, there were still countless hurdles to overcome like finding suitable venues, organising fuel, and dealing with the various environmental groups that were up in arms with the proposed race. But not only had Mike managed to deal with the multitude of potential disasters, he'd also managed to convince around twenty other individuals to give up huge chunks of their time to make it happen.

People like Rob and Annie Beakhust. Rob's role as Chief Scrutineer didn't just entail checking over the boats and managing his four assistants; Rob was instrumental in establishing the criteria for the various Classes. He started racing back in 1979, became Chairman of the Offshore Racing Driver's Association in 1990, and acted as Scrutineer at dozens of events. If anyone knew their job, it was Rob.

Mind you, his wife Annie (the stern head-mistress type who had kept us in line at the Driver's Briefing) was no stranger to this type of event either. As a self-confessed "race groupie" supporting Rob when he first started racing, Annie soon found herself getting embroiled in the Dark Arts of Race Control. She went on to organising the Race Safety at the legendary Cowes-Torquay-Cowes races for 16 years, and was involved in organising over 40 other offshore events. Between her and Rob's vast organisational experience and Mike Lloyd's naive enthusiasm, the three of them managed to overcome personality clashes and the paperwork nightmare that comes with the territory to somehow make this event happen.

It was around 8 pm when Mike Barlow finally sped into the marina car park, and with great fanfare the beautifully repaired bronze prop was lifted out of the boot of his car. Refitting it took less than two minutes, and after desperately ferreting out the hoist driver we were back in the water. Once again we made the slow, monotonous passage down through the harbour, until we eventually reached open water off Blockhouse Fort, and with more than a little trepidation Bob opened the throttles.

The two phenomenal Cummins QSB 380s built up to a roar beneath our feet, and the old boat pointed her bow skywards. As the speed built up her nose came down, and we were on the plane, running at around twenty knots. We were all deathly still, waiting for the vibration to return and end our race for good. But— nothing! The old girl ran smooth as silk, and with a big grin Mike told Bob to open her up— all the way to 28 knots.

We were rapidly losing the light by now, and by the time we reached the Needles there was nothing to see except far-off pinpricks of light. I was hugely disappointed; I had never seen these massive knife-edges of chalk before, and I was very much looking forward to it. Instead I had to make do with noting the flashes from the lighthouse and watching it slide by on the chart plotter.

Ocean Pirate's wheelhouse was conventionally laid out. To port was the helm with all the controls, dials and switches scattered across the massive expanse of dash. In the middle were the three steps that led down into the galley, saloon and forward bunks, and to starboard was the navigator's station. The most impressive feature was the Raymarine electronic chart plotter, and it was a source of constant fascination to whoever was sat in front of it. Hunched over the glowing screen, pecking at it like some demented crow, they would constantly fiddle with the settings, tinkering and fiddling obsessively. The boat was no stranger to state-of-the-art electronic gimcracks; when she went round Britain in 1969 she was one of the very few vessels fitted with a flash piece of kit called radar, and it proved its worth on the controversial Inverness-Dundee leg, which was run despite an impenetrable fog that could have easily ended in disaster for those that didn't have it.

One seemingly magical component that her present-day crew were especially enthralled with was the AIS feature.

A relatively new innovation, AIS stands for Automatic Identification System and was initially designed for large commercial vessels, although it is now starting to be used on smaller pleasure boats as well. There's a lot of technology behind it, but it basically means that if an AIS-equipped vessel shows up on the plotter, a small dialogue box pops up on the screen, relaying all the vital information about that vessel. Data like speed, size, type of boat and heading are all displayed, making it easier to figure out who you're dealing with.

Unfortunately the crew of *Ocean Pirate* were obviously besotted with this wondrous new innovation, and they spent many slack-jawed hours intently scrutinising every AIS-equipped vessel within a 100-mile radius. Which would have been fine, except we were in the middle of the Solent in pitch-darkness, and the weather was worsening by the minute. I would have felt much happier if my goggle-eyed crewmates joined me in peering out into the stygian darkness for signs of flotsam, jetsam and poorly-marked lobster pots. And the fierce glow from the screen was doing nothing for my night vision either.

I was definitely beginning to lose my sense of Fun.

To make matters worse, I had completely forgotten all about the guesthouse in Plymouth I had booked months earlier until my phone rang. It was the landlady, sweetly asking if I would be putting in an appearance anytime soon. Bugger. I grovelled pathetically and explained what was going on. "I'll be in quite late tonight," I told her hesitantly. "What time were you thinking of locking up?"

She was quiet for a moment, then told me she'd hide the spare key under the mat. She even gave me directions to my room, so I wouldn't wake anybody up in the middle of the night. God love that woman! If the world was filled with more wonderful people like Lesley Espin at the Firs Guesthouse, Plymouth, we'd all be immeasurably better off...

Mike had spent many thousands of pounds returning *Ocean Pirate* to her former glory, what with new engines, gearboxes, an outside helm for manoeuvring, bow thruster etc etc, but he had scrimped on the seals for the two large skylights in the wheelhouse so every time a large wave crashed over the bows a small waterfall of icy sea water flowed from the roof. Thanks to the boat's violent movement it was impossible to tell where the next waterfall would come from, so I decided to pull the zip up on my Gul waterproof jacket and hunker down.

This pragmatic approach also helped me to keep warm. Despite the two massive 5.9 litre engines roaring away beneath our feet, the wheelhouse was decidedly chilly, no doubt caused by the two big vents fitted to the aft wall that were locked wide open. Of course it was impossible to shut them, because that would have meant stepping outside to the aft deck to unlatch them, and that was clearly *verboten*. So was having a crafty smoke, and after five hours on board I was starting to crave nicotine like a junky lusts after smack. My only hope was that we would reach Plymouth soon, but it was becoming desperately apparent that "soon" was totally out of the question.

My intrepid crewmates had been gradually pulling back on the throttles as the conditions worsened. By now the wind and sea had built to a force six, and even a blind man could see that this forty year-old boat was struggling. Virtually every wave we hit was crashing into the screens, and the wipers might as well have been built out of Kleenex for all the good they were doing. We had slowed to around twelve or fourteen knots in an effort to save the boat from the worst of the beating she was taking, but it made little difference. I have seen such weather before, and realised that the boat's design would mean she'd handle it just as badly at 25 knots as at 5, so my personal impulse would have been to lean down on the sticks and grit my teeth, just like pulling off a plaster. But it wasn't my decision, so instead we dragged the misery out, mile after wretched mile.

We were now about twenty miles west of Portland Bill, pretty much smack-bang in the middle of Lyme Bay. There was a brief discussion amongst my ailing companions, and the decision was made to run for cover in Brixham, twenty nautical miles westwards, to wait out the weather. Personally, I would have preferred to open the taps and make for Plymouth (and that mystical key hidden under a certain B&B doormat). At 24 knots we would be there in two hours; but of course it wasn't my decision so we spent one and a half hours at fourteen knots instead, skulking into Brixham.

Mike and I had hugely opposing views of how to handle the situation due to our different opinions of what the Round Britain involved; in fact we were at polar opposites in our philosophies. The best way to describe it is by comparing the race to running the London marathon. My belief was that we might not be in with a chance of winning, but at least we should rise to the challenge and push ourselves to the limit. Mike was more like the lunatic who shows up at the start line dressed as a giant lobster. He had freely admitted to me earlier that he wasn't remotely interested in winning; instead he had come along to take *Ocean Pirate* round the UK as a homage to her glory days, when she took part in the original race back in 1969. It was, I felt, overly sentimental, not to mention taking anthropomorphism to the extreme.

But if I had to accept the fact that "it wasn't the winning, it was the taking part that counted", his reasons for running for cover was still fundamentally flawed— in six hours time the rest of the fleet would be setting off for the next leg, the 180 nautical miles round Land's End and across the Bristol Channel to Milford Haven. We, however, were still 40 nautical miles from Plymouth— almost three hours away at our current speed. At this rate we wouldn't be taking part in any race— we would be running almost half a day behind the rest of the fleet, and with one of the slowest boats in the competition there was little chance of catching up before Inverness. For all the racing we would be doing, *Ocean Pirate* might just as well have set off on her own.

At three in the morning most places are apt to look a little unwelcoming, and Brixham marina was certainly no exception. But much to my surprise we were hailed on the VHF by an annoyingly cheery voice who gave us directions to our berth, and he was on hand to take our lines as we manoeuvred our way into alongside the pontoon. He kept up a happy stream of jolly gibberish while I chain-smoked three cigarettes in the rain, ignorant to the fact that I would have gladly kicked his face into an unrecognisable pulp before dumping his lifeless body into the oily waters.

Instead I bit my tongue and slipped back inside the shelter of the wheelhouse. The four men had poured themselves nightcaps, but I was in no mood to put off the inevitable— I needed sleep, and badly. I threw myself down onto the padded bench that ran along the saloon table and was unconscious within moments.

Top– The crew of *Ocean Pirate*- Tom Brissenden, Mike Barlow, Paul Carter and Bob Pennington

Below– And they're off! The rest of the fleet races for Plymouth

Results- Portsmouth to Plymouth.

Distance: 130 nautical miles.

Pos.	Team/ Number	Class	Time	Overall position (Class)
1st	Team Silverline/471	RB2	2:34:57	1 (1)
2nd	Lionhead/22	RB3	2:50:48	2 (1)
3rd	Blue FPT/333	MC1	3:06:38	3 (1)
4th	Swipewipes.co.uk/ 43	RB4	3:07:21	4(1)
5th	Mystic Dragon/6	MC1	3:09:36	5 (2)
6th	Hot Lemon/2	RB3	3:09:50	6 (2)
7th	Seahound V/80	MC1	3:09:58	7 (3)
8th	Going Lean/7	RB3	3:15:16	8 (3)
9th	Hardleys/4	RB3	3:15:24	9 (4)
10th	Braveheart III/55	MC1	3:15:50	10 (4)
11th	Vilda/9	RB3	3:25:49	11 (5)
12th	Birretta/12	MC1	3:27:28	12 (5)
13th	Ikon/18	RB3	3:36:10	13 (6)
14th	Guttaboyz/33	RB3	3:47:08	14 (7)
15th	Sealbay/77	RB4	3:49:07	15 (2)
16th	Carbon Neutral/343	RB3	3:54:05	16 (8)
17th	Mr Mako/96	RB4	3:54:14	17 (3)
18th	Team Bandit/69	RB2	3:57:04	18 (2)
19th	Black Gold/10	RB4	4:06:33	19 (4)
20th	Power Products Marine/8	MC2	4:07:04	20(1)

Pos.	Team/ Number	Class	Time	Overall position (Class)
21st	Buro/15	MC1	4:08:28	21 (6)
22nd	GEE/185	HC1	4:17:52	22 (1)
23rd	Tequila/88	RB3	4:19:20	23 (9)
24th	Team Scorpion Dubois/ 16	MC1	4:20:08	24 (7)
25th	Seafarer/110	RB3	4:22 :44	25 (10)
26th	My Pleasure II/3	RB4	4:26:13	26 (5)
27th	Northern Spirit/5	MC2	4:31:53	27 (2)
28th	Relentless/47	RB3	4:32:28	28 (11)
29th	Team Pulsar-Vampire/ 102	RB4	4:33:11	29 (6)
30th	TFO/17	MC2	4:36:37	30 (3)
31st	Mud, Swell & Beers/14	RB4	4:54:11	31 (7)
32nd	Fugitive/130	MC2	5:08:28	32 (4)
33rd	Team Pulsar-Wolf/ 101	RB4	5:15:54	33 (8)
34th	Venturer/111	RB1	5:16:20	34 (1)
35th	Team 747/747	HC1	6:08:00	35 (2)
36th	Xanthus/1	HC1	6:25:10	36 (3)
37th	Wettpunkt.com/81	RB1	**DNF**	37 (2)
38th	Garmin Racing/72	RB2	**DNF**	38 (3)
39th	Blue Marlin/99	HC1	**OTR**	39 (4)
40th	Swordsman/68	HC1	**DNF**	40 (5)

DNS Denotes Did Not Start
DNF Denotes Did Not Finish
OTR Denotes Out of The Race
* Denotes maximum time allowance exceeded.

Pos.	Team/ Number	Class	Time	Overall position (Class)
41st	Team Blastoff/100	RB2	**DNF**	41 (4)
42nd	No Worries/11	RB3	**DNF**	42 (12)
43rd	Red FPT/177	CC1	**DNF**	43 (1)
44th	Team Jersey/45	RB4	**DNF**	44 (9)
45th	RIB International/144	RB4	**DNF**	45 (10)
46th	Cinzano/558	RB2	**DNF**	46 (5)
47th	**Ocean Pirate/323**	**HC1**	**DNF**	**47 (6)**

DNS Denotes Did Not Start
DNF Denotes Did Not Finish
OTR Denotes Out of The Race
* Denotes maximum time allowance exceeded.

Miles Jennings, Jan Falkowski, Drew Langdon and John Christensen celebrating their victory in the first leg

6.
Plymouth to Milford Haven.

Sunday 22nd June.

I had been asleep for all of what felt like 4 seconds when Tom's "hilarious" novelty ring tone brayed through my head. I was so mentally and physically destroyed that I couldn't identify the tune, but I felt certain it was from one of half a dozen bad 80's American TV shows— the General Lee's horn, perhaps, or the theme to Airwolf.

But I had (and still have) no interest in whacky mobile phone ring tones, so while Tom scrabbled to find his phone I resigned myself to the fact that three hours' sleep was to be my limit. Bright early-morning sunlight flooded the saloon, but I could clearly hear thousands of halyards rattling against aluminium masts. I decided to step out for a closer look at the weather and my new surroundings.

Even in the relative shelter of Brixham marina it was clear that the wind was still blowing strongly from the west. But there were barely any clouds in the sky, and the day looked like it would be a good one. Three smokes later I was ready to rejoin my crew mates who were starting to rouse themselves. Someone put the kettle on and I was suddenly glad to be on board; she might be one of the most unsuitable race boats in the fleet, but as a comfortable cruiser she made much more sense.

I couldn't help but to draw comparisons between *Ocean Pirate* and *Buzzi Bullet*, the boat that won yesterday's leg. Both boats measured around 40 feet, and both were powered by Cummins 5.9 litre turbo-charged diesels. But apart from those two similarities, they were as different as a hippo and a Ducatti. The *Silverline* boat, whilst being a couple of feet longer than *Ocean Pirate*, was less than half the width. Comparing the two on dimensions was like comparing a Ford Mondeo with a Formula 1 car— they might both be the same length, but no-one would ever confuse the two.

Even the engines, which on the face of it should be relatively closely matched in power output, were in fact miles apart. Despite the same 5.9 litre capacity, the *Silverline* units produced 480 horsepower each; 100 hp more than each of *Ocean Pirate*'s engines.

And as for weight differences: In P1 racing trim, the *Silverline* machine weighed in at around 4,500 kg. Mike, on the other hand, had made absolutely no efforts whatsoever to lighten the load, and he estimated *Ocean Pirate*'s gross weight to come in at around 11 tons— two and a half times what *Bullet* weighed. A quick look round the saloon revealed where it all came from— the shelves were still filled with books, the fridge was well stocked, as were all the cupboards. Mike had even set out with full fresh water tanks, adding around a ton to the overall weight of the boat. It was this last revelation that had finally hammered it home for me— Mike had about as much intention of racing as I did of flapping my wings and flying off into the sunset.

Having said all that, the cup of tea that appeared from the fully-stocked galley was better than any blood transfusion, and something Drew and the others on board *Buzzi Bullet* could only ever dream about. Suitably re-energised I went off in search of News.

I stretched the kinks out of my tired leg muscles by walking up to the marina office, where I found the same Prozac-happy guy as before. With my best fake smile screwed onto my face I asked if I could possibly blag five minutes on his computer to check my emails. He left me to it and I immediately logged on to the official Round Britain site to check out the full results list. But my brain wasn't up to making sense of it all, so I printed the page off instead to study at my leisure.

My next concern was keeping in touch with Rob at the magazine. I checked my phone and was shocked to discover that the battery was almost flat. Clearly all the panicked calls and texts of the previous day had taken their toll on my cheap Motorola, and it was in desperate need of a charge. When I got back to the boat Mike and the team were just winding down their plan of attack for the day. It consisted of "waiting the weather out". I was mentally grinding my teeth in utter frustration, and it spurred me on to get off that lackadaisical boat as soon as physically possible. But first things first— I would have to get a bit of juice into my phone. However after turning my bag inside out several times I couldn't find my charger anywhere. This was a disaster— my phone was my only link to the outside world, and without it I couldn't call in my daily updates to Rob, order taxis to the B&Bs I had booked all round the coast, and reassure my Beloved that I was still in one piece.

None of the others used a Motorola, so I resigned myself to a long trek into Brixham town centre to throw myself upon the mercy of its shops. As I stepped through the wheelhouse doorway Paul reminded me that it was Sunday. Just what I needed.

Luckily my feet were showing signs of recovery, and the slow walk into town was pretty bearable, raising my spirits dramatically. That, added to the warming rays of the sun, did me the world of good, and I started feeling slightly ashamed of myself for harbouring such ill feelings towards the aging *Ocean Pirate* and her equally elderly crew. I decided to make a magnanimous gesture towards my crew mates, and found a small bakery just raising its shutters. Two minutes later I was back on the street, clutching a bag of five fresh Cornish pasties.

My connection to Brixham is ludicrously tenuous, but a connection exists none the less. The town has been a fishing port since time immemorial, and the boat designers, builders and fishermen of Brixham built up a vast understanding of fishing boats. They led the way in the creation of the sailing trawler, which gave them access to the more bountiful waters further offshore. So the deep-sea trawling industry was born, and towards the end of the 18th century others were starting to understand the importance of the vessels coming out of this little picture-postcard town.

The Brixham trawlers were such an incredibly successful design that at their peak there were thought to be several thousand of them fishing the waters all round Europe, and in Scandinavia and the remote northern Faroe islands these sturdy craft were still earning their keep right up to the 50's.

In 1892, right here in Brixham, the keel was laid for *Leader*, a 100-foot sailing trawler. She fished in UK waters until 1907 before being sold to new owners in Sweden, where she worked the frigid waters until 1953. After that she became a training ship for the Swedish Cruising Club, until she was bought by a man named Don Hind, who sailed her to the west coast of Scotland. He renamed her *Lorne Leader* to reflect her new home— she would spend the next ten years or so exploring the islands and sounds around Oban as a charter boat.

And that's where I entered the story. My father in his role as Marine Engineer was asked to do some work on the boat, and being the sentimental romantic that he is he became quite attached to her, often dragging me with him to help with servicing the engine or installing two massive battery banks. He was so fond of the old Brixham trawler— one of only a handful left in existence— that when Don called asking for a couple of crew to help move her 10 miles to her new mooring dad wasted no time in throwing me into the car and racing down to offer our services.

There were four of us on board; Don, my father and I, and a journalist writing a feature for Time magazine. As soon as we had motored clear of the marina breakwater Don wasted no time in handing the helm over to me, despite being just a pup of 13 or so, and he ushered my dad and the journalist down below where there was a fine bottle of malt whiskey to take the edge of the chilly October wind. I was left to manhandle the 100 foot, 110 ton beast through narrow channels until, an hour and a half later, I had to drag the three drunkards from the warm saloon to help me pick up *Lorne Leader*'s mooring buoy.

And that was my tenuous link to this quaint, picturesque fishing town. I felt a weird camaraderie with the place, and instantly warmed to its narrow streets where shops sold ice cream and pasties to the thousands of tourists who descend on this place every summer.

But my bonhomie was starting to wear thin as I exhausted shop after shop in my futile quest to find a charger for my hateful Motorola. I was just about to turn it off in order to save the battery for when I *really* needed it when the treacherous little bugger started ringing.

"Hi Derek, it's Drew here. Where are you?"

Damn! I thought to myself. *I've got no time to listen to his bloody gloating.* "Drew! Hey, good to hear you buddy! Congratulations on the win yesterday. I'm in Brixham." I took a quick look at my watch. "Shouldn't you be getting ready for the race mate?"

"That's why I'm calling. The leg's been cancelled; they reckon the weather's too rough off Land's End, so we've loaded the boat onto the lorry and going to Milford Haven by road."

"Christ! Cancelled? OK, well, take care on the roads then. Hopefully I'll catch up with you in Wales." Now, in my defence I must just explain that my knowledge of the English coastline isn't the best. I had never had cause to study a map of the area, and since I wouldn't be doing any navigating during the course of the race I only had the most basic understanding of where everything was.

Drew was understandably quiet for a moment. "Uh, Derek? Since we'll be pretty much driving right past Brixham perhaps you'd like a lift?"

Wha-? "Really? Wow! That would be fantastic! Cheers Drew, I think you just saved my fucking life!"

We arranged to meet at the marina car park in an hour or so and hung up. I was so elated at being saved from certain doom that I almost skipped back to the boat, wolfing down my Cornish pasty on the way.

Back on board I proudly revealed my generous gifts to Mike and the crew, diplomatically ignoring the smell of fried bacon that hung in the air. "Here you go boys— breakfast! And what better than fresh, genuine Cornish pasties? After all, when in Rome, right?"

They stared at me oddly for a moment. It was Paul who finally broke the news to me. "What are you on about? We're not in Cornwall, we're in Devon you idiot." Well I told you English geography wasn't my strong point...

I told Mike about Drew's offer and we wished each other luck. I threw my gear into my bag and heaved it onto my shoulder, leaving behind three old men (and one relatively young man) to ponder the sky and shake their heads at the wind that continued to whistle through the rigging.

I felt on top of the world, and after grabbing a sandwich and a couple of coffees at a nearby café I stepped out into the brilliant sunshine to meet Drew. When he showed up, however, it wasn't in the lorry but in an Audi A2. His wife Judy was driving, and stuffed into the back seat was John Christensen. Drew popped the boot and we set about trying to cram my crap in with everyone else's. Once that was done I squeezed in the back beside John and soon we were on our way, bound for Wales.

On the way Drew and John filled me in on all the news. Whilst they had enjoyed a trouble-free run in the rough conditions -clearly Drew had been telling the truth all along about his preference for wilder water— others had not faired so well. Fabio had suffered the same humiliating fate as us, tapping the submerged concrete blocks off Southsea Castle. The damage to *Red FPT* was worse than ours, however, with a rudder, prop and shaft taking a bad clout, as well as damaging the cooling water intake. The boat had been lifted out at Portsmouth, and his small army of engineers were working flat out to fix her in time for the start at Milford Haven.

Another one of the favourites, *Wettpunkt.com*, had shot off the line at an alarming speed, but later had to limp into Torquay with engine problems. It turned out that the air intakes for the engines had been mounted facing the wrong way, allowing sea spray to be sucked into the engine. His shore crew were also frantically working on the boat, no doubt thanking the gods for the reprieve the bad weather gave them.

The crew of Team *747* would not have been so quick to thank the weather gods. As they powered their restored Fairey Spearfish out of the shelter of the Needles they took off after bouncing of a particularly nasty wave and landed badly. Or, more accurately, one of their crew landed badly. Mark Jealous, one of the four 747 pilots racing on board *Miss Daisy* badly injured his back despite the padding that the heavy Grabner lifejackets provided, and had to be dropped off at Weymouth to get checked out.

(Mark, a youthful 58, later told me his version of events: despite being in throes of agony, he vainly pleaded with his team mates that they throw him over the side and continue on with the race after giving the Coastguard his coordinates. With a straight face he assured me that he didn't want to be responsible for holding the team up. However, judging by the barely-hidden smiles from his team mates, I'm not entirely sure that Mark was being entirely truthful...)

But the biggest disaster had befallen the Supermarine Swordfish of Marcus Hendricks. *Blue Marlin*, the modern boat that qualified for the Historic Class because of her design, had hit something in the middle of Lyme Bay. The submerged object had punched a hole through her hull, and within ten minutes she had sunk to the bottom. Thankfully Marcus and his three crewmates managed to launch the liferaft, and a few minutes later were picked up by Jeremy Bennett and Tim Kary in *Tequila*, an 8.5 meter Scorpion RIB in the RB3 Class. It was a little eerie to think that whatever had sunk *Blue Marlin* could still have been blithely bobbing around in the same stretch of water where we had been blundering, blind and alone, at two that morning.

The opening leg was awash with boats suffering mechanical setbacks; Team *Blastoff* had no less than three debilitating electrical faults, forcing them to drop out of the leg. The Ocke-Mannerfelt batboat of Team *Jersey* also retired with electrical problems when the cable to the fuel pump chafed through. But they weren't the only team to suffer problems with their Mercury outboards; *Black Gold*, *No Worries* and *Northern Spirit* all reported various breakdowns of their engines, which would continue to plague them all throughout the race and keep the EP Barrus engineers very busy indeed. Tom and Charlie Williams-Hawkes on board their budget *TFO* had limped across the line with their faces black and the engine hatches wide open after they sheared off an exhaust manifold, while the youngest competitors in the event— 19 year old Tom Summerton and Joe Leckie on board *Mud, Swell & Beers*— managed to find their way into Plymouth without their electronic navigation after their GPS gave up the ghost.

One team who managed to beat the odds was *swipewipes.co.uk*. Nick Gilley and Jon Fuller had somehow managed to get their home-built Phantom across the line in an excellent 4th place, despite having had absolutely no time to test the boat whatsoever. I later discovered that they had only been launched literally a few hours before the start, and that they were continually tweaking and making adjustments to the boat as they went— with the race scheduled to cover over 1,300 nautical miles, they were in for a mammoth shakedown run.

But I struggled to muster any sympathy for other people's misfortunes; I was going to Milford Haven where I would have all day to find another ride to Bangor, get some hot food down me and get an early night in a warm, comfortable B&B bed. Yes sir, things were looking up!

Conditions in the back of the little Audi were even tolerable, right up until the point we had to stop to pick up Miles. Don't misunderstand me, I liked Miles. But there were now three of us jammed into the back seat, and getting comfortable for a quick catnap was proving to be impossible. Still, the banter was good and the weather was fine, and after a while my personal situation improved even more when Drew asked if I minded driving.

Drew is the only person I've met with the perfect solution for using SatNav in the car. He programmed it to take us to Milford Haven then threw it in the glove box. That way I could still hear the directions, but without the distraction of having to double-check the display. Genius. Sure enough, after a couple of hours we rolled into Milford Haven, and we spotted signs for the docks.

As we rolled down the pitted road things were looking pretty industrial, and there were no signs of any other racing boats, so when Drew spotted a young guy in a fluorescent green jacket sweeping the road he rolled down his window to ask for directions.

The lad was eager to help, despite suffering with a bad stutter. Drew explained we were involved in the powerboat race, but wasn't quite sure where we were supposed to be. As the lad began pointing us back in the direction we had just come from I suddenly realised he only had three fingers on his hand. I became totally fixated with those three digits; suddenly the rest of the world failed to exist as I stared, fascinated, at his hand.

Slowly I became aware of Drew looking at me. "Did you get that Derek? Back up to the main road, turn right and follow the signs for Pembroke Dock." He was trying to keep his face a mask of solemnity, but I could clearly see his eyes twinkling and dancing. He turned back to our guide. "Did you say it was the second road on the right?"

"No," came the reply, "you need to t-t-take the third t-t-turn. Just loo-loo-loo-look out for pe-pe-Pembroke Dock." By now the sniggering from the back seat was getting out of hand, so with a cheery wave Drew thanked him as I threw the car into a three point turn as fast as I possibly could.

Safely out of earshot we fell about laughing, tears blurring my view as I tore back up the road. "Did you see his hands?" laughed John. "Christ, it's a good thing the road we need is only the third on the right; any more and he'd have to take his socks and shoes off!"

As our laughs subsided Drew gently chastised us. "We shouldn't be so cruel. What a really nice guy, we shouldn't laugh at him. Unless he gave us totally wrong directions, in which case he deserves everything he gets!"

But our three-fingered friend was right on the money. We crossed the Cleddau bridge and cautiously threaded our way through a tired-looking Pembroke Dock until arriving, somewhat hesitantly, at the seemingly-deserted Admiralty Pier gates. We hadn't seen a single sign indicating where the race teams should gather, having gotten this far purely on luck and the stammered directions of a three-fingered road sweeper. But just as we were wondering where to try next a man in another high-visibility jacket stepped out of a small office just inside the gates.

"Are you here for that boat race thing?" he asked. When we told him we were he swung the tall metal gate open and waved us through.

About a hundred yards further down we came to a collection of pre-fab buildings that had obviously seen better days. And a little further was the beginnings of the fleet; half a dozen boats strapped to the backs of trailers and lorries, including *Buzzi Bullet*.

We clambered out of the car and stretched our aching limbs, tendons and sinew creaking and cracking in the watery sun. The impressive pier ran straight out into the Sound for about a hundred yards, then jinked left for a hundred more. It was, as the name suggests, an old Admiralty facility, and from 1816 to 1926 nearly two hundred and sixty Royal Navy ships were built and repaired in the area. After the Navy pulled out, the area was taken over, surprisingly, by the RAF, who found the location ideal for their flying boats. By 1943 this was the largest base for flying boats in the world, with a vast fleet of Sunderlands and Catalinas.

Given its importance, there was also a massive Army presence in the town, but in the late 50's the RAF started drastically scaling down its operations, and with it went the British Army— and the town's fortunes. Despite the oil refineries that sprouted from the industrialised landscape along the Sound, it was clear that Pembroke Dock had fallen on tough times, a fate illustrated by the shabby Portacabins and sheds that lined the pier.

I dumped my bag on the concrete with the others (something I was going to bitterly regret later) and went off to explore our depressing surroundings. I spotted the 38-foot Fountain of Team *Blastoff* sitting by a ramshackle shed and wandered over to take a closer look. Her entry was the third instalment of a family tradition that went back almost forty years.

In 1969 Richard Griffith and his wife Sue entered the first Round Britain race in *Samanda Thuz*, a Swedish-built cabin cruiser. Then, for the 1984 race, they entered *Everest Forever*, a much sportier Sunseeker XPS 34. For the 2008 race they had pulled out all the stops, and *Round Britain Challenger* was, on paper, a strong contender. But a quick scan of my print-off of the first leg results told a different story. Team *Blastoff* were showing right at the bottom of the results table. This was, I later discovered, due to a string of electrical problems— problems that would eventually prove insurmountable.

The sleek, aerodynamic engine hatch was propped up, and from deep within the confines of the engine bay I heard a familiar West Country tirade. Rob Jenkins, the Race Marine mechanic I'd met at the P1 race in Italy, was apparently not very impressed with the boat's twin 500 horsepower Mercury engines, judging by the prolific stream of profanities he was hurling in their direction.

"What's up Rob? Lost your contact lens?" I grinned.

"Eh? Oh, alright there Derek? No, it's the bloody electrics mate. Poxy piece of crap's been one fucking nightmare after another. 'Ere, you ain't seen Steve about anywhere have you? He's buggered off with the van somewhere."

I told him I hadn't, and left him to his electrical gremlins. By now my stomach was beginning to growl, and I kept an eye out for some sort of food-dispensing place— a burger van, café, anything, but there was nothing promising in sight. That's when I remembered I had stocked up on goodies at a service station earlier in the day. I had biscuits, crisps and a couple of bottles of juice stashed in my bag, which was right next to the *Silverline* lor-

The lorry was gone. The Audi was gone. And, worst of all, my bag was gone. I frantically looked round to see if the small pile of bags had been moved: I checked doorways, lean-to sheds, and even under other cars and vans, but to no avail. I was terminally fucked.

When I packed up my gear on *Ocean Pirate* I had thrown everything into my holdall: camera, credit cards, my notebook with phone numbers and addresses, everything.

Frantically I called Drew, one of the few numbers I'd stored in my phone, and to my eternal relief he told me all the bags were in the back of Steve's van. So where was Steve? "He's with us. We decided to try and get the boat launched back at Milford marina instead of waiting for the cranes at Pembroke Dock. We won't be long." And with that cheery promise he hung up.

I was hugely relieved by that bit of news, but that didn't fill my stomach. It also meant that I was missing out on some great photos, because the vast open space at the base of the pier was starting to fill up with more and more boats, vans, lorries and pick-ups, and the confusion would have made for some great shots.

When the Race Organisers had seen the weather forecast for that morning, they had made the tough decision to cancel the second stage. 60 mph winds and seas in excess of 6 metres were nobody's idea of fun, especially when rounding the Lizard, where tidal streams merge to create perilous conditions. Rather than wait it out and run a day behind schedule, the Organisers had decided that the fleet should make its way to Milford Haven by road. Which was fine for the likes of *Silverline*, *Red FPT* and the rest of the big teams with bespoke trucks and a professional shore crew, but for the vast majority this required hiring haulage companies specialising in boat transportation. On a Sunday.

They then faced another dilemma. The two mobile cranes that had been specially hired had not yet materialised. This was because they were expecting to be lifting boats out of the water later on in the day; boats that were still supposed to be racing across the Bristol Channel, not showing up on the backs of lorries that charged by the hour and couldn't offload their cargo any other way. Drew had tried to play it canny; seeing that the cranes weren't in place yet, he decided to launch *Bullet* at the marina across the Sound, where we had encountered the digit-deficient stutterer. Unfortunately it turned out that he wasn't the only one with that bright idea.

Several hours later Admiral Pier was starting to lose any faint vestiges of charm it might have held for me. I had seen everything there was to see, including the old slipways and dry dock, the dilapidated buildings, the shiny race boats, the stressed crews, and even watching the Rosslare ferry leaving the terminal a few hundred yards away was no substitute for Food, a Shower and Bed— my three fantasy objects of desire. I had called Drew several more times to chase him up, but every time he fobbed me off with "soon, soon".

There was one nugget of good news. Earlier I had told Rob at the magazine that I still needed a ride for the next day's leg to Bangor. He had promised me he'd do his best, and a little while later he called me back with a lead.

"Good news Derek! You know Team *747*, the airline pilots with the restored Fairey? One of their guys got badly injured yesterday; you can probably take his seat."

"Fantastic! I'll give them a call. Cheers matey!" I admit, I shouldn't have been so glad about another man's misfortunes, but I had a job to do damnit!

This potential lifeline threw up a couple of major problems though. Firstly, I didn't have their phone number, and secondly, my phone had finally bought the farm. Luckily for me, I knew exactly where I could find the answer to my first dilemma.

Race Control had set up shop in a poky Portacabin halfway along the pier. With my collar up to ward off the worst of the icy wind that rattled windows and stirred up little dust-devils I painfully hobbled over. (Yes, by now my feet were once again howling in protest at my relentless rambling, and all my high-powered painkilling drugs were safely stowed in my bag.)

I was greeted by the stern face of Annie Beakhust, the fearsome woman who had called us to order during the first Driver's Briefing all those months before. After recounting my tragic tale to her (and several curious onlookers) she decided to give me a chance.

My phone conversation with Jonathan Napier, the boat's owner, was quick and pleasingly fruitful— he would be more than happy to have me on board, provided of course that I had all the right paperwork for Race Control. I assured him everything would be legit, and hung up.

As I handed Annie's phone back to her I told her— with a wave of relief— that I would be signing in as crew with Team *747* for the next day's leg, and she rattled through the paperwork like the pro she was.

That was one problem sorted, but by now it was after 8 pm and exhaustion was slowly turning my brain to mush. In one of the disused buildings I came across a small group of drivers, mechanics and other assorted ne'er-do-well's who, for various reasons, were stuck on that Godforsaken pier with nothing to do. They had scraped together a motley assortment of chairs and had tried to make themselves comfortable as best they could. I joined them, glad to be off my feet and out of the unforgiving wind.

Discarded in a corner lay an old Yellow Pages, at least six years old. Out of sheer boredom I leafed through it, then decided to entertain myself by reading the entries under "G" for "Guesthouses". To my astonishment I thought I recognised the name of the B&B that was supposed to be my refuge for the night. One of the guys leant me his phone, and I called the number.

There were so many variables: what if I'd gotten the name of the guesthouse wrong? What if they had changed their number? What if-?

"Hello?"

"Oh hi, I'm sorry to bother you. This might sound a bit weird, but do you still do Bed and Breakfast?" I asked cautiously.

"Why yes, of course we do. Did you want a room?" she asked me.

"No, well, yes actually. What I mean is, I think I might already have a room booked with you for tonight. My name's Wynans."

There was a pause. "Yes, here you are— a single room for the 22nd. I was beginning to think you weren't coming Mr Weenams. It's almost half past eight you know."

"It's 'Wynans' actually. Yes, I know it's getting late, but the thing is, I've been held up. I shouldn't be much longer though. Half an hour or so at the latest, I hope."

She didn't seem happy, but she said she was would "wait up" for me. I almost felt bad, until I rechecked my watch— 8:25. *What time did these people go to bed?* I wondered.

But time passed, and there was still no sign of Drew or Steve in his van. Without cash or credit cards I was stuck, and I hadn't even paid for my room in advance, so there was no point trying to find the guesthouse. I called my intended landlady twice more that night— once a little after nine, and again at ten o'clock. That last conversation did not go well.

"Now look here. I run a decent establishment, and I don't think I want any weirdos under my roof, thank you very much!"

"Huh? Weirdos? What weirdos? I'm not a weirdo," I spluttered.

"Well you certainly sound weird."

"I'm not weird, I'm just really tired. Listen, you've got to take me in— I'm an ordained priest for Christ's sake!" I pleaded.

"I'm sorry, but I have to insist that you stay well away from my home. I can do without odd guests like you!" And with that the bitch hung up on me. I was too tired to be outraged by this point, just bewildered. Where was the humanity? The sympathy? The trust? What a difference between this miserable old harridan and the faceless angel of Plymouth, who had offered to leave the front door key under the mat. Was this the true face of British guesthouse hospitality?

Sometime after 11 I got bored and took a stroll back up the access road to the big steel gates that barred the entrance to the pier. There were two men inside, idly gossiping and chain-smoking hand-rolled cigarettes. We chatted about this and that, and then-

-and then I was in the lobby of the Cleddau Bridge hotel. I genuinely have no idea how I got there. I didn't even know where I was; all I can remember is sitting in a wonderfully comfortable chair in the bar (which was closed), then looking up to see Drew, John and Steve walk in. Steve admitted that his van was outside, and I grabbed the physically-shattered mechanic and literally dragged him outside so that I could be reunited with my belongings.

Back inside I had to face the realisation that I had nowhere to sleep. Then John, that beautiful, balding Kiwi, told me that one of his Cummins colleagues was stuck in Plymouth. That meant that the guy's hotel room was up for grabs! Woo-hoo! Of course there was a downside— the hotel was a couple of miles away. Still, it was a bed for the night, so while John called the hotel to let them know I would be taking the room I tried to get the receptionist's attention to ask her about a taxi.

The harried-looking girl behind the desk fended me off with a raised hand and an abrupt "In a minute!" She was in the middle of some sort of dispute with the well-spoken man next to me, and with nothing better to do I eavesdropped on their discussion.

"Now listen," the man was saying, "I'm trying to tell you that I don't want this room."

"But sir, I've been trying to tell *you* that it's not your decision. It's not your room, it's reserved for a Mr Brown." (I can't remember if that was his actual name; for the sake of the story that's what I'll call him.)

"Yes, I know that. Mr Brown won't be needing the room tonight. He's still in Plymouth." At the mention of "Plymouth" I took another look at the man. It was Ed Williams-Hawkes, he of the eye patch and *Wettpunkt.com*'s navigator.

"I don't care where Mr Brown is sir, he's the only person who can cancel the room," countered the exasperated receptionist.

Ed was getting really wound up now: "Bugger Mr Brown, *I* was the one who booked the bloody room! *I'm* the one who's paying for it! Mr Brown is working for *me*!"

It took a while, but slowly a couple of synapses in my brain fired half-heartedly. "Hi Ed, having trouble?"

He turned to me like I was a total stranger. Which, to be perfectly honest, I was. "Oh hi. Yes, I'm trying to tell this woman I want to cancel a booking, but she won't let me."

"Yes, I heard. Listen Ed, perhaps I can help you out. As it happens, I'm looking for a place to crash tonight. How about you sell the room to me?"

The man's mind was clearly faster than mine. I had barely finished my sentence when he said "Done! How does 85 quid sound?"

"Ed, you got a deal. Can I square you up later?"

That made him hesitate for a second, but finally he relented and we shook hands on the arrangement. All this had taken place right in front of the receptionist, but as suavely as I could I turned to her and said "Good evening, my name's Mr Brown. I believe you have a room for me?"

She handed me the key card with a queer look in her eyes, like a rabbit hypnotised by a cobra's swaying dance. I signed the proffered slip with a flourish and turned my back on the poor girl, immediately ignoring her and hoping she wouldn't push for identification.

My lofty retreat was almost ruined by the sudden appearance of a waiter bearing a tray of magnificent-looking sandwiches. With a flourish he dropped the platter onto a table, where Ed and his cohorts ripped into the mound of triangular delicacies like a pack of hyenas devouring a still-kicking impala.

This was almost too much for me to take. I stood, spellbound, as the gang of heartless wolves literally annihilated the sandwiches in under a minute. I think I saw someone chew twice, maybe three times, but certainly no more than that. With bulging cheeks they stuffed tuna and cucumber morsels into their pockets, and with several more clutched into each hand they magically scattered to all four points of the compass, scurrying off to digest their meal in the comfort of their rooms.

Ed saw me staring (perhaps the light dancing on the ribbon of drool creeping from the corner of my mouth caught his attention) and beckoned me over. "There's still some left; help yourself." And with that, he was gone. To be fair, the whole world had suddenly vanished as far as I was concerned. Three or four battered little triangles of bread had survived the holocaust, their once-pristine whiteness now besmirched by the remnants of their fallen comrades' fillings. A cheese and pickle sandwich had a dollop of tuna on it the size of a large grape, but I wolfed it down regardless, my neglected taste buds too grateful to object. Another had no filling at all, just two sad little triangles clinging together, nothing more than a thin smear of margarine uniting them. I didn't care; I devoured them with even less restraint than the *Wettpunkt.com* boys. (It wasn't until much later that I found the forgotten crisps and biscuits in the bottom of my bag, crushed to a fine powder.)

After demolishing the leftovers I felt a damn sight better. Belatedly I turned to thank Ed for his generosity, but he had already gone. In fact, everybody had disappeared, even the bewildered receptionist, so I dragged my bulging holdall onto my shoulder and walked the three or four miles to "Mr Brown's" room.

7.
Milford Haven to Bangor.

Monday 23rd June.

My internal alarm clock went off around seven the next morning, which was just as well since I'd forgotten to arrange a wake-up call. A strip of glorious sunlight cut like a laser through the gloom, and with hope in my heart I leapt out of bed— well, limped out of bed— and threw open the curtains. We had been blessed with another gloriously sunny day, and it even seemed that the wind had dropped— perfect racing weather.

I dallied too long in the shower, revelling in the powerful spray of hot, soothing water, screaming only a couple of times as soapy water stung the open blisters on my feet. Suitably refreshed I treated my feet to more padded plasters and creams, got dressed in clean clothes and hauled my gear along mile after mile of anonymous corridors. Or at least most of my gear. My shiny new Toshiba laptop, safe and secure in its own padded bag, was nowhere to be seen. I could only hope that it was still rattling around in the back of the Race Marine van, nestled between starter motors and cylinder head gaskets. But I was oddly grateful to have (temporarily) lost it; it was one less thing to lug around from pillar to post.

Most of the restaurant tables were taken up by teams enjoying a civilised breakfast, but the queue at the buffet table was mercilessly short and I had piled my plate full of food in no time. I joined Nik Keyser of Team *Cinzano*, who were running the aluminium Don Sheade-designed CUV. This boat had made quite a name for herself in the 1980's, winning the Cowes-Torquay-Cowes four times, and finishing second in the 1984 Round Britain. This time round, however, things were not looking quite as promising. Electrical trouble with the two Ilmor petrol V10 engines meant that she failed to complete the first leg, but Nik was hopeful that the problem had been rectified.

Nik finished the last of his coffee and excused himself, leaving me to gorge on toast, corn flakes and tea. I had become so engrossed in breakfast that I hadn't noticed that the room had cleared, and when I finally looked up I virtually had the room to myself. Looking for a safe spot to smoke my post-breakfast cigarette I wound up in the lobby, which was packed with racing teams gathered round little mounds of luggage. It seemed that just about everyone was on the phone, probably to the guy standing just a few feet away, and I threaded through them to escape to the solitude of a little open-air courtyard.

Sitting on a bench sucking sweet, sweet tobacco smoke into my lungs I wondered about how Mike Barlow and the rest of his crew were getting on in Brixham. Had they left for Plymouth yet, or had they somehow found a lorry to transport them by road to Milford Haven? I couldn't even call them to ask; my phone was now nothing more than a paperweight.

I checked my watch and found to my amazement that it was almost eight o'clock. The morning's briefing was due to start at 8:30, and I hadn't even booked a taxi yet. I dropped my cigarette butt in the ashtray and stepped back into the lobby, which was suddenly almost deserted. In the space of five minutes at least fifty people and their piles of bags had vanished into thin air.

I walked over to the receptionist (glad it wasn't the same girl from the previous night) and asked if she could book me a taxi. She managed not to laugh in my face, explaining that she'd already tried for other guests, but all taxis were fully booked for at least another hour.

Bugger! Why was everything going sideways on me? The tough part of this job was supposed to be the racing, not the simple stuff like getting something to eat or booking a cab!

I started unashamedly pleading with the half-dozen or so people left in the lobby to give me a lift down to Admiralty Pier, but they all shrugged apologetically, saying their cars were already dangerously overloaded. I stood outside the front door, miserably smoking another cigarette and mournfully watching as taxis turned up, filled to the brim with people and equipment, then drove off.

I went back inside, looking for new faces to hassle, but it was looking hopeless. I was just mentally preparing myself for the two mile walk when a total stranger ran up to me. "Quick, follow me!" he urged, then grabbed hold of my sleeve and literally dragged me outside. A car stood outside, engine running and one of the back doors open. "Get in!" he yelled and threw me into the back seat.

I was so stunned by this sudden event that I didn't have time to speak. *What the hell is this?* I wondered. *Am I being kidnapped here?* I hadn't even finished my thoughts when my mystery kidnapper slammed my door shut and thumped on the car roof, signalling the driver to catapult off, tyres screeching.

I was half sitting on top of someone else, who was in heated conversation with a girl in the front seat. Nobody even registered my presence. "Did you get the forecast?"

"Yes, I printed it off earlier. It's looking quite good; yesterday's force 9 has dropped away to a force 4. They're predicting a slight to moderate sea state," the girl replied. "Quite a change from yesterday."

My companion in the back seat seemed relieved. "Excellent. We should have a race today."

I decided to make my presence known. "Thanks for the lift guys. You saved my bacon there. Who are you with?"

"We're RYA. Glad to help out a competitor. What happened, did your team mates leave you behind?"

I explained my situation, and the car went quiet. They were clearly shocked at my lack of organisational skill, but luckily we rolled into Admiralty Pier before they had a chance to openly mock me.

We piled out of the car and I thanked them again for their help, then shouldered my bag to seek out Team *747*. I found them at Race Control, signing in for the day. Jonathan Napier looked like the stereotypical British Airways pilot he was, with silver hair and a friendly face. He greeted me with a warm handshake and introduced me to the rest of the crew.

Cormac Lundy and Andy Fielding were also B.A. pilots, but it would have been harder for me to guess it. The two men were balding, and stood noticeable shorter than their driver, Andy especially. And Cormac's broad Northern Irish accent and bawdier sense of humour set him apart from the others, making me think that perhaps he had just transferred from Ryanair.

We introduced ourselves as we walked; the briefing was about to begin. We filed into another ramshackle building, where a dilapidated room was slowly filing with other teams. The room was bereft of any furnishings or fixtures, apart from a laptop hooked to a projector that pointed at one blank wall.

Mike Lloyd again called us to order, starting his briefing with the news we all desperately wanted to hear. "Gentlemen, good morning. I'm pleased to see that you all made it here from Plymouth, which is wonderful news, because today we <u>will</u> be racing!" There was a cheer from the crowd. "Now, before we get into the details, I'd like to remind you all that you must not, under any circumstances, enter the exclusion zones. We will be monitoring every one of you via Marine-Track, and anyone who crosses over into one of these zones will be heavily penalised. Do I make myself clear?" There was a muttered rumble of understanding.

When Mike and his colleagues started organising the race almost two years before, they encountered a huge wave of objections from assorted wildlife protection organisations who were concerned of the threat to marine wildlife from fifty sets of razor-sharp props and phenomenally quick hulls. In a radical display of compromise and cooperation the Race Organisers and the various objection groups agreed to a series of exclusion zones, keeping the fleet clear from areas where local wildlife was considered to be most at risk. The decision seemed ludicrously obvious to me, but I was amazed to discover later that this was the first time in the history of offshore racing that anybody had attempted such a thing.

Mike then introduced us to a nervous young man who represented the Pembrokeshire Coast National Park. He cleared his throat, then started off by telling us all how excited everyone in the area was to be able to witness the wonderful spectacle of nearly fifty powerboats racing out of Milford Haven. But things quickly went sideways on him from there.

He punched a button on the laptop, and the stylised logo of a sea-gull over a dolphin flashed onto the wall. "Here in Pembrokeshire we are blessed with a wonderful array of stunning wildlife." This was beginning to sound like a well-rehearsed talk at a local primary school. "Not only do we have some beautiful and very rare plants-" a photo of a straggly-looking weed was projected on the wall— "but the area is also home to lots and lots of exciting wildlife." The weed was replaced by a cute little rabbit, possibly munching its way through the previous rare plant.

This was too much for some to take. Unsurprisingly, it was Ed Williams-Hawkes who was the most vocal. "Oh for God's sake! We're here to race, not to get a lecture on bloody rabbits!" His was the loudest of half a dozen or so objections, but Mike quickly stepped in to quieten him down.

"That's enough! This man has very kindly taken the time out to explain some of the area's rich wildlife; the very least you can do is shut up and let him finish!" The vast majority sided with Mike, and applauded to show their agreement. This made the wildlife guy even more nervous, but he bravely continued with his spiel.

I tuned out as he stammered his way through his little presentation. I had to agree with Ed on this one; we weren't here for a wildlife appreciation talk, we were here to *race*. Undoubtedly this little chat about seagulls and flowers was part of the Race Organisers' deal with the wildlife crowd, but there was a time and a place for that kind of petty finger-wagging, and half an hour before 200 miles of furious racing across the Irish Sea wasn't it.

Our wildlife expert hadn't done himself any favours either. Instead of opening with a picture of a cute wittle bunny-wunny he should have shown us a flock of thousands of guillemots sitting on the surface of the sea, or a pod of whales breaching. In a manic voice he should have howled: "Imagine you're doing eighty miles an hour when *BAAAM!!!* you plough into a flock of ten thousand birds! Or a pod of sperm whales suddenly surface right in front of you— *SMACK!!!* Those buggers can weigh up to 57 tons and grow up to 80 feet long! Imagine what hitting one of those would do to your boat!"

If he had started out like that, eyes wide and spittle flying from his lips, he would have had every man in the room hanging on his every word. We would all, as one man, have stopped breathing and leaned forward so as not to miss a single manic syllable. Tell a powerboat racer his wife had just been arrested for performing a sex act with one of the Queen's Corgis in front of visiting Heads of State at a Royal garden party and the best you'd get out of him would be a shrug. But tell him that his boat could potentially be irreparably damaged by an underwater obstacle and you'd have his full and undivided attention.

I was woken from my reverie by the sound of more applause, and our relieved-looking speaker thanked us and switched off his projector. Courtesies over, we got back to the small matter of the race to Northern Ireland. Gary Manchester, a very angry man in charge of the starting procedures, wasted no time in berating everyone for the piss-poor start at Portsmouth.

"Today we will be starting in two groups again. So all the boats in MC1, MC2, RB4 and the Historics will leave first. You are going to run three abreast behind the Start Boat right down Milford Sound. Once we reach the muster area you will approach the Start Boat one by one, so that I can check your race numbers against my list. Do <u>not</u> move off until I have signalled you to do so. Once I have told you to move off, you will join the rest of the fleet in circling counter-clockwise. Does everybody know what "counter-clockwise" means?" We cleared our throats and stared at the ground, but Gary wasn't asking a rhetorical question. "Does everybody understand what that means?" he asked again, raising his voice. The room responded with muttered yeses, and I almost laughed out loud at the bizarre spectacle of over one hundred men being bollocked like a bunch of naughty school children. He seemed satisfied by the response, then went on. "The Start Boat will then run roughly north to south, showing the yellow flag. That is your signal to follow me, but you must <u>not</u> overtake until I have hoisted the green flag. Is that clear?" There was a rumble of consent which Gary took as a mutual Yes. "Good. Once the first fleet is away, I will return here to pick up the second group and we'll do it all again. Any questions? No? Good." And with that he handed back to Mike, who gave us the weather forecast, reminded us once again to avoid the exclusion zones or else, and gave the start times for the two packs— 11 o'clock for the first fleet, and 11:30 for the second. The race starts had been delayed by three hours to give the stragglers a chance to get launched and fuelled after the chaos of the previous day, and it bought some teams crucial time to prepare for the 200 nautical mile crossing.

Briefing over for another day, we all filed out into the sunshine. I had signed in with Race Control the previous evening, so Jonathan took me down to the boat to get my gear ready for Scrutineering. Not only did Rob Beakhust and his band of Scrutineers check over every boat before each leg, they also had to make sure that each crew member was carrying all the right safety equipment. I laid out my racing clobber on *Miss Daisy's* deck for the Scrutineers to look over. I had my drysuit, a knife, pack of personal flares, medical compress and my stylish orange helmet. Guy Childs, one of the Scrutineers, took a quick look at my gear and shook his head.

"Where's your lifejacket? And your whistle? And who are you racing with today, Team *747*? 'Cos if you are, you'll need to change the numbers on your lid." And with that he walked off, shaking his head at my stupidity.

Jonathan told me he didn't have a spare lifejacket for me, and panic set in again. But I spotted the *Silverline* boys further down the pontoon so I jogged down and caught Jan's arm.

I explained the problem and he told me to speak to Ian, who was languishing in the cab of his truck. I almost kissed him when he dragged a spare Grabner from under a pile of bags and dirty clothes, and when he fished out a roll of black electrical tape I almost cried with joy.

The heavy duty lifejacket had a whistle secured to it by a bit of mouldy string, and with the electrical tape I could fashion the number 747 to stick on my lid. Everyone had to have their team's number clearly marked on the top of their helmet, so that they could be easily recognised from the air if they should find themselves paddling around the ocean for whatever reason. My lid still bore *Ocean Pirate*'s number, so I peeled off the vinyl 323 and replaced it with a crude, but legible 747. *Thank god the numbers were all straight lines* I thought; *I'd hate to be on a boat that was all eights, twos and fives.*

Once again fully legit to race, I hunted down Guy and proudly showed him the Grabner and my handiwork. He grunted and put a tick next to my name. I was set to go once again, and with only minutes to spare.

Jonathan had the decency not to brandish a list of Dos and Don'ts in my face; instead he quickly went over some basic safety instructions with me, but with time against us he stopped after a few moments. "Tell you what Derek, you seem halfway bright. Just do what we do and you'll be fine." With that he gave the thumbs-up to Fred Kemp and Mike, Jonathan's dad, who made up Team *747*'s shore crew. They cast us off, and as I struggled to get my Grabner and helmet on we slowly motored out to the centre of the channel.

As we waited for the rest of the first fleet to join us in clear water we all commented on what a great day it was turning out to be. The Sound was like a millpond, there were a scattering of fluffy cumulus clouds dotted around the rich blue sky, and the wind was negligible. Today was going to be a Good Day.

Things looked up even more when, like a curious dolphin, a boat with similar lines to our own *Miss Daisy* appeared and studied us from a distance. Immaculately turned out in crisp white with a blue cabin, she bore the number 290 and the word "Bovril" on her hull. This was *Miss Bovril II*, one of the boats that competed in the first Round Britain. She had raced alongside *GEE* (who had joined us in the Sound) and *Ocean Pirate* (who hadn't shown up yet) when she had finished a very respectable 15th overall. She wasn't racing this time around, but she had kept her original livery as a badge of honour.

Miss Daisy, the Fairey Spearfish that was about to whisk me over 200 nautical miles across the Irish Sea, was 30 feet of retro loveliness. Jonathan had restored her to serve as a high-speed cruiser on the French Riviera, where her classic lines matched the 40 knots her two Cummins engines produced. (By curious coincidence, these were the same spec engines that had powered my last fateful ride, *Ocean Pirate*.)

Jonathan had been inspired by a film of the 1969 race, when a fleet of five Faireys had entered, with four of them taking 3rd, 4th, 5th and 6th place overall. When he heard on the grapevine that there was to be a race in 2008 he wasted no time in signing his 30-year old boat up, but he was under no illusions regarding prizes. When I asked him my standard question— "Are you entering to win or to ex-perience a race?"— he answered with refreshing honesty.

"I don't think we stand much of a chance, to be honest. We're one of the slowest boats here. But we'll pick our fights; I think we'll probably give *GEE* a good run for her money!"

Indeed. But the competition already had a lead of almost 2 hours on the smaller boat, thanks to the detour Jonathan was forced to make when Mark Jealous was injured on the first leg. There had been fur-ther complications that day, when sea water had gotten into the fuel tank via the breathers. Fred Kemp had moved them, but only time would tell if the modification would do the job.

That wasn't to say that *GEE* was running a faultless race. Even be-fore the race had begun the team, made up of the three Clayton brothers amongst others, had been sailing pretty close to the wind: she wasn't launched until the 18th of June, just three days before the start. During desperately brief sea trials it became clear her trim tabs were playing up, and her props weren't delivering full speed. Frantic work remedied the faults in the nick of time, but even then they weren't problem-free, with the tabs failing again during the first leg.

Looking back at the pontoons at the base of Admiralty Pier, I spot-ted the unmistakable shape of *Red FPT*, repaired and ready to race once again. Further along was another unmistakable outline— *Buro*, the Botnia Targa 42 owned by Peter Vanhauter. She really stood out amongst her racing contemporaries, but I was glad to see her here none the less— the more the merrier I thought, and to hell with stereotypes. The same could be said for the much-maligned Scanner RIB *Braveheart III*. This team, made up of Scottish trawlermen, had surprised everyone by placing their shoe-shaped boat ninth on the first leg, the rough conditions proving that she wasn't just a Med boat.

Slowly more and more of the first fleet made their way out to the middle of the channel, and finally the Fountain Start Boat fired up its engines and led us down Milford Sound towards open water and the muster area.

That eight mile run down Milford Sound was one of the most in-credible experiences of my life. Twenty-two of us weaved our way down the Sound, the roar of our engines merging with that of our fellow competitors and the wind whistling past our helmets. We thundered on, jinking left and right to negotiate the narrow channel between the long finger piers where oil tankers discharged their valuable cargo. At twenty knots, and (roughly) three abreast, navigating through these bottlenecks was an exhilarating experience, made even more dramatic by the wakes of those in front. We were constantly surfing, pointing first one way and then another.

Jonathan was battling heroically, spinning the wheel from lock to lock as he tried to keep us clear of the boats around us, who were all trying to cope with the same conditions. Jonathan, looking for clear water, drifted to the right, letting the *Power Products Marine* Phantom take our port side. Alongside them was the *Braveheart* RIB, and we gave them all a happy wave. Further back was the incongruous shape of *Buro*, keeping close to their Belgian country-mates on the Buzzi-designed *Birretta* RIB.

As if trying to keep position in a column of twenty-two powerboats wasn't enough, we also had "civilians" to contend with. Our route down to the Irish Sea was lined by yachts and motorboats, a floating corridor of curious spectators, their boats rocking violently in the continuous wake. We waved at our guard of honour with the panache of movie stars on the red carpet, feeling slightly ridiculous and a little guilty for creating such havoc, but the smiles and waves from our victims quickly laid such concerns to rest.

It was a magnificent spectacle, and after my aborted start at Portsmouth two days before it gave me my first real taste of what powerboat racing was all about. And I wasn't just a spectator; I was a competitor, a participant— I was a racer. OK, in reality I was nothing more than moveable ballast and an unknown writer who might get the team's sponsors a bit of coverage in *MotorBoat & Yachting* magazine, but those poor bastards hanging on for dear life on their viciously-swaying dayboats didn't know that. To them I was another of those strange, mysterious beasts who are called "brave", "stupid" and "crazy" in equal measure.

There were also a few unwitting obstacles in the shape of three or four yachts. Blissfully unaware of the hellbroth fast approaching from astern, the "rag and stick" brigade were rudely awoken from their gentle pursuit as a snaking mass of noisy powerboats overtook them, and opposite the lifeboat station at Angle where the channel was particularly narrow the combined wake of our fleet set one yacht rocking in spectacular fashion. We waved friendly apologies and mouthed "Sorry!" at the poor buggers frantically clutching at railings and rigging to keep from being thrown overboard.

Finally we rounded Thorn Island and we dropped off the plane, slowly passing by the Start Boat so that Gary Manchester could check we were all present and accounted for. We had slowed to a crawl, and it became apparent that the mirror-smooth water at Admiralty Pier bore absolutely no resemblance to the big sloppy swell that now rolled in from the Irish Sea.

We idled past the Start Boat, and with Gary's nodded approval we motored off into West Angle Bay, on the southern side of the estuary, to join the dozen or so boats that were now executing a beautiful holding pattern. Like a shoal of sardines being corralled by a pack of sharks, they slowly circled anticlockwise around an invisible axis. We joined them seamlessly, and it was a truly wondrous thing to witness and to be a part of. There were no sudden bursts of throttle or frantic spinning of helms; the whole thing was effortless and inspiring, despite the six-foot waves that tried to knock us all off course.

Jonathan must have read my mind as I watched some of the smaller boats like Team *Jersey*'s little batboat being thrown about. He tapped my shoulder and said: "Don't worry about getting wet today; *Miss Daisy* is a really dry boat in a sea." Of course no sooner had the words left his lips when a rogue wave slapped into the starboard bow and doused us all in icy seawater. The look of total embarrassment on Jonathan's face was priceless, and he apologised to me like he'd just run over my dog. But I wasn't fazed; we were powerboat racers after all, not fair-weather boaters out for a Sunday afternoon run. It would take more than a dribble of icy water to get me down (although if it happened too often I would be forced to reassess my opinion...)

We were almost all in position, and the adrenaline was starting to jangle our nerve endings. We checked and double-checked the straps of our lids and bulky lifejackets. Andy went through the waypoints on the plotter one more time. Jonathan carefully studied the gauges, making sure the engines were running sweetly. And I— well, I generally got in the way and asked stupid questions.

Jonathan sat on the one-man bench seat to port, while Cormac and Andy took the longer seat on the starboard side. In front of them was the closed door that led to the cabin below, with a tiny head compartment to the left, opposite a small galley, with two bunks further forward.

I decided to sit on the deck behind Andy and Cormac's bench seat. Here I could brace my back against the coaming and wrap my right arm around the seat base. Although from here I couldn't see dead ahead, I was able to see everything to port, astern, and— with a bit of neck-craning— everything to starboard.

We were still slowly circling, waiting for the last boat to clear the Start Boat. Somebody said something like "That's the last of them: won't be long now!" and my heart rate cranked up a notch. And at that precise moment, as I looked south-westwards towards open water and our imminent route, I saw one of the most bizarre things I've ever witnessed.

From behind the rocky headland of St Anne's Head appeared a two-masted sailing ship, a surreal throwback to the time of Nelson and Blackbeard. Despite showing no sails, she glided serenely across the mouth of the estuary, looking so incredibly out of place that I hesitated in saying anything, lest I was suffering from some adrenaline-induced hallucination.

But the terse voice of Gary Manchester over the VHF confirmed that I really was seeing what I thought I was seeing, telling us that we'd have to wait until the unidentified vessel had cleared the entrance. Blissfully unaware that she was holding up twenty-odd fired-up racers she smoothly carried on her course, hugging the coast to destinations unknown.

After three or four minutes she finally slipped behind the southern headland and we were free to race. The Start Boat thundered past us, Guy hanging on to the yellow flag for dear life as the wind tried to rip it from his grasp. The fleet pointed their noses south-westwards, and as the Start Boat turned and raced towards open water (Guy now showing a green flag) we laid on the power and followed. As Jonathan opened the throttles the two Cummins engines beneath me changed pitch from a grumble to a roar, and then from a roar to a deafening howl as the green flag went down.

I had decided to squat for the start so that I could see ahead. My peripheral vision picked up other boats hurtling across the sea, but my attention— everybody's attention— was focused down a narrow tunnel that correlated with our course for the next five hundred feet or so. When the Start Boat backed off and turned to fetch the second fleet, we didn't notice. Unless something crossed our intended path we barely registered it.

Despite the intoxicating thrill of setting off at speed with twenty other likeminded lunatics, my haunches were starting to burn. I decided to sit back down on the teak decking, hanging on to the base of Andy and Cormac's seat for dear life.

Thundering across a seven-foot swell at 40 knots in a thirty foot boat was a magnificent spectacle; unfortunately the numbers also added up to a lot of time spent airborne. I was spending a great deal of time floating weightless several inches above the deck; which was fun, in an amateur-astronaut kind of way, but we all know that what goes up must come down, and smashing my skinny arse onto the deck repeatedly was already growing tiresome. I tried to wedge myself in by forcing myself backwards against the coaming, but there was nothing for my legs to brace against so I only succeeded in banging my spine against the fibreglass with every ferocious landing.

It seemed that despite their thinly-padded seats, the rest of the team were also taking a battering. Jonathan had little choice; he pulled back on the throttles a little, slowing *Miss Daisy* to around 28 knots or so. But unknown to us, damage had already been done.

We were now no more than ten minutes into the race, and as the teams followed their own courses the fleet scattered. It seemed that *GEE*'s track was pretty close to our own, and it was reassuring to be able to look back and right to see her high bow following along.

It was even more reassuring when suddenly, without any warning, the small wooden mast holding the VHF and GPS aerial fell backwards into the cockpit, the securing bolts having rattled loose from the violent pounding.

Jonathan immediately throttled back as Andy and Cormac wrestled with the two-foot long mast and its appendages. To lose either the radio or the GPS that was instrumental in guiding us across miles of anonymous water would have been a disaster. Of course every boat carried a spare compass, charts and hand-held VHF radios (not to mention a satellite phone for emergencies), but the chances for error were much greater when navigating with paper charts, and nigh-on impossible at speed.

Cormac ducked into the cabin and emerged a moment later with those two finest inventions— Duck tape and cable ties. We were frantically trying to strap everything back together when I suddenly felt a presence looming over my shoulder. I turned around and nearly crapped myself when I saw the forty foot bulk of *GEE* looming just a few yards behind us. She had dropped off the plane and was slowly motoring towards us to make sure we were OK. Jonathan gave the Clayton brothers a big thumbs up, and we wildly waved them past— there was no need for them to lose precious time worrying about us.

The *GEE* team opened the throttles and powered past us, waving enthusiastically. Their concern for us was heartening, and perfectly demonstrated the camaraderie that was beginning to pervade all aspects of this event. Today the Historics Class was made up only of *GEE* and Team *747*, the other boats missing this particular leg for various reasons. But instead of *GEE* taking full advantage of our temporary weakness, they chose instead to slow down and offer to help.

It took us a few more minutes of bodging before the mast was considered fit for purpose, and as soon as it was Jonathan wasted no time in opening the taps and chasing down the white smear in the distance that was *GEE*.

It was strange to see everyone fan out and disappear so quickly, especially when you consider that we had to avoid the exclusion zones that kept us well away from concentrations of marine wildlife. The zone stretched roughly from Skokholm island to the Smalls, two tiny clumps of rock some twenty nautical miles to the west of our starting point. This forced us to run westwards straight out into the Irish Sea, only turning northwards once we were clear.

But in the empty expanse of ocean we could just make out the tiny, fast-moving specks that were our race mates. One particular speck in front of us was growing larger by the second, and the lack of white water at her stern indicated she was barely moving. As we closed the gap it became clear it was *GEE* lying dead in the water. Jonathan turned towards her and began to slow down, but her crew waved us away, indicating that whatever the problem was, they had it under control. We had repaid the favour: Karma 2, Competitive Spirit 0.

Just before Jonathan opened the throttles again I decided to shift.

My arse-cheeks would be black and blue the next morning, and I did-n't fancy adding a splintered coccyx to my rapidly growing list of ail-ments. A little further aft the deck dropped down about a foot or so, and where it stepped there were two stainless steel mounts that came up about three feet. I stood between them and held on, and instantly discovered a much easier, painless method of travelling. With legs slightly apart I could balance easily, and by having my knees bent a little I found I could ride out the slams and crashes as we bounced off wave after wave.

Things improved even further when we finally cleared the Smalls and turned northwards. We were now running in the shelter of Ire-land, and slowly the sea dropped to virtually nothing. We still bounced over lazy rollers, but they were now only a couple of feet high at the most, and we managed to keep the props in the water pretty much constantly. The smoother it got, the further Jonathan opened the throttles, and we were soon screaming towards Bangor at 40 knots— top whack for this thirty-year old boat.

We were now slap-bang in the middle of the Irish Sea, and except for the giveaway white rooster tail of one of the top end boats in the distance— *Wettpunkt.com* perhaps, or *Blue FPT*— we had seen no other signs of life. And suddenly I felt a little odd. No matter where I looked, there was not a single sign of human activity. I couldn't make out the vaguest sign of land in any direction, even though we were now blessed with near-perfect weather. And although the second fleet had been released only half an hour after us, we had only spot-ted that one lonely rooster tail far off in the distance. The horizon was also bereft of trawlers, ferries or pleasure boats— we were to-tally alone. Up until that moment I didn't know what it felt like to suf-fer from agoraphobia, but after that day I think I have a rough idea.

It was hard to feel apprehensive for long though, because with the cheery smiles and thumbs-up from Andy, Cormac and Jonathan I couldn't help but shrug off any weird thoughts I might have been brewing. For a while I scrabbled forward to join the boys in a clumsy lunch of crisps and biscuits (crisps, by the way, are about the worst thing to try and eat on a speeding boat), and Cormac kept me enter-tained with jokes at Andy's expense.

"Here, did you know that all this pounding is making us shorter?" he shouted in his broad Ulster accent.

"Actually, yes," I replied. "I was reading up on it; it's a known fact that in long-distance races, crew actually lose up to half an inch!"

Cormac was grinning from ear to ear by now. "Did you hear that Andy? Half an inch he says!" And turning to me, he went on: "Andy's terrified— he's only just tall enough to be an airline pilot. If he winds up half an inch shorter he'll be out of a job!" Cormac and I shared a good laugh at that, but it looked like Andy failed to see the funny side.

"Relax Andy," I yelled, "you could always hang upside down somewhere for a couple of days when we're finished— get yourself stretched out again." It was hard to tell if Andy appreciated my advice— at the time I hadn't yet realised that Andy's sense of humour could sometime be drier than a camel's jockstrap.

As we rocketed across the desolate emptiness of the Irish Sea I did a quick spot of mental arithmetic. The leg from Milford Haven to Bangor was 200 nautical miles. At forty knots, that meant we'd be there in exactly five hours. But the distance of 200 nm was based on a perfect course. We would probably go over that slightly, and we hadn't been able to run at top speed for the entire leg. Throw in a margin for error and I arrived at a guesstimate time of between five and a half and six hours. Provided nothing went wrong, that was...

Over the years the popularity of racing powerboats has waxed and waned, just like any other niche sport. It first sprung to prominence in the early 1900s with the wealthy upper classes. With time on their hands, money to burn, and an insatiable need to relieve the boredom of being rich and idle, they sought out new ways of finding excitement and adventure. They found it in building and racing ever more powerful boats, utilising the new petrol engines whose performance and reliability were improving almost weekly. As the engines improved it became clear that the design of the wooden hulls also needed to be developed, and during that time the advances in hull design leapt forward at a staggering pace.

The displacement hull had been around for many years, but suddenly the advent of the internal combustion engine highlighted its limitations. In a flurry of mathematical and engineering brilliance, new hulls were produced in a relatively short period of time: planing hulls, hard chines, sharp V hulls that flattened out, even stepped hulls were created (although this particular innovation was very much a dark art with a plethora of opposing opinions: some insisted that any more than two steps were a waste of time, whilst others felt that the more the merrier, with some hulls boasting up to a dozen steps).

It was around the same time that designers started experimenting with different drives, and once again it was these first pioneers that paved the way for what we still use today, nearly a century on. V drives, stern drives and even surface drives first saw the light of day in the 1910s and 20s.

This evolution would never have taken place if it wasn't for the competitive spirit of the wealthy racers whose names are now synonymous with the sport: names like Gar Wood, Hubert Scott-Paine, Henry Segrave, Kaye Don and Marion "Jo" Carstairs are the very foundation stones of powerboat racing today.

(Ah, these names! They stir the racer's blood and evoke mental black and white film-reels of quick smiles on oily faces; starched collars under white overalls and firm sportsmanlike handshakes. But the stories behind the names... Gar Wood, for example, refused to race unless his two lucky charms– teddy bears stolen from his wife– were securely tied to the boat's engines. Marion Carstairs was an infamous lesbian, shocking the world with her insistence on wearing men's clothes, while Segrave had recovered from terrible injuries in the First World War to go on and set a new land speed record– in 1927 he had thundered across Daytona Beach at 203 miles per hour. Whenever these people encountered any form of obstacle or boundary they would shoulder it aside, thrusting their way through using nothing more than the sheer force of their will. They were a unique group of individuals, and it seems obvious that they would have excelled in any discipline. The powerboat racing community was incredibly fortunate that they had chosen the unpredictable surface of the sea as their battlefield of choice.)

But what were they racing for? National pride, for one thing. In 1903 Sir Alfred Harmsworth– a wealthy publisher– established the Harmsworth Trophy in an attempt to make powerboat racing as popular and successful as motor racing was starting to become. It worked— and the sport's popularity slowly grew on both sides of the Atlantic. In 1931 an estimated half a million spectators crowded along the banks of the Detroit River to witness one particular race between Kaye Don in *Miss England II* and the American Gar Wood in *Miss America IX*. (It ended badly for the Brits– *Miss England II* flipped and sank, although Don was unhurt.) It was during preparations for this now infamous race that both boats broke the magical ton– first Wood, and then, a few days later, Kaye Don topped 100 miles per hour.

When the Second World War rolled around all these jolly indulgences were put on hold as everybody focussed on the job at hand, although the specialised skills of Scott-Paine and Wood were utilised by the military to develop Motor Torpedo Boats. After the war the Harmsworth Trophy was re-instated, but in those austere years interest had waned, especially in the rarefied air of international competition.

It wasn't until the late Fifties that the sport started to make a comeback with the introduction of the Miami-Nassau race. It was, on the whole, very much an American affair, and the majority of competitors weren't wealthy industrialists; rather they were racing car drivers in search of a suitably adrenaline-filled hobby to supplement their 9-5.

The situation returned to form when Sir Max Aitken, a wealthy English newspaper publisher, took part in a Miami-Nassau race. He and his wife Lady Violet were so enraptured by the experience that they vowed to bring a similar event to Britain, and in 1960 he announced that he would be organising a race from the Isle of Wight to the English coast. The next year, in 1961, the very first Cowes-Torquay powerboat race was run.

The basic premise for competing craft was initially very simple, with the rules based on cabin cruisers widely available at the time. The theory behind it was not only to make the sport more accessible to the man in the street, but also to encourage mainstream manufacturers to develop their existing models, with some success.

The late Sixties saw the original Cowes-Torquay distance double as teams were now forced to return to Cowes, making the event a true marathon at around 230 miles. This was also the golden age of modern racing, with other countries also establishing their own events. And, most pertinently, 1969 saw the inaugural Round Britain race–one of the toughest, longest offshore races the world had ever seen.

But by the mid-Seventies the sport's popularity once again dipped, and Aitken's original desire to see everyday cabin cruisers racing competitively became diluted as manufacturers started producing more specialised machines.

(This throws up a tricky conundrum: did the sport's popularity wane because it was getting so elite, or did it become an elitist environment because only a small group of people still took part? This is a real "chicken & the egg" question, and if anybody can give me a definitive answer, I'd be happy to hear it.)

Regardless of the reasons why, powerboat racing was once again falling out of the spotlight. When the second Round Britain race was held in 1984, the field was made up of a handful of thoroughbred racers and a gaggle of ill-prepared amateurs, and the event barely made the news. But *this* race was turning out to be something quite different. A fleet of nearly fifty boats was virtually unheard of in recent years, and since the rules stipulated that the dominant catamaran hulls were banned it made for a much more competitive race than the 1984 event. It was starting to look like powerboat racing was making a resurgence, and not before time.

I had been pondering these things as we zipped along the Irish Sea at forty knots, my mind lost in the days of Wood and Carstairs. But slowly I started to sense a change of atmosphere on the boat, and I turned my attention back to the present.

Jonathan and Andy had been deep in discussion, and when Andy ducked below for a second before coming back with an almanac clutched in his hand I knew we had a problem. We had been running along the Irish east coast for about half an hour or so, and by shouted conversations I knew we were just a few miles from the finishing line at Bangor. The two men consulted the almanac, and as Andy wrestled his phone from his pocket Jonathan eased back on the throttles.

As he made his was aft to where I stood with a stupid expression on my face he quickly explained. "I don't think we have enough fuel to make it. Give me a hand lifting the hatch so we can have a look."

We opened the hatches and knelt down to squint through the Perspex covers. The tanks were virtually empty! "OK, we'll have to go in to refuel somewhere. Derek, as soon as we get alongside the fuel pontoon get the filler caps off. Cormac, you're on fenders. Don't bother tying up; just hang on to something. Andy, how are we doing?"

Andy was still talking to someone on the phone but he threw Jonathan a quick thumbs up. We dropped the hatch covers again and Jonathan took the helm. "Well?"

"Copeland Marina. Donaghadee. Two miles that way," he pointed.

Jonathan wasted no more time; he pointed *Miss Daisy* in the direction of a small town in the distance and opened the taps once again. But here was a real dilemma— should he run flat out to minimise the damage to our time, or should he take it easy to eke out the few litres of fuel we had left? He compromised, and ran for Donaghadee at 20 knots.

As we chewed our fingernails Cormac decided it was time to offer some of his own local knowledge. "Now Jonathan, Andy, when we get there don't say a word, OK? Just let Derek and me do all the talking. With your poncy English accents you're likely to get us all shot."

The two of them stared at him incredulously, but he managed to keep a straight face. I decided to join in the fun. "Cormac's right. He's a local boy, and I'll be safe enough because we Scots get on fine with the Irish. But you two are deep in bandit country, so unless you want the boat to mysteriously catch fire, just keep quiet."

For a long, long moment Jonathan believed every word we said. Then he finally twigged that we were winding him and Andy up, and despite the tense situation he managed to break into a smile.

We barrelled into the little marina and found the fuel pontoon straight away. Jonathan spun the boat round so that we were facing out and Andy and Cormac threw out a couple of fenders. We hadn't even kissed the pontoon yet, but Jonathan was already yelling orders to the two bemused marina staff. "Diesel! 100 litres in each tank! Please tell me you'll take a cheque?"

One guy passed me a fuel hose and I yelled Go! as soon as the nozzle was in the general vicinity of the filler. It was a shock to see just how little fuel was left— we were way past running on fumes, by now those Cummins were running solely on memories. As the precious liquid pumped into that tanks— slowly, soooo slooooowly— Jonathan was frantically scribbling a cheque. I heard someone saying "That's one hundred litres" and I whipped the nozzle out of one tank and into the other, then yelled Go! again.

The whole thing was done in under ten minutes, and probably closer to five. It wasn't quite Formula 1 territory, but by marine standards it was pretty damn quick. The two marina guys gave us big friendly waves and wished us luck as we raced out of the marina again, probably slightly over the permitted limit.

Out in open water we spotted the big RIB *Seafarer* thundering towards Bangor. We were now pitifully close to the finish line, just six miles round the headland. Then, as we approached the narrow channel between the Irish mainland and Copeland Island I spotted the *Silverline* boat, clearly having difficulties. It looked like they had lost steering or perhaps an engine, because every time they gunned the throttle the boat just turned her bow to starboard.

But they were in no imminent danger, and help was literally just around the corner. There was plenty of clear water between them, us and the shore, so without missing a beat we roared past them and made the turn eastwards into Belfast Lough.

We skirted Ballymacormick Point and suddenly we were faced with a bewildering assortment of civilian boats. There were a couple of plastic cabin cruisers and three or four small RIBs all waving excitedly. It was all very nice and friendly, but where the fuck was the finish? We needed to cross the line between a boat flying the RYA flag and a marker buoy, but in the confusion it was impossible to make out where that was. We were all shouting at each other, desperate to know if anyone knew where the finish boat was, and Jonathan ended up sweeping through the gaggle of spectators at full speed and looping round to come in again. Finally we spotted a chequered flag being hastily unfurled from one nondescript fly bridge cruiser, and we realised we had crossed the line.

To say I felt good was an understatement. I was euphoric, having finally enjoyed my first full-length leg in actual racing conditions. My body had taken a battering, but at that moment I was blissfully unaware of my aches and pains. I should also have been feeling tired after spending six hours trying to keep my balance in a bucking boat, but that too was temporarily pushed to one side whilst I shared in the team's mixture of relief and jubilation. As we slowly nosed our way through the gap of the sea wall into the magnificent Bangor marina we congratulated each other and formally shook hands.

Marina staff directed us to a temporary berth by the fuel pontoon, and as we made our way into the heart of the complex we spotted other race boats already tied up, mechanics busy with servicing, checks and repairs. We tied up *Miss Daisy* and shut her hardworking engines down.

Just next to the marina building stood a little portable office that was serving as Race Control, and as Jonathan signed in I took a look at the results sheet pinned to the wall.

Once again one of the prototype Goldfish RIBs had excelled. On the first leg *Lionhead* had taken second place; today her sister boat *Guttaboyz* had won it. *Wettpunkt.com* had overcome the engine problems of the first day to take second, and third into Bangor was *Mr Mako*, a Pascoe RIB.

The times showed the difference in performance between those at the front and the Historical boats; *Guttaboyz* had covered the 200 nm in three hours and thirty-five minutes, whilst we had been at sea for five hours fifty-six minutes. And *Miss Daisy* claimed to be the fastest Fairey in the world! Still, at least we weren't last— we were shown as 28th, with at least a dozen boats still to come in, including *GEE*, Team *747*'s closest rival.

Jonathan had finished signing in, and as he stepped over to check out the results Gill, she of the unnatural red hair, turned her attention to me. "Oh hi Derek. How was your day?"

"Excellent Gill, really amazing."

"Good, I'm pleased. So, who will you be racing with tomorrow then?" she asked with an innocent little smile.

Her question totally threw me for a moment. "Uh, I'll be with, um,-"

Jonathan leapt in to save me. "Actually Derek, we'd be more than happy to have you along with us again if you're stuck."

God love that man! "Really? Fantastic! Yes, if you're sure you don't mind...?"

With that settled I turned to Gill with a haughty expression. "I think you'll find I'll be racing with my good friends in Team *747* tomorrow Gill. All right?" And without waiting for an answer I turned and stepped out of the office, my feelings still smarting from her insinuated insult.

By now the fuel pontoon had almost cleared, so we went back to the boat and motored across to fill the tanks— all the way this time. Cormac's brother Brendan had joined us, and had brought refreshments in the form of six bottles of Stella. We all gratefully accepted a bottle, and once we were securely tied up and the fuel pump was running we all looked around for a suitable bottle opener.

I was smacking the neck of my bottle against a steel ladder with no real chance of success when one the crew from *Buro* called me over. They had just joined us on the pontoon, and while his team-mates finished tying the Botnia Targa up he took the bottle from me and with a magical fluid movement handed me my beer back— minus a top.

I've always been like a child when it comes to sleight of hand stuff, and this little trick totally blew me away. Hey guys! Check this out— he just opened my bottle by magic!" By now the others were getting frustrated by the lack of bottle opening devices on board, so it was more my brandishing of an open bottle that caught their attention, rather than the promise of a magic trick.

Cormac was closest, and he handed the bottle across to me. I passed in across to my new Belgian friend, and with a Gallic "allez-*pouf*!" he popped the top. He'd been too quick for me, and I'd missed how he'd done it. Luckily there were still four more bottles to be opened, which were passed down in quick succession. And then I figured it out. He was using his wedding ring as an opener, levering the tops off between it and his finger. Genius! Proof at last that that little ribbon of battered gold was good for more than just scaring off attractive women!

After refuelling we cruised round to the boat's overnight berth, then I slung my bag over my shoulder and wished the *747* boys good night. Now that all the adrenaline and euphoria of the day had worn off, I realised I was absolutely shattered. Six hours spent standing on a bucking deck had torn open my feet again, and my leg muscles had turned to lead. Wearily I trudged back up the steps and past the marina office, looking for a payphone so I could call a cab.

But before I got a chance to have a look around I spotted *Buzzi Bullet* sitting on the back of her lorry. I walked over and found Ian Brown up to his elbows in oil.

"Hi Ian, what happened? I saw her a couple of miles from the finishing line, going round in circles it looked like."

"Oh hello mate, I didn't think I'd see you here! Looks like the boys have knackered a gearbox. They've got no drive to one shaft, so we'll be up all night trying to sort it. You didn't pass Miles did you? He was supposed to be getting checked out by the doc."

"No, why? What happened?" I asked.

"He got thrown about a bit coming across the Irish Sea; looks like he's banged up a couple of ribs."

"Jesus! Well I hope he's OK. Tell them I said Hi will you? I'm off; I need my bed."

Ian laughed. "Yeah mate, you look like shit!" With that cheery comment I wished him luck for the long night ahead, and I staggered off in search of a taxi.

Then it suddenly dawned on me— I still had to call in my daily report to Rob, and to reassure my Beloved that I had survived another day. I stopped a stranger and asked if there was somewhere nearby that sold phone chargers, and she pointed me up Main Street where she told me I would find an Asda. I cast an apprehensive eye at the steep road. She caught the look on my face and reassured me. "Ah, don't you worry yerself. It's just a wee walk; you'll be there in no time at all." And with a cheery pat on my arm she turned and left me to face what looked like the Eiger by myself.

Of course it really wasn't that steep, but the combination of exhaustion, stress and shredded soles made that long arduous trek feel like a never-ending torment.

When I reached the supermarket I made a bee-line for their mobile phone section. I searched through the racks of chargers, but couldn't find one to suit my phone. *Screw it* I thought to myself. *Just buy a new one and be done with it!* I picked up a Pay As You Go phone and gave the cashier £50, making sure that the receipt went straight into my bag. *The fucking magazine got me into this shit, they can bloody-well buy me a new phone* I thought angrily.

As soon as I was outside I ripped the box open and carefully transferred the SIM card from my crappy Motorola into my shiny new Nokia. When I turned it on, however, all I got was a message stating "SIM card incompatible". So I took it out and tried again. And again. By now I felt like crying, so I pulled myself together, jammed everything back into the box and went back inside the supermarket.

The girl behind the counter seemed eager to help me, but she couldn't figure out why my SIM card wouldn't work either. She suggested that I try another phone, but her manager overheard her and blundered into our conversation. He wanted to know what the problem was, and so I explained the whole sorry mess to him.

"Huh." he said when I was done. "So why don't you just buy a universal charger?"

I looked at him blankly, and he explained that they sold phone chargers with a whole range of different adaptors to suit every phone. He sent the girl off to find one, and when she returned he studied the back of the packaging. "Now then, let's have a little loo— Aha! Here we are sir, Motorola. I think you'll find this is just what you'll be needing." I thanked him and he glided off, no doubt looking forward to pasting another gold star in his diary that night.

I paid the girl for the adaptor and stepped back out into the magnificent evening sunshine. Just along from Asda was a pizza restaurant, and I went in to give my feet a reprieve. The teenager behind the counter told me he wasn't open yet, but I replied that I just needed to sit down for ten minutes. I took his noncommittal shrug as permission and I dropped into a chair next to a power socket. After grappling with the god-awful plastic packaging I finally managed to scatter a dozen tiny little adaptors all over the table, earning me a glower from my host as he wrapped cutlery on the other side of the room. But no matter how hard I tried, I couldn't make any of them fit my bastard phone.

People who know me will attest to the fact that I've never been very good at controlling my temper, and as my frustration with the fiddly little phone adaptors grew, so did my rage. Finally I could take no more of my phone's inanimate insolence and I threw the hateful bugger across the room, where it smashed into the far wall with a delicious crunch. "Worthless piece of drivelling *SHITE!*" I yelled out after it, totally losing the plot.

The poor guy who had let me in hurried over, wanting to know what the fuck was going on. I immediately apologised and tried to calm down; the last thing I needed was some horrible scene with a 18 year old kid in a deserted pizza place. I sucked in plenty of calm, refreshing air and explained to the guy about the problems I'd been having with my phone, and to his credit he managed to see my side of it.

He fetched my miraculously undamaged phone and gently tried to make one of the adaptors fit. Suddenly it lit up and it started to charge— it was a genuine miracle! It wasn't the right connector, but he found that if he jammed it in and pressed it to one side he could make a reasonable connection.

I nearly cried again, this time in relief. I gratefully accepted his offer of coffee, which I sipped while sweet, precious electricity trickled into my phone. When I slipped out fifteen minutes later I left him a tenner under my cup as a thank-you, then called my guesthouse for directions. Instead my cheery landlord told me not to be daft; he would come and fetch me himself. I told him where I was, and five minutes later he rolled up to the pavement.

Billy was an absolute gentleman, even heaving my heavy bag into the boot for me. The guesthouse was only a couple of streets away, but in the quiet comfort of his old BMW I almost fell asleep.

His wife Mary was just as welcoming, and she could tell I was in no fit state for idle chit-chat. She showed me to my room, where I barely managed to call Rob with my progress report before plugging in my charger and passing out fully clothed on the bed.

Below– *Miss Bovril II*, a veteran of the 1969 race, now a spectator

Top– *Power Products Marine* with *Braveheart III* in the background

Below– *Blue FPT, GEE* and *Pulsar-Wolf* running down Milford Sound

Results-
Milford Haven to Bangor.

Distance: 201 nautical miles.

Pos.	Team/ Number	Class	Time	Overall position (Class)
1st	Guttaboyz/33	RB3	3:25:52	3 (2)
2nd	Wettpunkt.com/81	RB1	3:29:07	33 (2)
3rd	Mr Mako/96	RB4	3:45:12	9 (1)
4th	Team Bandit/69	RB2	3:59:02	10 (1)
5th	Hot Lemon/2	RB3	4:04:25	4 (3)
6th	Hardleys/4	RB3	4:05:24	5 (4)
7th	Blue FPT/333	MC1	4:05:38	2 (1)
8th	Braveheart III/55	MC1	4:07:41	6 (2)
9th	Vilda/9	RB3	4:09:22	7 (5)
10th	Sealbay/77	RB4	4:09:48	11 (2)
11th	Lionhead/22	RB3	4:11:56	1 (1)
12th	Venturer/111	RB1	4:21:04	22 (1)
13th	swipewipes.co.uk/ 43	RB4	4:24:03	12 (3)
14th	Seahound V/80	MC1	4:29:23	8 (3)
15th	Team Scorpion Dubois/16	MC1	4:33:42	18 (5)
16th	Birretta/12	MC1	4:39:58	13 (4)
17th	Carbon Neutral/343	RB3	4:42:41	15 (7)
18th	Power Products Marine/8	MC2	4:44:36	17 (1)
19th	Northern Spirit/5	MC2	4:46:49	20 (2)
20th	Seafarer/110	RB3	4:47:07	19 (8)

Pos.	Team/ Number	Class	Time	Overall position (Class)
21st	Fugitive/130	MC2	5:04:18	27 (4)
22nd	Tequila/88	RB3	5:09:29	21 (9)
23rd	Going Lean/7	RB3	5:11:53	14 (6)
24th	TFO/17	MC2	5:16:10	24 (3)
25th	My Pleasure II/3	RB4	5:18:19	23 (4)
26th	Team Pulsar-Vampire/102	RB4	5:35:47	25 (5)
27th	Relentless/47	RB3	5:37:21	26 (10)
28th	**Team 747/747**	**HC1**	**5:56:29**	**32 (2)**
29th	Team Silverline/471	RB2	6:03:43	16 (2)
30th	Buro/15	MC1	6:18:40	28 (6)
31st	Team Pulsar-Wolf/101	RB4	6:26:22	30 (6)
32nd	GEE/185	HC1	6:26:29	29 (1)
33rd	Mud, Swell & Beers/14	RB4	6:57:37	31 (7)
34th	RIB International/144	RB4	**DNF**	38 (10)
35th	Team Jersey/45	RB4	**DNF**	39 (9)
36th	Black Gold/10	RB4	**DNF**	35 (8)
37th	Team Blastoff/100	RB2	**DNF**	41 (3)
38th	Garmin Racing/72	RB2	**DNF**	40 (4)
39th	Mystic Dragon/6	MC1	**DNF**	34 (7)
40th	Red FPT/177	CC1	**DNF**	42 (1)

DNS Denotes Did Not Start
DNF Denotes Did Not Finish
OTR Denotes Out of The Race
* Denotes maximum time allowance exceeded.

Pos.	Team/ Number	Class	Time	Overall position (Class)
41st	Cinzano/558	RB2	**DNF**	47 (5)
42nd	Blue Marlin/99	HC1	**OTR**	44 (4)
43rd	Xanthus/1	HC1	**DNS**	37 (3)
44th	No Worries/11	RB3	**DNF**	45 (12)
45th	Ikon/18	RB3	**DNF**	36 (11)
46th	Ocean Pirate/323	HC1	**DNS**	46 (6)
47th	Swordsman/68	HC1	**DNS**	43 (5)

DNS Denotes Did Not Start
DNF Denotes Did Not Finish
OTR Denotes Out of The Race
* Denotes maximum time allowance exceeded.

Below– *Miss Daisy* cooling her props, Bangor

8.
Bangor to Oban.

Tuesday 24th June.

They say Saint Patrick dreamt of seraphim when he spent the night in Bangor some 1600 years ago, which is why the area is also known as the Vale of Angels. Perhaps it's just as well that he wasn't caught up in the middle of some demented powerboat race, because "Glade of Unconsciousness" just doesn't have the same ring to it.

Waking up on that glorious Tuesday morning was a real struggle for me, and by the time I had made it downstairs I was running late— again. Fortunately Mary, my landlady, was an understanding soul and she wrapped a bacon roll in Bacofoil and called a taxi for me while I sipped scalding hot tea.

Down at the marina there was no sign of the Race Organisers, so I took a stroll down the pontoons to see if my crewmates from Team *747* had arrived at the boat yet. They hadn't, but on my way down I had noticed the *Silverline* boat was tied up on one of the pontoons. Since she was back in the water I assumed that Steve the Race Marine mechanic had managed to fix whatever the problem had been, so out of curiosity I set off to find someone who might know more.

Eventually I bumped into Ian and his son Josh, who were just preparing to set off for the ferry terminal at Larne, 30 miles away. Ian told me that they had worked through the night welding a drive coupling on the boat, and he was looking forward to the ferry crossing to Stranraer on the Scottish mainland so that he could catch up on some sleep before the long drive up the coast to Oban.

He also managed to hit me with a thrilling bit of news— there might be a seat for me on the boat! I left them to it and set off in search of Drew.

When I finally caught up with him it was back at the Marina office, where a large crowd of racers had gathered for that morning's briefing. Jan, John and Miles were also there, and after a quick greeting they turned back to hear what Mike had to say. Drew and I went into a private huddle, whispering so as not to interrupt Mike.

"Hi Drew, Ian said you might have a seat for me today?"

"That's right. Miles is still suffering with his ribs, so he's going to sit this leg out. You're more than welcome to join us if you like."

"That'd be great! Cheers Drew!"

With that taken care of, there was still the small matter of letting Jonathan know the change of plans. I caught sight of him and the rest of the *747* team right at the other end of the crowd, and I muscled my way through to get to him before Annie did.

At every briefing Annie would go through her list of teams, asking each one in turn to confirm who would be on board that day. Since many teams rotated their crew, it was essential that Race Control knew exactly how many would be on each boat for each leg in case of an accident— it would be potentially catastrophic if a boat sank, and the rescue services didn't know there had been an extra crew member on board that day.

Annie had already started working her way through her list as I frantically jostled my way through the crowd of bemused competitors, muttering "Excuse me, sorry, coming through, watch yourself!" as I went. Annie got to Jonathan seconds before I did.

"Team *747*, who's racing today? I've got Jonathan, Andy and Cormac. Is that right?" she called out.

Jonathan gave me a quick "Morning Derek" before telling Annie in a loud clear voice: "We've also got Derek Wynans with us again today."

"Actually mate, Drew's offered me a spot on his boat," I whispered. "Do you mind?"

"Eh? No, that's fine. Actually Annie," he trumpeted again, "Derek now won't be joining us— it'll just be the three of us."

Annie fixed me with a glare. "Jumping ship are you?" she asked cynically.

The crowd was watching us closely, and I felt a bead of sweat trickle down my temple. "Hi Annie, yes, I'm riding with the *Silverline* guys today. If that's alright with you."

She now turned to pick out Drew. "Is that right? Are you taking Derek?"

The crowd turned its head like spectators at a tennis match, curious about this new development. "That's right. It'll be myself, Jan, John and Derek. No Miles today," Drew replied.

She gave a little "Humph!" of displeasure and made a scribble on her clipboard. Then she dismissed us by calling to the next team on her list, pointedly asking them if *they* were making any changes to their line-up. They smugly replied they weren't, and Annie gave me a look as if to say: "See? They know not to mess up my system!"

The briefing ended, as always, with a weather forecast for the day ahead. There was a gentle north-westerly blowing, with sea states said to be "moderate, easing later". Conditions looked to be good, and I was looking forward to the 115 nm run to my home town. This leg would be one of the shortest, and on board *Buzzi Bullet* it was also guaranteed to be one of the quickest— provided nothing went wrong.

Once the briefing was over I was free to apologise to Jonathan, Cormac and Andy for dumping them just half an hour before the start. But there were no hard feelings, and they wished me well on the *Silverline* boat.

With that taken care of, I scurried back to Drew and the boys to find out exactly what had happened to the boat yesterday, and how they had managed to fix it.

Drew explained that they had burnt out the rubber coupling that was fitted between the gearbox and the drive shaft on the starboard engine. This rubber coupling is designed to absorb the sudden shock that occurs every time the props enter or leave the water when the boat is running hard in rough conditions. The sudden load (or lack of load) on the drive shafts could damage the gearbox and possibly the engine, so a damper is fitted to take the worst of the force. Yesterday one of the couplings had finally had enough and the tough rubber had physically melted away, leaving the boat virtually helpless. She had eventually made it into Bangor just after us, drastically dropping her in the overall results table from first to 32nd overall and second in the RB2 Class.

They had worked through the night to strip the coupling down and had hired a local welder to physically weld the two ends of the coupling together. This meant that *Buzzi Bullet* was now back in the running, but without the rubber to absorb the sudden shock of the props spinning clear of the water and then suddenly hitting resistance again as they re-entered, Drew would have to take it easy in rough seas.

All this was relayed to me rather hurriedly, as the race start was not far off. I dragged my holdall into the marina's changing room and set about getting kitted up.

This was the first time I would have to rely on my full wardrobe of protective racing gear. On *Ocean Pirate* and *Miss Daisy* I had been warm enough in jeans, a t-shirt and jumper, with my wonderfully comfortable Gul jacket keeping me dry from the occasional splash of rogue spray. But on *Buzzi Bullet* I would need something a little more substantial.

I stripped bollock-naked, magnanimously ignoring the envious stares from the other men who were getting changed, and pulled on the thin and gossamer-light leggings and top that made up my base layer. Then I strapped on the sturdy knee supports and kidney belt, essential for surviving the boat's bone-jarring ride, before climbing into the clumsy drysuit. I dug my gloves out of my holdall, and dumped a pair of jeans, t-shirt and my sadistic trainers into my drybag, along with my newly-resuscitated phone and trusty tobacco tin.

I now had my bulky Grabner lifejacket and gloves in one hand, with my holdall and drybag in the other. I waddled down the pontoon and dumped the drybag and Grabner next to the *Silverline* boat, then hurried along to *Miss Daisy*, where Jonathan, Cormac and Andy were just preparing to head off to the muster area. They kindly agreed to take my holdall to Oban for me, and we wished each other luck before I headed back to *Bullet*.

I just had time to stow my drybag in the bottom of the boat before John cast us off, and as he scrambled on board Drew dropped the engines into gear and Jan guided us out of the marina, weaving through the three massive breakwaters that protect the 600 or so berths from the worst the Irish Sea can throw at it.

I had just finished the laborious struggle of clipping the emergency kill-chord round my leg when Drew's voice came over the intercom.

"Guys, can any of you hear the trim tabs clicking?" We all held our breath, listening to hear the tell-tale electrical *click click click* that usually sounded over the intercom when the trim tab switches were operated. Nothing.

"Shit. OK, Derek, can you give John a hand getting the engine cover up please? John, take a look, see if you can spot anything," Drew asked us. Now I tried frantically to unclip the kill-chord from round my calf again and unstrap my helmet so that I could turn around to undo the catch that secured the engine cover. Somehow John had managed to undo his before me, but after a moment or two the hatch was up and John had disappeared into the engine compartment head-first, just his ankles showing.

After a minute I suddenly felt Jan banging on my back: because John and I had removed our lids we couldn't hear that the tabs had started working again. Jan threw me a big thumbs-up and pointed at John. I grabbed one flailing foot and dragged him out of the engine bay, then we dropped the hatch and re-secured it before starting the whole kill-chord-reattachment process all over again. Once I got my helmet on I overheard John telling Drew that he had found a loose connection on one of the batteries, probably a result of the work done the previous night.

Drew's decision to take the Cummins engineer on every leg now made perfect sense; I'm pretty sure I would have struggled to find and cure the fault as quickly as John had, despite my mechanical training, and his presence on board had made the difference between racing and a very uncomfortable and slow crossing to Oban. Realistically, I think that Drew would have opted to turn back to port to effect repairs rather than risk the perilous 115 nm leg without working trim tabs.

As I had discovered in Italy a few months earlier, the tabs were essential for negotiating the tight corners of a P1 circuit, letting Jan either slide the back end out, or keeping it tightly tucked in, depending on how he wanted to get round the marker buoys. In long-distance endurance racing, however, corners are few and far between, and often a driver can cover dozens of miles without having to make a course change (unless something gets in the way, like a lobster marker or another boat). A change of direction usually happens when the boat passes a headland, and then it's usually done without the flamboyance and dramatics of a tight circuit turn.

So why the importance of the trim tabs in endurance racing? Well for one thing, they're essential to getting the boat's hull up on the plane. With the tanks stuffed with fuel, not to mention all the safety gear and spares on board, a thoroughbred racing boat will struggle to get up enough speed to get up onto the plane, that magical point where the bow drops, the stern lifts and the whole outfit becomes a light, balanced arrow slicing through the water. Up until that point, they tend to be cumbersome, clumsy creatures, wallowing around with their bows pointed skywards at ridiculous angles so steep that the drivers can't see past them to know where they're going.

This is where the tabs are vital. A press of a button activates an electric ram which angles them downwards, and the flow of water pushing against them physically lifts the stern of the boat up. As the stern lifts the bow drops, and suddenly the boat is transformed into a lithe, efficient machine. But the tabs aren't just vital to get a boat planing. As the race progresses fuel is burnt, and the boat's balance point changes. The tabs are then used to re-trim the boat, keeping her riding level.

Trim tabs are also useful when the boat is meeting waves at an angle. By using just one tab (they're always fitted in pairs, but can be activated independently) a skilful driver can lean the hull of the boat away from the waves. Although it looks odd to see a motorboat heeled over like a sailing yacht, it makes for a much more comfortable ride, since the waves are presented with less hull to smash against. This isn't much of an issue on board the streamlined *Buzzi Bullet*, but for the older designs like Team *747*'s Fairey and *GEE* the tabs were vital, and when they failed it made their race incredibly uncomfortable, forcing them to slow down on several occasions.

John had gotten the repair done just in time; the Start Boat raised the yellow flag and Drew opened the throttles as Jan pointed the bow towards the west. As we picked up speed to keep pace with the Start Boat we gently edged towards the northern shore of Belfast Lough, with just a few boats between us and the town of Whitehead in the distance.

Then the green flag dropped and we were away! Despite a six-foot sea running Drew didn't hang around, and we were soon leaving the rest of the pack behind. Once clear of the Irish mainland Jan pointed *Bullet* northwards, aiming for the western tip of the Mull of Kintyre some 30 miles over the horizon.

Once again the pack seemed to split and splinter as everyone followed their own slightly different courses, but before everyone went their different ways I had a good look round at the slightly reduced fleet.

Today we were missing eleven boats— of the six boats in the Historic Class, only *GEE* and *747* had made it across to Ireland, with the rest of the Class making their way to Oban or Inverness to rejoin the race from there. (Apart from *Blue Marlin* of course, which was lying 350 feet down on the bottom of Lyme Bay.) Also missing were Team *Blastoff*, *Garmin Racing* and *Cinzano*, all struggling with persistent mechanical setbacks. The RIBs of *Ikon* and *RIB International* had also failed to make the crossing, but most disappointing of all was the news that Fabio Buzzi had retired *Red FPT* just twenty miles out of Milford Haven. Not only had he pulled out of the leg because of mechanical problems, but he had pulled out of the entire event. This was a real pity, as the boat's iconic status and Fabio's legendary reputation had helped to promote a great deal of interest in the race. I could only hope that by now we had managed to generate enough public interest, and that the race itself would be able to hold the public's attention.

As we bounced across the sea our course merged with that of *Venturer*, another Buzzi creation. This forty-foot RIB, with its black tubes and white hull, looked incredible as it leapt from wave to wave. Its two Seatek diesel engines put out an astounding 1500 horsepower combined, over five hundred more than we could muster, and yet we spent a good ten minutes running side by side, just a dozen yards or so separating us as we tore up the ocean at over seventy miles per hour while a helicopter overhead recorded the fight for posterity.

Slowly, inch by inch, we crept ahead of them, before they eventually started encountering the turbulence of our wake and had to alter course to find undisturbed water, falling further behind as they did so.

Throughout it all I had been my usual quiet self; totally engrossed in the exhilaration of the fight and doing my best to avoid being a nuisance. Suddenly Drew's calm voice sounded over my headphones. "Are you all right back there Derek? You're very quiet."

"What? No, I'm fine Drew. Just keeping a low profile," I replied.

Jan chuckled in my ears. "Did Drew wake you up there?"

The very idea of falling asleep at 65 knots in the back of *Buzzi Bullet* as we pounded across six-foot seas was utterly insane. "Yeah, I was just drifting off. This gentle rocking is so relaxing," I joked.

While the ride wasn't as smooth as all that, it was pretty comfortable, once you got the hang of it. With my feet firmly planted on the rubber decking and my hands wrapped round the orange grab bar at chest height, I found the going pretty easy. The knee supports were doing a good job of keeping my knees from falling apart, and the tight constraints of the kidney belt stopped my spine from compressing too much every time we landed hard. It was a shame that Miles hadn't managed to come to grips with the right stance yet. In the big swell out of Milford Haven yesterday he got thrown sideways, bruising his ribs badly. So while we charged north, he flew south for some intensive physiotherapy in order to be fit for the next racing leg, which would be Inverness to Edinburgh in three short days.

Some people will tell you that slow is good— and it may be, on some days— but I am here to tell you that fast is better. I've always believed this, in spite of the trouble it's caused me. Being shot out of a cannon will always be better than being squeezed out of a tube.
Hunter S Thompson, Song Of The Sausage Creature.

Thompson was talking about motorbikes when he wrote that, but so what? The first time I read those words I immediately knew exactly what he meant; those lines resonated deep inside me then, and they still do so now. Safely installed within *Buzzi Bullet*'s Kevlar hull, I was totally at peace and as content as I've ever been. Snug and secure, surrounded by the padded foam bolsters and my own thick lifejacket I crashed over the waves, legs flexing and my hands resting lightly on the grab bar in front of me. Occasionally the boat would take off from the top of a large wave and I would become weightless for several seconds at a time. Whenever that happened all would go strangely quiet, save for the roar of the wind and the silver props whipping freely through the air. But the calm always had an edge to it, and even as my feet levitated briefly off the thick rubber padding I would already be preparing for the jarring impact as we crashed back into the water. Sometimes the impact would be brutal, the force threatening to buckle my knees and throw me to the deck, but more often than not the hull would kiss the sea with the tenderness of a lover's caress, gliding back into the water like a naked body sliding under silk sheets.

In a world where a person's rights are constantly being eroded and restrained, it is getting harder and harder to find the freedom to just open the taps and go all-out in a half-crazed attack on gravity and the rules of physics. On the city streets we're under constant surveillance from thousands of closed circuit cameras, and out on the so-called "open road" that isn't really "open" any more we daren't mash the throttle into the carpet for fear of falling foul of a dizzying array of speed traps. Provided we ever get to clear stretch of road at all, that is. And even in the vast emptiness of the sky we're restricted in where we go by ever-more stringent no-fly zones where we can expect to be literally shot down if we dare to defy these hysterical rules.

But not so at sea. Sure, there are certain places where a man can't go nuts, but that's almost entirely a matter of common sense, not the result of some paranoid delusion that everyone is hell-bent on mass destruction. Once you're clear of sandbanks, rocks and busy shipping lanes, you can throw those levers forward and lean on them with all your might. There are no speed restrictions out in open water, no mini-roundabouts or "traffic calming measures" that do little to calm *me*. Instead, there's nothing more than that old cliché of Man and Machine against the Elements. Out here the only things determining your speed are your engines and the size of your balls. Nothing else matters. Nothing else should ever matter. Once it was the birds who represented utter freedom from oppression. Today, the last refuge of the speed-nut and the free spirit is the sea.

My euphoric battle against Nature and Gravity went on for minute after magical minute until we were about a mile off the south-western tip of the Mull of Kintyre, the land shrouded in a thick mist as always. Fortunately out at sea the visibility was fine, which meant that Jan could see that we were heading into a patch of very confused water.

Here the gap between Ireland and Scotland was no more than 12 miles, and it meant that as the tides changed billions of tons of water trying to flow through this natural bottleneck swirled and eddied around the tip of the Mull, which jutted out into the channel. We had reached it just as conditions were at their worst, and Jan's course, calculated to be the quickest possible route from Bangor to Oban, put us right in the middle of a patch of wild and unpredictable sea.

I heard Jan telling Drew to back off a little, but suddenly it was too late. We fell awkwardly off one particularly big wave, and the bows buried themselves into the face of another. The impact threw us all forward, but even as the spray hit us Drew was back on the throttles, powering *Bullet* through and out the other side. Normally this strategy would work, but in a very rare miscalculation Drew had misjudged the size and confusion of the waves, and he unwittingly powered us straight into the base of an even bigger wave.

As we ploughed into it a solid wall of icy green water thundered along the deck and into the cockpit, throwing Jan and Drew backwards. Jan's helmet connected with mine, and a millisecond later the fluid mass of the wave hit John and I. As gallons of seawater flooded the cockpit the intercom shorted out, deafening us with a sudden squeal of feedback. Miraculously Drew had yanked the throttles back immediately, saving us from any further danger.

All four of us battled to undo our helmets so that we could make sure everyone was OK. Once we established that no-one had been injured, Drew and Jan checked the gauges on the dash to make sure the engines were undamaged. Thankfully they had escaped unscathed, and their quiet rumbling behind my back was hugely reassuring.

Then Jan noticed that the plotters weren't working properly. They still displayed the coastline, less than a mile off our starboard beam, but nothing else— heading, speed, course; they were all missing from the waterproof displays. A quick glance across the deck told Jan all he needed to know.

The antennae for the GPS was contained in a small plastic housing, about eight inches in diameter and an inch thick. It was bolted flush to the deck just in front of the Plexiglass windscreen with four bolts and plenty of silicone sealant. Or at least it used to be; now there was nothing left of it. Even twenty feet back from the bow, the wave was powerful enough to have ripped the entire unit clean off the deck. I, however, had managed to cling on, and had just survived my very first "stuffing", which is the proper term for burying a boat into the base of a sodding great wave and trying to impersonate a submarine. It wasn't glamorous, it didn't make me sexy, but it did mean

I could finally say that, for a little while, I was a powerboat racer.

(I would later discover that we weren't the only team to fall foul of the confused seas off Kintyre. Tom and Charlie Williams-Hawkes on board *TFO* would also suffer a dramatic stuffing, but they did it in their 25 foot Revenger. Fortunately, they too managed to get away with it, but with only one engine and being some 15 feet shorter than *Buzzi Bullet*, I know which boat I'd rather stuff into a wave.)

Luckily Jan had a laminated chart taped to the dashboard in front of him in the event of just such an occurrence, and since we had a fair idea of where we were we strapped our lids back on and Drew hit the throttles once more.

As we got closer to the shelter of Islay to port the sea flattened out, and now Drew could throw the throttles wide open, confident that the props would stay submerged and wouldn't put any undue stress on the welded drive plate. But as we screamed past the Skerries off Islay's south-eastern shore we were navigating mostly by guesswork. Then I spotted a white smudge three or four miles ahead of us.

"Hey guys! Is that a rooster tail up ahead?" I yelled between Drew and Jan.

They took a second to follow my pointed arm, then Drew raised a thumb in acknowledgement. He shouted a muffled "Well done!" and Jan made a slight correction to put us right on the other boat's tail.

Slowly we started catching up to the mystery boat that had served as a beacon to us, but as we gained ground I suddenly spotted movement across to my right and realised that we in turn were being stalked. Creeping up the eastern side of the Sound of Jura were two RIBs, their rooster tails giving away their position. Although I couldn't make out who they were yet, after watching them for a minute or so it was obvious that they were hauling us in. I tapped Drew on his shoulder and pointed, but all he did was shrug— we were running flat out, and there was nothing we could do about their advance.

As we cleared the northern tip of Jura there was no time to marvel at the deceptive calm of the Gulf of Corryvreckan, where some of the world's largest whirlpools are to be found when the tide is right. We were now right on the tail of our unwitting guide, which turned out to be *Blue FPT*. Jan cut across her wake and put us on her starboard side, which would give us the racing line for the next turn to the northeast, once we cleared Easdale island.

As we thundered side by side up the Sound of Luing I noticed that Drew and Jan were constantly stealing sidelong glances at *Blue FPT* as she skimmed across the water, admiring how this brute of a machine carved through the sea. By now the intercom was starting to dry out a little, and through the crackling and hissing I could hear the two men discussing the incredible-looking Buzzi-built boat.

"She really rides well, don't you think?" asked Jan.

"Yeah, really nice," Drew replied. "But she could go faster I reckon. What engines does she have, do you know?"

"Ah, three engines putting out over 1400 horsepower I think," said Jan. "Do you think it's the props?"

"Yeah, that's what I was thinking. Needs tweaked props. She'd be good for 85 knots easy, I'd say."

Their keen eye and technical knowledge was to be applauded, and I admired their ability to analyse and diagnose whilst racing across the sea at killer speed. But this was my old stomping ground, and in my fishing days I had laid fleets of prawn creels in these very waters. I was painfully aware of the very real risk of catching a rope here, and I anxiously scanned the sea ahead for the tell-tale orange buoys, pointing between Drew and Jan whenever I caught sight of one in our path.

By now the adrenaline was really up and pumping again— we were edging ahead of *Blue FPT* despite her three Fiat Powertrain engines that put out 460 horsepower each; we in turn were rapidly being hauled in by the RIBs of *Lionhead* and *Venturer*; and there was a helicopter just a few feet above our heads, filming the whole thing.

As we rounded Easdale island and turned northeast to line up with Kerrera Sound we were clear of *Blue FPT* and pulling away. But it wasn't enough; with only seven miles to go before the finish line a grey blur whipped past us. *Lionhead*, the prototype RIB from the Norwegian Goldfish factory, overtook us easily, doing well over eighty-five knots to our eighty. Shortly afterwards the distinctive outline of *Venturer* pulled alongside and then passed us, in a reversal of our previous encounter in the rougher waters of the Irish Sea.

We thundered down the Kerrera Sound, desperately looking for the finishing line. I couldn't see the boat with the chequered flag anywhere, and clearly neither could Drew as he continued right into the heart of Oban Bay at full throttle. But Jan had spotted it, and knowing that we had crossed the line he pulled Drew's throttle hand back to bring us to a stop.

We sat there, dead in the water in the middle of Oban Bay, gently rocking on our own wake. I had never come into my home port at such a phenomenal speed before, and the whole thing was quite bewildering. Once again I felt that rush of euphoria, knowing that I had just managed to complete another leg— and this time pretty high up the leader board. It seemed my three team-mates had more important things to worry about however, as they stood on the narrow side decks and pissed into the bay.

Oban is a small fishing port on the Scottish west coast, its horse-shoe-shaped bay protected from the worst of the weather by the island of Kerrera, lying just half a mile offshore. A mile further out is the Isle of Mull— a vast, hulking island that bears the brunt of the Atlantic storms, and the last landfall between Oban and Newfoundland's rocky shores, nearly 2,000 miles away.

The town was once fuelled by the vast shoals of herring that thrived in the rich Atlantic waters, but as the fishing industry slid into decline in the 1970's so too did the town's fortunes, but the resurgence of its popularity amongst the tourists threw it a dubious lifeline.

Caledonian MacBrayne have made Oban an important hub for the islands off the Scottish coast by building their ferry terminal in the town. Visitors to Colonsay, Tiree, Coll and Mull have little other option than to take the ferry from Oban, especially during the winter months, when the sparsely-equipped air fields on the islands are frequently closed due to bad weather. Because of the many ferry routes that stem from the town, Oban has been calling itself the "Gateway to The Isles" for some time now, and rightly so.

But I know from personal experience that Oban isn't all sunshine and smiles. In the winter months the spending tourists stay away in droves, and everybody who depends on visitors for their income pull down the shutters and hunker down, peering out at the storms that lash the west coast through chinks in their curtains before withdrawing back to the warm solitude of their homes. Winters can be cold, depressing times here, with weeks passing by without a single dry afternoon. Of course this is just as likely to happen in the spring, autumn, or even the summer months, but when you're down to less than six hours of daylight a day it seems even worse somehow.

But today was a fine, sunny day. Tourists, like flies, only come out in the sunshine and there would be plenty of them out today. On a day like this it would be madness not to head for the highest point in town, where McCaig's tower overlooks the bay.

Back in 1897 a local banker and megalomaniac by the name of John McCaig generously decided to help out the local stonemasons, who were struggling to find work during the interminable winter months. He designed a massive circular structure, some 200 meters across, to be built by the unemployed stonemasons. By happy coincidence, it was also intended to be a permanent reminder to the town of just how fabulous he and his family were, and no doubt the completed building would have lived up to his expectations. McCaig had planned the building to resemble Rome's coliseum, with a museum, art gallery and another tower planned. Undoubtedly his biggest egomaniacal project, the commissioning and erecting of huge bronze statues of himself and his family, never came to fruition. Perhaps if he'd been alive today he'd have had his likeness carved into the hillside instead, but Mount Rushmore was still several decades away.

When he died in 1902 work on the tower stopped. His sister had contested the will, and the project was abandoned. Curiously, when his sister died nine years later, she left clear instructions in her will that her brother's vain-glorious statues be built and placed in the tower, just as he had originally wished. But the Scottish Court of Session overruled the plans because: "They would turn a respectable and creditable family into a laughing-stock to succeeding generations." Some might say that it was already too late, with the tower commonly referred to by locals as "McCaig's Folly".

Overlooked by this vast testament to frivolous wastefulness, dozens of powerboat racing teams roared into the bay. Perhaps a cynic might have seen a connection, but not me— I was still euphoric at the dramatic crossing, and in no mood for philosophy.

Everybody had expected the finish to be close, considering how short the leg was. But it was still a surprise when I found out later just *how* close it had been. *Wettpunkt.com* had beaten everyone in, with a time of 1 hour 43 minutes. Taking second place was *Lionhead* in 1 hour 46 minutes. And then it got really close. *Venturer* came third in 1:48.13, *Relentless* in fourth just ten seconds later, with us in fifth just twenty seconds after that. *Guttaboyz* crossed the line in 1:49.23, beating *Blue FPT* across the line by a mere sixteen seconds. It was incredible to think that after nearly two hours of racing across a mix of sea conditions, only three minutes and thirty seven seconds separated second place from seventh. It was even more surprising given the diversity of the boats; from the massive triple-engined hard boat of *Blue FPT* to the 29 foot RIB *Relentless* and everything in between. Given the miniscule differences in time, it was obvious that stuffing the boat off the Mull cost us dearly— it probably lost us second place— but we wouldn't know the exact times until later, and by then it wouldn't matter anyway. That Was Then And This Is Now, right? Right.

As we motored towards the Northern Lighthouse Board pier to join the boats that had beaten us in I dug into my drybag for my phone. I gave my wife a call, and she left the café where she had been sipping coffee to jump in a taxi to meet me. We tied up alongside *Wettpunkt.com* and scrabbled up the seaweed-covered steel ladder onto the pier.

I was still buzzing from the excitement and frantically dug around for my tobacco tin. It was gone! With a sickening realisation I remembered that I had thrown it into my holdall, which was currently bouncing around *Miss Daisy*'s cabin. It would take another hour or so for her to cross the finishing line, so in the meantime I would have to do what I seemed to be doing a lot of lately— I started begging.

Annoyingly everyone seemed to be health fanatics, so I offered to sign us in with Race Control to keep my mind of cigarettes. As I scribbled my signature next to Team *Silverline* I heard the unmistakeable click of someone working a lighter, so I scurried outside to find Ed William-Hawkes lighting a Hamlet.

"Ed, how are you? Cracking leg eh?" I opened. "Look, you wouldn't happen to have a spare cigarette on you, would you?"

"Actually, I do. Hang on a second." He opened his packet of cigarillos and for a second I thought he was going to offer me one. But to my huge relief he instead pulled out a single cigarette. "I always keep a spare for a friend of mine, but you can have it," he said.

What a top man! First a hotel room, then left-over sandwiches, and now this— I was really taking a shine to him, despite the uncomfortable way he would fix me with a cold stare from his one good eye.

I thanked him and sucked the harsh blue smoke deep down into my lungs. Emergency taken care of, I walked up to the security gates just in time to see my Beloved clamber out of a taxi. The security guard made to stop her walking into the compound, but I waved him away and gave my wife the first hug and kiss since... six days ago? Had it really been that long? She looked fantastic as always, and I chattered away to her like a stoat on speed as I took her down to the pier to meet the *Silverline* boys and to see the boat in the flesh.

Introductions made and small-talk done, I stepped behind a lorry to change out of my sweaty drysuit and base layer and into the jeans and t-shirt I had stuffed into my drybag. I bummed a cigarette from her and called Rob, jabbering away about close racing and stuffing and helicopters and pissing into my hometown bay.

With my work done for the day I decided it was time for a hard-earned beverage. There would be no racing the next day; instead the entire fleet would make for Inverness either by road or the Caledonian Canal, where they would enjoy two days off to recuperate and carry out vital repairs before setting off for Edinburgh on Friday morning. Today was only Tuesday— plenty of time to secure a ride down the east coast.

I made a quick phone call to order a taxi, then told Drew and the others to meet me in the Oban Inn when they got *Buzzi Bullet* loaded onto the truck, passing on the phone number of a local taxi firm.

The Oban Inn had been serving booze to fishermen and sailors since 1799, which was probably why it was one of the few pubs in Oban where I felt at ease. The management had refused to conform to 21st century décor standards, choosing to avoid designer-look leather sofas and bleached-blonde oak coffee tables. Instead the floor was made up of slabs of slate so dark that they seemed to swallow what little light there was, and the smoke-stained wooden panelling on the walls was barely any better.

The staff seemed to match the overall scheme perfectly; with dark, brooding eyes and old scars etched onto their faces— and that was just the barmaid. It was the kind of place where asking for a skinny latte would get you knifed, and returning a pint because the glass was dirty would be tantamount to calling the barman gay. It was my kind of pub, and I hoped my powerboat-racing friends would like it.

My Beloved and I had barely sipped our drinks and cracked open the salt & vinegar crisps when the others started arriving; it appeared that Drew and Jan had told everyone to meet up here. As the pub filled I met my obligations as a host of sorts, and in retrospect it would have been quicker just to dump all my money on the bar and be done with it.

As the afternoon wore on we were joined by Rob and Steve of Race Marine and Richard, Sue and Dorian Griffith, who had transported their problematic Fountain *Round Britain Challenger* from Milford Haven to Oban on the back of a trailer. A little later I got a call from Jonathan to say they had just crossed the line, and I told him where to find us when he'd put *Miss Daisy* to bed.

At one point I was deep in discussion with John Christensen about something or other, and suddenly I remembered a voicemail message I had received at some point during the leg. It was a little indistinct, but it was clearly Mike Barlow on *Ocean Pirate,* and his anger was unmistakeable.

There were four teams racing with Cummins engines— *Silverline, GEE, 747* and *Ocean Pirate*. With the exception of *Silverline*, all the engines were brand new units, and so Cummins had agreed to have a team of mechanics with spares ready at every port to make sure the engines performed as they should. Unfortunately when *Ocean Pirate* suffered a fuel fault halfway up the Irish coast she was forced to head into Dun Laoghaire, a couple of miles south of Dublin. Naturally there weren't any Cummins mechanics nearby— they were either 80 miles north, in Bangor, or just leaving Milford Haven, 100 miles across the Irish Sea.

But Mike didn't seem to grasp the simple logistics involved, and he chose to vent his spleen on my uncaring voicemail. He wound up his tirade by telling me that if I should bump into John Christensen I was to tell him that "'Cummins' is a seven-letter word for 'shit'", and he would be peeling the Cummins Mercruiser Diesel stickers off the boat at his earliest convenience.

This little tale reminded John that he need a new phone, as the screen was broken. And that in turn reminded me that I still had a brand-new Nokia in my bag, which was worthless to me because it refused to accept my SIM card. With impeccable timing Jonathan walked into the pub and delivered my bag, and moments later John was the proud new owner of a mobile phone with matching receipt, and I was suddenly £50 richer.

By now the pub was buzzing with activity, and over the clatter of conversation I shouted in my Beloved's ear that I was absolutely starving. We stole out and made for a half-decent eatery across the road, where I made a pig of myself by devouring a steak almost before the waitress had a chance to put my plate on the table. I had left the pub with good intentions— a quick bite to eat and then back to the banter in the bar— but suddenly I was fighting to stay awake, so instead we jumped into a taxi and escaped to the solitude of our isolated little cottage.

Top– *Wettpunkt.com* charging towards Oban

Below– The first of the boats tied up in Oban

Results-
Bangor to Oban.

Distance: 113 nautical miles.

Pos.	Team/ Number	Class	Time	Overall position (Class)
1st	Wettpunkt.com/81	RB1	1:43:05	30 (2)
2nd	Lionhead/22	RB3	1:46:02	1 (1)
3rd	Venturer/111	RB1	1:48:13	18 (1)
4th	Relentless/47	RB3	1:48:23	22 (9)
5th	**Team Silverline/ 471**	**RB2**	**1:48:43**	**12 (1)**
6th	Guttaboyz/33	RB3	1:49:23	3 (2)
7th	Blue FPT/333	MC1	1:49:39	2 (1)
8th	Going Lean/7	RB3	1:54:59	11 (6)
9th	Birretta/12	MC1	2:02:37	9 (4)
10th	Braveheart/55	MC1	2:03:03	5 (2)
11th	Hot Lemon/2	RB3	2:07:10	4 (3)
12th	Hardleys/4	RB3	2:08:30	6 (4)
13th	Sealbay/77	RB4	2:14:25	10 (1)
14th	Team Jersey/45	RB4	2:15:33	35 (8)
15th	Northern Spirit/5	MC2	2:15:47	21 (2)
16th	Seahound V/80	MC1	2:16:35	8 (3)
17th	Carbon Neutral/343	RB3	2:17:01	13 (7)
18th	Vilda/9	RB3	2:17:30	12 (1)
19th	Seafarer/110	RB3	2:20:34	20 (8)
20th	Power Products Marine/8	MC2	2:23:49	16 (1)

Pos.	Team/ Number	Class	Time	Overall position (Class)
21st	No Worries/11	RB3	2:30:31	36 (11)
22nd	Tequila/88	RB3	2:30:56	23 (10)
23rd	Team Scorpion Dubois/16	MC1	2:36:02	19 (5)
24th	Fugitive/130	MC2	2:38:31	26 (4)
25th	TFO/17	MC2	2:50:56	25 (3)
26th	My Pleasure II/3	RB4	2:55:19	24 (4)
27th	Team 747/747	HC1	2:58:48	33 (2)
28th	GEE/185	HC1	2:59:05	28 (1)
29th	Mud, Swell & Beers/14	RB4	3:05:25	32 (7)
30th	Team Pulsar-Wolf/101	RB4	3:06:05	31 (6)
31st	swipewipes.co.uk/ 43	RB4	3:15:04	17 (3)
32nd	Team Bandit/69	RB2	3:15:38	15 (2)
33rd	Buro/15	MC1	3:18:02	29 (6)
34th	Mr Mako/96	RB4	3:22:11	14 (2)
35th	Team Pulsar-Vampire/102	RB4	3:33:41	27 (5)
36th	Mystic Dragon/6	MC1	3:36:15	34 (7)
37th	Black Gold/10	RB4	**DNS**	37 (9)
38th	Ikon/18	RB3	**DNS**	38 (12)
39th	Xanthus/1	HC1	**DNS**	39 (3)
40th	RIB International/ 144	RB4	**OTR**	40 (10)

Pos.	Team/ Number	Class	Time	Overall position (Class)
41st	Red FPT/177	CC1	**OTR**	41 (1)
42nd	Garmin Racing/72	RB2	**DNS**	42 (3)
43rd	Team Blastoff/100	RB2	**DNS**	43 (4)
44th	Blue Marlin/99	HC1	**OTR**	44 (5)
45th	Swordsman/68	HC1	**DNS**	45 (4)
46th	Cinzano/558	RB2	**DNS**	46 (5)
47th	Ocean Pirate/323	HC1	**DNS**	47 (6)

DNS Denotes Did Not Start
DNF Denotes Did Not Finish
OTR Denotes Out of The Race
* Denotes maximum time allowance exceeded.

Below– *Blue FPT* overtaken by *Silverline*

9.

Oban to Inverness.

Wednesday 23rd June.

My small croft lies in a forgotten glen half an hour out of Oban. My nearest neighbours are over half a mile away as the crow flies, and the nearest streetlight is over four miles away. Why am I telling you all this? So that you can get some idea of how completely dark and silent things get when I turn off the lights and go to sleep. For the last five days I had been trying to sleep in strange beds, surrounded by a perpetual orange glow and constant traffic noise. But now, for one brief night, I was allowed to sink into a deep and undisturbed sleep, temporarily excused from the exhausting stress of having to hop from boat to boat, constantly worrying about bags, hotel rooms and food.

When I awoke I felt like I'd slept for a week. I spoiled myself with a leisurely breakfast, and right on time my taxi rolled up to take me into Oban. From there I caught a minibus to Fort William (enduring one of the most pedantic, irritating drivers in the process) and then a coach for the two hour trip to Inverness.

Whenever the road ran alongside one of the lochs or stretches of canal that link the west and east coast of Scotland I kept an eye out for powerboats sporting race numbers and sponsorship stickers. While teams who enjoyed the luxury of their own trailers or lorries took the soft option of travelling to Inverness by road, about a dozen or so boats, mostly the Historics, had elected to make the journey on their own bottoms. This entailed getting to the slip at Oban by 5am, where a specially laid on ferry would transport them to the marina on Kerrera island. From there the boats would run northwards to Fort William at the top of Loch Linnhe, where Neptune's Staircase marked the western end of the Caledonian Canal.

The canal is an astounding piece of industrial engineering. It was designed by Thomas Telford, one of Scotland's most prolific and talented civil engineers. Telford was born in Dumfries-shire to a poor farming family, and spent his childhood working as a shepherd. At fourteen he landed a stonemason's apprenticeship, and by twenty-five he had moved to London to work on Somerset House. He had a powerful desire for continual self-improvement and a keen eye for detail, facets that weren't lost on his superiors. Two years later he was in charge of the construction of Plymouth Docks, and from there he went from strength to strength. By the time Telford died in 1834, he had designed and built Ellsmere canal and Pontcysyllte aqueduct, the Menai Straits suspension bridge and the Gotha canal in Sweden. But it was in Scotland where he was at his most productive: 32 churches, over twenty harbours, 920 miles of road, 120 bridges, and, his most impressive feat, the Caledonian Canal.

The Caledonian Canal runs from Fort William on the west coast of Scotland to Inverness on the east, and links the Atlantic and North Sea. When it was opened in 1822 it meant that boats no longer had to round the perilous Cape Wrath and Pentland Firth, where countless ships had floundered on the inhospitable shores. Instead they could now travel the sixty miles from coast to coast in perfect safety.

To be fair, it wasn't too tricky for Telford to link the two coasts; geography had already done much of the hard work for him. Running along the Great Glen are (from west to east) Loch Lochy, Loch Oich and Loch Ness, and between them they already cover 38 miles. All Telford had to do was link them all together with another 22 miles of canal and 29 locks to cope with the changes in elevation. It has to be said that the end result, combining Victorian engineering and Nature's grandiosity, is absolutely stunning. I have travelled the canal myself, and once spent nearly two months zipping across Loch Ness at 40 knots while working on a film with Werner Herzog, and I was deeply envious of the dozen or so boats that would be crossing the lochs flat out.

The previous night I had been offered several seats to traverse the Caledonian Canal; with Team *Blastoff* on their troublesome Fountain, on board *Miss Daisy*, and even on board the Start Boat, which belonged to the Head Honcho at *Silverline* Tools. But I couldn't face the idea of getting out of my pit for a 5am start, so I turned down the chance to cross Loch Ness at over 100 mph, instead opting for a lie-in and the sedate comfort of the coach.

At the first Driver's Briefing at Southampton, Mike Lloyd had made a big deal about having come to a special arrangement with British Waterways Scotland, who manage the Caledonian Canal. He claimed that teams who chose to travel to Inverness via the canal were to be given "special dispensation" to run flat out across the lochs, and he touted it as a "unique privilege". That was utter bollocks; unlike many of England's congested lakes, there are no speed restrictions on Loch Lochy, Oich and Ness, only through the canals. The truth was that any half-bright Yahoo with a 100 knot powerboat could spend all day hurtling up and down Loch Ness' 23 mile length with no repercussions other than an aching jaw from the perpetual smiling he'd be doing and a massive fuel bill.

I got into Inverness around lunchtime, so after a quick bite to eat I grabbed a taxi to my digs. To say the room was small would have been an understatement. I was faced with a dilemma; either I was in the room, or my bag was. There was no third way. When I discovered the en-suite bathroom I finally managed to come up with a compromise— with a heavy foot I found that my bag fitted into the shower cubicle. Just.

With that taken care of I ventured out into the world and made for the Muirtown Basin, the marina where the fleet would regroup. The three Goldfish RIBs were there, looking military-crisp in their smart grey covers, as were some of the smaller RIBs, who had been trailered up earlier that day and launched by the 20-ton crane. But where were the big boys?

I found Mary and Gill at their new Race Control office, temporarily commandeered from British Waterways. After enduring the usual mockery from them for a couple of minutes I found out that the race had taken over an abandoned warehouse just a few minutes' walk away, where teams could work on their boats undercover. I thanked them by stealing their last copy of the results sheet for the Bangor to Oban leg and wandered off to find somewhere quiet.

As I mentioned earlier, *Wettpunkt.com* had taken first, followed closely— extremely closely— by *Lionhead*, *Venturer*, *Relentless*, *Silverline*, *Guttaboyz* and *Blue FPT*. Dean Gibb in *Going Lean* came in in eighth, and the two-man Belgian team on board *Birretta* were ninth. Bobby Cowe and his team— the only Scottish entry out of 30 British competitors— managed tenth, beating such notables like *Seahound V* and *Sealbay* into town.

I was pleased to see that Jonathan and the other pilots of Team *747* had beaten their Class rivals *GEE* into Oban, taking 27th place. But towards the very bottom of the sheet I was puzzled to see the Pascoe RIB of *Mr Mako* lying in 34th. The reason for my confusion was because Jamie Edwards and John Lindsay had been third into Bangor the day before, so they clearly had plenty of pace. (It turned out later that somehow a blob of silicone had found its way into their fuel tanks, occasionally blocking the line. This was a problem that would hinder them several more times during the race, costing them valuable time.)

The old B&Q warehouse had been totally overrun by the fleet. In the carpark outside four or five boats rested on their trailers or on the back of lorries as mechanics pored over engines, gearboxes and stern drives. It was here that I finally got a true sense of the size and determination of the shore crews that worked so hard for absolutely zero recognition.

When it came to dishing out silverware, there would be no less than seventeen trophies to be awarded, as well as awards for the winning boat in each Class. Of those seventeen, only two could be considered as recognition for the incredible job the support crews did. Of course without the invaluable help of the mechanics, gophers and fixers that worked astounding hours every single day of the race hardly anybody would have made it round, but whilst this was widely acknowledged verbally there seemed to be little in the way of official appreciation.

Blastoff, the troublesome Fountain entered by the Griffith family, was once again deemed fit for use, and was being prepared for launching at the Basin. Once back in the canal, Dorian and Richard planned to make the long journey through the town for trials on Loch Ness. But to reach the loch, they would have to pass through seven lock gates, one swinging bridge and seven miles of canal with a strict 5 knot limit— a hell of a trek for sea trials on Loch Ness.

Inside the warehouse I found the heavy hitters. *Blue FPT* sat on the back of her lorry, engine covers closed and surprisingly free of mechanics and engineers. Not so for another Buzzi design— *Wettpunkt.com*, which had taken up residence right at the very back of the shed. Her mechanics were hard at work doing technical stuff, but their self-imposed isolation away from the rest of the teams was slightly intimidating, so I decided to leave them to it.

The two business-like RIBs of Team *Pulsar* were also undercover, the single Suzuki 300 outboards of *Vampire* and *Wolf* needing nothing more than a simple service. I was amazed to hear that *Vampire*, one of the smallest boats in the race, had also elected to travel by sea from Plymouth to Milford Haven on that cancelled leg. They had made it to Admiral's Pier just in time for the Driver's Briefing, and after a quick splash of fuel they had joined the start and crossed to Bangor with the rest of the pack— one hell of an achievement, especially in a 25 foot RIB.

Elsewhere in the disued warehouse men were busy working on the Ocke-Mannerfelt bat-boat of Team *Jersey*, their damp gear hanging on jury-rigged clothes lines, and *Power Products Marine*, the 28 foot Phantom getting some much-needed TLC.

I walked over to the familiar boat of Team *Silverline*, where an exhausted-looking Ian was tidying away tools. "Alright Ian, packing up already?" I asked.

He gave me a wry smile. "I wish. I don't know why I'm putting my tools away; I'll be needing them again soon enough." He nodded at the ladder leaning against the boat and I clambered up to have a look for myself.

Ian and John had wasted no time in whipping out the starboard engine and gearbox in order to replace the coupling they had damaged coming across from Wales to Bangor. The temporary weld had held, but they couldn't risk running with it down the east coast. We still had 720 nautical miles to cover; 792 statute miles across the North sea. But finding spares had proved tricky; even as Ian was explaining the situation to me his phone rang. It was his son Josh— he had just landed at Dusseldorf and wanted to know who was supposed to be meeting him. He had flown out to pick up the replacement parts, but he only had thirty minutes on the ground before his flight back to the UK boarded, and now his German contact had failed to appear.

I left Ian and Miles to their frantic international phone calls, then spotted the Race Marine van parked in the corner. I jumped in the back and quickly found my laptop bag, sandwiched between a 25 litre can of oil and a pack of twelve oil filters. After another little wander I decided to find a restaurant for a decent meal followed by an early night. I stepped outside and phoned for a taxi, but as soon as it arrived someone came running out of the warehouse, pleading to steal it. I let him take it, and the driver promised to come back for me.

I sat on the cracked cement pavement and leaned back against the cool brick wall of the building, pulling my battered old tobacco tin out of my pocket as I did so. As I rolled a cigarette I idly wondered how long I'd actually owned my tin— ten years? Twelve? I couldn't remember; the thing had been with me since forever, and was showing the scars of too many drunken nights and careless dunkings into the sea. Over the years the green lettering of the Golden Virginia Tobacco Company had been faded and scratched into oblivion, both accidentally and on purpose. Just a few months before I had tried to hide its dull grey surface by wrapping it entirely in Duck tape, but now the tape was starting to peel and tear, making it look even more wretched. I didn't care though, it still served its purpose perfectly. Not only did it hold a clump of tobacco and a pack of green Rizla papers, it also served as a pillow, a paperweight, a straight edge and, on occasion, a weapon of sorts.

When my taxi driver returned twenty minutes later, he started asking me about the race. What was going on? How long was it? How many boats were taking part? Clearly the Race Organisers had once again failed to inform the local media, and in a rare display of goodwill I offered to give my driver a quick tour of the boats in the warehouse.

He was clearly awestruck at the small but impressive display of boats, and I spent five minutes or so acting as PR Man, recounting our exploits to date and explaining where we'd be going next.

For the average man in the street powerboat racing probably conjures up mental images of exotic machinery plastered in gaudy sponsorship stickers, beautiful scantily-clad models frolicking under an azure-blue sky, and handsome, rugged millionaires stepping out of their Lamborghinis and into their boats, stopping only to smile at the Press and to playfully slap a model's firm young buttocks before roaring off to do battle with the ocean and other equally rugged racers. And, to be fair, there is an element of truth in that kind of stereotype, especially in the higher echelons of the sport. P1 and Class 1 racing bear the closest similarity to the glamour and glitz of better-known motorsports such as Formula 1 and Moto GP, but further down the scale things are often very different.

There are an endless variety of Classes in powerboat racing; in the UK alone the RYA, which is the UK's governing body for watersports, oversees no less than twenty-six different Classes, which run the gamut from Zapcats to P1. While this gives the casual appearance of a heavily-subscribed sport, the sad truth of the matter is that for many of these Classes there are often less than half a dozen entrants, and often merely showing up can guarantee a team a podium finish.

By and large, the people who race in this plethora of categories are regular nine-to-five types who like to occasionally pit their weekend toy against like-minded individuals; in that respect it's much the same as taking the family Focus down to Santa Pod for a blast down the quarter-mile drag strip. In both cases there's usually not much required in the way of modifications, safety equipment is more common sense than high-tec, and usually the car or boat escapes unharmed, safe to carry on its more mundane duties afterwards.

With this type of "run what ya brung" racing, there is little in the way of reward, either financially or aesthetically. The boats are typically towed and launched from their own trailer hitched to the back of the family car, and the "grand spectacle" of the dry pits and launching area is eerily similar to any other summer Saturday by the seaside. There are no teams of mechanics swarming over the engines, no sponsored VIP areas and sadly no 18 year-olds parading around in skin-tight Lycra.

Instead, expect to see an overweight middle-aged man squeeze into a Grabner as his buddy tightens up the engine's spark plugs with a Halford's tool set. Our brave driver's wife will have set up her folding garden chair at a strategic point, and from here she can split her attention between the bee-like whining of racing outboards and her copy of Heat magazine.

And, no matter how heroic his racing, back on shore the winner can often count on no more than a token symbol to reward his bravery— a tin plate, perhaps, or a cheap trophy with his team name crudely engraved on the faux-bronze plaque.

Even in this race, widely considered by many teams as the jewel in the crown of European powerboat racing, there was little in the way of decadence in a sport that, by its very nature, is decadent. With the sole exception of the first start in Portsmouth there were no banners advertising the event, no marquees where sponsors could woe VIPs, and a distinct dearth of eye-candy. This was mainly due to the fact that the Organisers had failed to find a major sponsor for the race. Without a major sponsor, there was little to advertise, and so our coming and going from town to town went largely ignored by the Press, whose involvement in the race would have made a massive impact on public interest.

(Months afterwards I spoke to dozens of competitors who bemoaned the lack of publicity, not because they wanted to further their own sponsors, but because they all felt that their accomplishments were worthy of recognition— regardless of how well or how poorly they were doing in the results tables. Many found it galling that this incredible race was being conducted in a virtual vacuum, since for so many of them it represented a gargantuan investment of their own time and money, and they risked their lives on a daily basis for, at best, a silver dish.)

I had done my best to explain some of this to my driver and we were just heading back to the taxi when Drew bounded over. Would I mind if we gave him a lift to the nearest hardware shop?

I said Sure and we jumped in the car, our driver seemingly honoured at being asked to chauffeur one of Europe's finest powerboat racers.

Drew was in search of nuts and bolts, but they were an odd length, and we spent over half an hour ducking in and out the side streets of Inverness's industrial estate before he finally found what he was looking for. When we dropped him off back at the boat he offered to pay for the fare, but I waved him off. "After all," I told him, "you gave me a lift to Milford Haven. Consider us even."

As we passed a supermarket I suddenly remembered that I had yet to make good on my promise to Mike on *Ocean Pirate*. The price of my seat had been a bottle of malt whisky and a bottle of gin, so I made my taxi wait for me while I dived inside to mount up even more debt on my smouldering credit card. With that taken care of my driver dropped me off at an excellent little pub overlooking the river, and after a perfect steak and three pints of the black stuff I wandered back to my ridiculously small room to fight with the furniture for supremacy.

Below– Scorpion RIBs in formation on Loch Ness

Top– *Swordsman* and *Blastoff*

Below– *Team Jersey* get their laundry done

10.
Inverness Lay Day.

Thursday 24th June.

On the morning of the official lay day I took a leisurely stroll round the Muirtown Basin, which was now starting to show a full complement of race boats. All the teams who had travelled the Caledonian Canal had arrived the previous evening, but the journey hadn't been without its dramas.

The Fairey named *Swordsman* had somehow clouted a prop on one of the lock walls, and her exhausted crew had worked through the night to repair the damage. The *Braveheart* team had rolled up their sleeves and helped out, both with their time and their equipment, to get the Historic Class boat fixed as quickly as possible, and if it hadn't been for their help *Swordman*'s prospects would have looked bleak indeed.

Another boat to damage her prop and shaft was *Miss Daisy*, the Fairey entered by Team *747*. But they hadn't even made it as far as the canal; while en route to Fort William the boat had smacked into a submerged rock off the northern tip of the island of Lismore. They had gone back into Oban to be hoisted out and inspected, and a frenzied plan of attack was thrown together.

While Fred Kemp and Jonathan's dad Michael had another stab at getting the boat to Inverness (this time on one engine) Jonathan would fly down to Southampton to pick up a new shaft and prop. This launched a great rumour round the pits— I was assured by three or four different people that British Airways, who employ Jonathan and his team-mates, refused to let Jonathan on board because the prop and six-foot shaft were considered "offensive weapons". Naturally this resulted in a lot of eye-rolling and head-shaking, but of course it later turned out to be a total myth— in fact Jonathan travelled with Flybe, who were only too happy to help out— provided that they were allowed to use the story for their in-flight magazine.

I felt slightly guilty when I heard about Fred and Michael's mishap off Lismore, because they had offered me a ride up the canal on the Tuesday evening. I had turned them (and others) down, preferring to go for the lie-in and coach option instead. But if I had taken them up on their offer, I would have been able to warn them about that treacherous patch of water, where the rocks are barely visible on all but the lowest of tides.

Or maybe I would have chosen that precise moment to take a piss off the stern of the boat, and we would have hit the rocks anyway, resulting in the same damage to the boat and my credibility totally shattered.

Braveheart's generous assistance to the *Swordsman* boys also worked in *Miss Daisy*'s favour— by the time the damage was repaired to *Swordsman* the Team *747* boat was limping into the marina, and as one Fairey was craned into the water, the other was craned out to take her place, supported on the hard by the same blocks and supports.

This time it was the turn of the boys on *GEE* to come to the rescue. One of their crew, John Guille, had been on hand in Oban to help with the initial damage appraisal, and in Inverness it was John and *GEE* team-mate Nathan Ward who would work late into the night alongside their rivals to replace the damaged parts. It was also they who spotted that two engine mounts were badly damaged, preventing the new shaft from lining up properly, and with a generator and lights borrowed from the *Braveheart* team they would work through the night to get her fixed for the next day's long leg to Edinburgh.

But on that bright morning there was still no sign of *Miss Daisy*, her progress up the canal painfully slow as she limped north-eastwards on one engine, and I was blissfully unaware of their problems. I had my own problems to worry about— I didn't have a ride for the next day, so I gave Rob at the magazine a call. As we chatted I realised that the original plan— joining Drew, Jan and Miles on *Silverline*'s *Buzzi Bullet* was now completely unattainable. One of their engines was still out, with the boys waiting impatiently for Josh to fly back from Germany with the new parts. Drew had become convinced that John should travel on board on every leg, and with Miles getting professional help for his damaged ribs he was likely to retake his seat, meaning no seat for me.

While Jonathan had been extremely generous in letting me join his band of 747 pilots on *Miss Daisy*, I was reluctant to abuse his hospitality. The same could be said for Mike Barlow and *Ocean Pirate*, which had finally caught up with the fleet in Fort William and had joined the convoy to travel up the canal. Plus, it had become painfully apparent that the team was most definitely not one of the "Winning At All Costs" brigade, and although I could understand their philosophy I wasn't sure I could agree with it.

Slowly a plan began to form while Rob and I kicked ideas about. During the three racing stages I had joined three different boats— why not try to keep the pattern going? "Can you imagine it?" I enthused to Rob. "Racing every leg on board a different boat? Do you realise that this has never been done before? Good God man, I'll be making history!"

Rob could see the merits straight away. "Why not? The original plan has already been blown to shit, we might as well work it to our advantage. But that still throws up the original question— what about tomorrow?"

As I pondered the question my eyes idly scanned the waterfront. "Well, if you're feeling cunning, how about getting me a seat with the Norwegians on one of their Goldfish RIBs?" I suggested as I spotted the two grey boats alongside one of the pontoons.

There was a moment's silence, then Rob spoke up. "Leave it with me, I'll see what I can do."

I hadn't been serious about trying to get a seat on the Goldfish boats, but Rob had hung up before I got a chance to tell him I was kidding. *Lionhead* wasn't just leading the RB3 Class, but it was also currently first overall. The sister boat *Guttaboyz* was also incredibly competitive, lying third overall— no way would the Goldfish team let some gibbering imbecile set foot on board either of their boats, adding excess weight to such finely-tuned craft.

In anticipation of the imminent Bad News phone call, I set about trying to organise my *real* seat for the 210 nautical mile leg to Edinburgh. Tomorrow's stage was the longest of the entire race, and we would be running eastwards into the North Sea before rounding Kinnaird Head at Fraserburgh and turning south. After passing Peterhead, Aberdeen and Dundee we would finally swing westerly at Fife Ness, heading up the Firth of Forth and the two landmark bridges that crossed it. Such a long, hazardous passage would not be easy, so a smart man would be wise to target one of the more comfortable boats in this race.

I found the Belgian crew of *Buro* enjoying lunch in the boat's well-appointed wheelhouse. Peter Verhauter, the boat's owner, was very laid-back and easy-going, and readily agreed to take me along on the next leg. I thanked him profusely and left them to their meal, buoyant at the knowledge that I had sorted out my ride for the next day on board the Botnia Targa, one of the oddest— but comfiest— boats in the racing fleet.

Thinking ahead, I decided to try and organise a seat for one of the future legs. This seemed to be the ideal time, since the mood amongst the teams was a little more relaxed now that everybody had a little more spare time to take care of the boats and themselves. I spotted the RIB of Team *Scorpion Dubois* and went over to introduce myself to the navigator and driver, Sarah Fraser and Amanda Knowles. We exchanged cordial greetings before I cut to the chase.

"Listen, I was wondering if you might like to let me join you for one of the legs." The two women went a little quiet, so I tried to sweeten the deal. "It would give your sponsors a great bit of publicity in *MotorBoat & Yachting*", I added hopefully.

"Actually Derek, I think not. We've already had plenty of coverage in the media, and we're kind of trying to prove a point."

"Oh yeah? And what point is that then?" I asked, confused.

"Well, we're the only all-girl team, so we'd prefer not to have any male involvement. I hope you understand."

"Um, alright. How about if I strap on a wig then?" I was nothing if not determined.

The two women didn't see the funny side. "Sorry, but no. We're trying to show everyone that women can do just as well as men in a race like this, so..."

I gave up and started walking away, then spotted something incongruous. There were two guys from the shore team working on the boat. On the women-only boat. It would appear that sisters weren't really doing it for themselves after all. I pointedly watched as the men did whatever they had been asked to do on the boat, hoping to catch the girls' eye, but neither of them even glanced in my direction, foiling my plan to raise an incredulous eyebrow at them and exposing them for the hypocrites they really were.

Of course I could have gone back and confronted them, pointed out that their Girl Power veneer was about as convincing and sincere as a politician's apology, but what would have been the point? If I could see through their charade within a few minutes, then no doubt the rest of the fleet would have too. So instead of getting into an argument about their lack of feministic backbone I just shook my head sadly and walked away.

A couple of berths down from Team *Scorpion Dubois* I noticed a bit of activity. Declan Curry, the chubby business presenter of BBC's morning news programme was interviewing the Clayton brothers next to their Historic Class boat *GEE*, so I wandered over to listen in.

Declan had been following the fleet round the UK off and on, reporting not on the race specifically, but using it as a lead to discuss the status of the various ports we were visiting. I'd seen him around before, but this was the first time I'd seen him engaging with any of the teams face to face.

Of course by the time I got there they were already finished, and he shook their hands and wished them luck. As he and his film crew packed up, I walked across to chat with (I think) Paul and Mark, two of the three Clayton brothers.

But first, it's important that you understand that I was in no way acting like a journalist. Throughout the entire event I spoke to people like a normal human being, interested only in the kind of stuff everyone else might be interested in. My brief from the magazine was outrageously simple— they only wanted my impressions, perceptions and emotions as I experienced the race; they would let their real journalist Ray Bulman do all the proper reporting.

So I greeted the two men by asking how things were going for them so far. They were friendly and open, but as we chatted one of them asked: "So which team are you with then?"

"Oh, I'm not with anyone in particular," I replied frankly. "I'm with *MotorBoat & Yachting* magazine. Actually, I was going to ask if you'd consider letting me tag along on one of the legs?"

The two men physically stepped back, their eyes wide. "What? You're with a magazine?" Anybody who witnessed their reaction would have been forgiven for thinking that I had just offered to rape their first-born children.

"Uh, yeah", I replied, a little startled by the fear in their voices. "I've been hopping from boat to boat, and I thought-"

"God, sorry, but we can't talk to you", one of them stammered. "We've done a deal with another magazine. I don't think they'd want us talking to you."

"OK, well, forget about the lift then." I tried to change the subject, hoping to calm them down a little. "So how's your scrap with Team *747* going? I was with them on the leg from Milford to Bangor, and-"

"No, sorry, but we really can't discuss anything with you", interrupted the other one. "It's this exclusivity deal we've got with the magazine. You understand, right?"

Their paranoia was starting to wear thin, but I tried to engage with them as normal, regular people one last time. "Jesus! Well, if it makes you feel any better, I promise not to mention anything to my editor, OK?" I tried to placate them, but it was clearly far too late. As I stepped forward with my palms open in supplication they hastily shuffled backwards to keep me at a safe distance. I sighed. "OK, fine, I won't ask you anything about the race." They didn't seem reassured, and I swear one of them glanced round to see if he'd been spotted talking to someone from a rival magazine. "Let's change the subject then— have you got any idea what the weather's supposed to be like for tomorrow, because I can't find a forecast anywhere."

I got another nervous smile, followed by: "Look, I'm sorry, but we really can't talk to you. We don't want to get into any trouble."

"What? You don't want to tell me the weather forecast in case you get into trouble? You know what? Forget it. You guys are seriously fucked up. Have a good race, and maybe you'll speak to me when this is all over, OK?" They were pitifully grateful at my decision to leave, and as I walked away I was shaking my head sadly at their insane paranoia. *Christ!* I thought to myself, *it's not like I'm Jeremy fucking Paxman or anything!*

The next boat along was *Ocean Pirate*, so I stepped on board and politely rapped on the wheelhouse door before letting myself in. Mike and the rest of the crew were chatting happily in the wheelhouse, and I congratulated them on having caught up with the rest of the fleet. "I bet you thought I'd forgotten our arrangement," I told Mike as I handed him a carrier bag containing a bottle of Lagavullin and Bombay Sapphire gin. He told me that he never doubted me with a smile, but I could see in his eyes he was surprised I'd finally paid my fare. The mood on the boat lifted even further, and pleased to have spread a little happiness I wished him luck and step back into the sun.

I wandered over to a burger stall that was doing a roaring trade, and while my hand-made burger sizzled intoxicatingly on the hotplate my phone rang.

"Derek, I've got some great news for you!"

"Hi Rob, I've got some pretty good news myself. You go first."

"Be at the Goldfish boats at six o'clock tonight. They've agreed to take you along, but first they want to meet you."

I was utterly gob smacked. Somehow that marvel of a man had gotten me onto the quickest boat in the fleet, and all in under an hour! "Jesus Rob, you're a fucking legend, do you know that? Nice one matey! Actually, I didn't think you'd do it, so I've blagged a spot with the Belgians on their Botnia Targa" I told him. "I guess I'd better try to change it for the Edinburgh-Newcastle leg instead."

We talked a little more, and he laughed in amazement when I told him about the Clayton brothers' reaction to me, but by then the kid on the burger stall had waved to tell me my lunch was ready, so I cut the conversation short and set about devouring my burger.

Having gorged myself I settled down in a quiet sunny spot to finally try to make sense of the adjusted overall results sheets I'd picked up at Race Control.

Lionhead, one of the two prototype Goldfish RIBs, was leading the race from the dark horse entry of *Blue FPT* by only a miserly thirteen minutes— not bad after nearly nine hours and over 370 miles of racing. Just a handful of seconds behind was the second Goldfish RIB *Guttaboyz*, who were nearly twenty minutes ahead of the experienced father and son team Mike and Dave Deacon on board *Hot Lemon*. Surprising everybody (including themselves) were the trawlermen on *Braveheart III*, the much-maligned RIB which was in a solid fifth, demonstrating ably that this event wasn't purely about speed. The boat was proving to be incredibly reliable so far, and if they could keep out of trouble and maintain their respectable pace there was a strong chance that the inexperienced Fraserburgh crew could prove to be the biggest upset of the race.

Other teams that stood out included *Birretta*, a pair of Belgians in their 33 foot Buzzi RIB, who were holding their own in ninth, a respectable result indeed for this amateur team. My friends in the *Silverline* team weren't doing so well, however. Their mechanical breakdown just a few miles short of the Bangor finishing line had cost them dearly— from first on Day One down to twelfth halfway round. Their plight was yet another indication of just how incredibly important reliability was in an endurance event.

Others learning this lesson the hard way included *Venturer*, the 40 foot RIB we had battled with on the Bangor to Oban leg. They had suffered with a blocked water intake on the first leg and problems with dirty fuel on the second. But when everything was working fine she was damned quick, and if Buddha had smiled on Andy Macateer and his crew the team would have been a lot further up the listings than eighteenth.

But by far the most unexpected name towards the bottom of the list (retirements notwithstanding) was *Wettpunkt.com*. Lying way, *way* down in thirtieth overall, Hannes Bohinc must have been grinding his molars into a fine dust. By rights he, his navigator Ed Williams-Hawkes and his co-driver Max Holzfeind should have been challenging the Goldfish RIBs for a top three position— after all, Fabio Buzzi himself had been reported as saying that *Wettpunkt.com* was the best boat he had ever built, and at a rumoured £1.5 million I should bloody-well hope so too! But when the two Isotta-Fraschinis started sucking in seawater instead of air during the first leg it created a monstrous mountain for the Austrian and his team to overcome.

The airline pilots on board the Historic Fairey of Team *747* were showing as being 33rd overall, which initially didn't look too bad out of a fleet of forty-seven starters. But on closer inspection, I noticed that they were the last of the boats who had completed all three stages without any major mechanical breakdowns (although they did lose time on the first stage when they had to put an injured Mark Jealous ashore, then struggled in the last stretch with dirty fuel.)

For many teams, fighting for outright victory was never on the cards. Instead, they would be aiming for first place in their own Class; a much more realistic prospect which would still yield a great deal of kudos— and a nice bit of tin for the display case to boot.

For the Historics, it was shaping up to be a two-way fight between *GEE* and the boys of Team *747*. *GEE* had a one hour and forty-five minute advantage over the classic Fairey, but that was far from insurmountable.

In the rest of the fleet, time differences were just as small. *Venturer* and *Wettpunkt.com* were the only boats in the RB1 Class, and with Bohinc's chances of an outright win looking unlikely, his best chance of a trophy lay with beating Andy Macateer, who was over three hours ahead of him.

The RB2 Class was also down to two serious contenders— Team *Bandit*, the taxi drivers in their monstrous-looking Hunton RIB versus Team *Silverline*, one of the most experienced crews in the race. But despite their impeccable pedigree, the *Silverline* boys only had half an hours' lead over their Class rivals, and with four more stages left to run, it was imperative that they and the boat kept it together.

The current race leader *Lionhead* had little to fear. The second boat in its RB3 Class was the sister boat *Guttaboyz*, trailing by no more than 14 minutes. But with *Hot Lemon*, *Hardleys* and *Vilda* all within an hour of the race leader's time, it looked like this Class would bear watching more than any other.

Another Goldfish was leading the RB4 group. *Sealbay* was a private entry, but that didn't mean that Frederik Selvaag and Eirik Jaer weren't being well looked after by the factory team. So far their lead over *Mr Mako* and *swipewipes.co.uk* was a shade over one hour, but only time would tell if the Norwegian-built RIB would be able to resist the pressure.

The dark horse that was *Blue FPT* might have been second overall and leading the MC1 Class, but it was being stalked by another, even darker horse. The novice team of Scottish trawlermen on board *Braveheart III* were within half an hour of the Greek entry, and at the same time showing an incredulous fleet the merits of their unusual-looking Scanner RIB. It might have been built for the Med, but this standard production boat was clearly unfazed by the UK's rough waters. The Fraserburgh boys would have to keep on their toes though— only half an hour behind them was Chris Strickland on *Seahound V*, and with a trophy cabinet groaning under the weight of silverware from previous endurance races, Chris and his team would be undaunted by the prospect of the next four days.

Finally, the MC2 Class. The 28 foot Phantom of *Power Products Marine* was leading the Class of four, but *Northern Spirit* were within twenty minutes of stealing the position. Tom and Charlie Williams-Hawkes were one and a half hours behind the Class leaders, but less than ten minutes ahead of *Fugitive*, which left them no room for error whatsoever.

And as for the Classic Class, well, with its only entry (*Red FPT*) loaded up onto a truck and on its way back to Lake Como to lick its wounds, it looked like that particular bit of tin would have to go back to the silversmith, who would whip off the inscription plaque and sell it to some second-rate golf tournament for Best Dressed Caddy.

It was Guy Childs, one of the Scrutineers, who drew me back to the real world. "Come on mate, you're missing the barbie!" I had completely forgotten all about the barbecue the Organisers had laid on, even though the marquee just across the marina was in plain view.

"Cheers Guy, I was miles away." As we walked towards the smell of grilling meat I asked Guy if he could check my gear out later. We agreed to meet by the Goldfish boats at six that evening, which worked out nicely with my rendezvous with the team, and as he joined the line for a burger I headed for the beer table.

It might have been tepid, but the cans of McEwans lager were really hitting the spot, and as I was reaching for my fifth I overheard one of the competitors complimenting Mike Lloyd on the spread. Then my blood ran cold. "No problem Dave, but remember it's only one beer a head OK? We're not made of money you know." I casually grabbed my last tinny of the day and made a discrete exit.

Enjoying the pleasant afternoon outside the tent I bumped into Peter Verhauter, and asked if he'd mind if I joined *Buro* at a later stage. He was completely understanding, although he seemed a bit perplexed why someone would rather ride in an open, uncomfortable RIB instead of a warm, dry wheelhouse boat. As we chatted I noticed that although Peter's English was very good indeed, he was struggling with finding the right word occasionally. Since I'd been cursed with Dutch parents, I invited him to try me in that language instead. He was shocked at discovering my dirty little secret, but it meant that he could express himself more clearly whenever he was stuck in

English. Unfortunately for him, I picked up most of my Dutch in Rotterdam's rough docks district, so I was dialectically obliged to inject one curse for every two normal words.

So there we were, a Belgian and a Dutch Scot, drinking beer in Inverness in the middle of the world's toughest powerboat race. And then the Norwegians arrived.

Fortunately they had included an Englishman amongst their contingent, and it was he who had somehow managed to single me out.

"Derek? Hi, my name's James Sydenham; I believe you're going to join us on *Lionhead* tomorrow?"

As is usually the case when you need to make a good impression, I struggled to shake his hand. With a beer in one hand, a burger dripping fat in the other, and a half-smoked roll-up in the corner of my mouth I doubt I came across as a Professional— especially if he'd heard me murdering my mother tongue a few moments earlier. *Fuck. If he speaks Dutch I've had it!* I thought, but instead I carefully set my beer down and wiped a greasy hand on my jeans before shaking his proffered hand.

"James! Really good to meet you!" I gushed. "Listen, thanks for letting me tag along tomorrow, it's a real privilege."

"You're very welcome, but it isn't me you should be thanking." He nodded at two of his companions. "This is Pål Sollie, and his brother Henrik. Pål designs the boats, and Henrik is in charge of selling them. They agreed to let you join us for a leg."

I shook their hands and thanked them, feeling clumsy and stupid. All three of them were friendly enough, but they seemed to exude an overpowering aura of Cool that was almost tangible. It was as if they were detached from everything, observing the rest of the world from a bemused distance. They were too sharp to be Valium freaks, but perhaps they had gotten their hands on some new, exotic drug that killed the pain everybody else was feeling. Or maybe it was all just a front, and when we fired up our engines tomorrow morning they would be just as wired and jittery as the rest of us.

While the two brothers observed the Human species interacting amongst themselves (no doubt making mental notes to be compared later) James, the more sociable of the three, told me how lucky I was to be joining the winning boat. Apparently there was a queue of people jumping up and down to experience the RIB's speed and handling for themselves, but so far they had all been turned down.

Christ only knows why they were willing to let some jabbering loon join them on the longest leg of the race. Perhaps *MotorBoat & Yachting* was far more powerful than I had ever imagined. Or perhaps they had read my daily blog on the magazine's website and concluded that I was nothing more than an excitable madman; too overcome with the whole drama to write a damning review if their boat turned out to be a pig.

The truth of it was, I didn't give a flying fuck why they chose to take me over anybody else— I was joining the current front-runner of the Round Britain Powerboat Race, and to buggery with the politics behind it. And if the boat *did* turn out to be the aquatic version of a Princess Ambassador (which was highly unlikely, given the current standings) I'd waste no time at all in slagging it stupid to anyone who'd listen.

James hadn't been asked to join the Goldfish factory team just because he looked the part— he was their sole UK dealer, based at Salterns Marina in Poole, Dorset. He was also an accomplished powerboat racer, having spent several years racing V24 bat-boats. When I asked him if he thought the team could hold on to the lead, he was dismissive.

"It really doesn't matter what happens. The fact is, we're here to test the boats. If we go home tomorrow, we'd be satisfied with what we've already achieved."

"But surely you're not *just* here to give the boats a good thrashing?" I asked him. "Don't tell me Pål and Henrik wouldn't like a shiny trophy for the office?"

That got a wry smile out of him. "Well yes, of course it would be nice. But as far as we're concerned, we don't have anything to prove any more." And that was pretty much that as far as he was concerned, so I dropped it and we chatted idly about other things for a little while.

We were soon interrupted by the announcement that the briefing was about to get underway, so we all squeezed into the marquee to try to hear what was being said. Without the benefit of a PA system Colin Stewart, the bearded Officer Of The Day, was struggling to make himself heard, so I muscled my way forward to get a better listen.

It seemed that once again the environmentalists had struck, forcing the Organisers to move the start line a whopping ten miles out in order to protect the local seals, whales and dolphins. What's more, the run out to the starting point would be more of a stroll, with boats forbidden from planing. This caused an outcry, especially from those with thoroughbred racing boats; until they started planing the boats would travel with their bows pointed skywards, making it almost impossible to see where they were going. The only way round this was to drive in a zigzag, a potentially lethal manoeuvre in some of the narrower stretches of the Moray Firth, made even more dangerous by the announcement that the Organisers wanted a repeat of the three-abreast line we executed leaving Milford Haven.

But despite the complaints, we were told that this was how it had to be. There were ominous rumblings, but nobody— not even Ed Williams-Hawkes— felt like smacking their heads against the brick wall of Stupidity so the briefing was quickly hurried on.

We were told that we had another environmentalist in our midst, but fortunately he had decided not to rile us with another patronising lecture (probably after being warned of his comrade's fate in Wales), so instead he just offered a cheery wave as Mike introduced him. We were then told how the helicopter and plane chartered to ferry the Organisers from port to port were being used to look out for any whales and dolphins in the Firth, so that the Organisers could take the necessary steps to avoid us crossing their path. Again, nobody saw the sense in pointing out the damage a sodding great whale could do to a boat, which was yet another missed opportunity as drivers gently faded out of the conversation.

People soon perked up again when the start time was announced— 6am! This was because the fleet would have to negotiate the Clachnaharry Works lock, the swinging railway bridge and the Clachnaharry Sea lock just to feel salt water under our hulls. Then it would be the long and potentially dangerous plod up the Firth, under the Kessock bridge and then threading the needle where the channel narrowed drastically between the historic Fort George on the eastern shore and Chanonry Point on the west. Here only half a mile separated the two points, and if that sounds like a lot then it just shows that you've never seen over forty powerboats running roughly three abreast at eight knots before, weaving wildly from side to side so that they can see past their bows to figure out where they're going.

As the briefing wound down I realised that it was after five. I found James and promised I'd be at the boat for six, then grabbed a passing taxi back to my digs to pick up my racing gear for Scrutineering.

Guy was just finishing Scrutineering the first Goldfish boat when I arrived. Before starting on the second boat he took a minute to check my gear over, pulling me up on a missing whistle and the wrong numbers on my helmet. Again. Another taxi got me to Caley Marina who have a fantastic chandlery, where they sorted me out with a new whistle and a handful of plastic stick-on numbers— 22 for *Lionhead* and 15 for *Buro*. Suitably sorted I rushed back to the boat, where a chuckling Guy and a bemused Norwegian team watched me sort out my gear. Finally Guy gave me the all-clear, and I stepped onto *Lionhead* to check out my ride for the next day.

The first thing that struck me about the number 22 boat (and the identical number 33 *Guttaboyz* boat alongside) was how much they looked like military craft. The tubes were dark grey, with slightly lighter hull and topsides. Set into the front of the console was a large rectangle of deeply tinted glass, which could be opened by the press of a button. Two electric rams first pushed the glass outwards, then raised it, exposing a very handy storage area where the team had stowed their helmets, lifejackets and so on. It was a very slick and well-designed piece of engineering, something that was repeated all over the boat.

James took great pleasure in showing me the orange key fob that started the two Yanmar 380s remotely, their engine hatches also operated by electric rams. But when I walked round the console and saw the magnificence of the dash, I was left virtually speechless.

This truly was a thing of great beauty. The single-spoke wheel was sculpted out of aluminium, as were the formidable-looking gear and throttle levers that looked as if they controlled the spinning of the planet itself. Behind the wheel, laid out on the same pale grey fibreglass, were sombre black gauges with sparkling chrome bezels, and a Raymarine plotter nestled beneath the low coaming that served as a wind break.

There was an identical plotter to starboard, neatly angled forward, but instead of regimented lines of gauges there was instead a row of rubber switches that controlled all the electrical components on board. And instead of a gorgeous wheel, there was an aluminium grab bar mounted along the dashboard's leading edge.

The seats also looked like beautifully engineered works of art, minimalist yet practical. Height-adjustable and fitted with a damping system, I was looking forward to travelling in comfort and style the following day.

As the boys secured the smart grey canvas covers across the boat I wished them a good night and told them I'd see them the following morning— at a deeply unsocial 5:30— then wandered off to sign in with Race Control ahead of the morning. I was fully aware that mornings are definitely not my forte, and the chances of me forgetting to take care of the paperwork were pretty high.

"Evening ladies," I ventured. "Not too late for me to sign in is it?"

Gill and Mary lifted their eyes from the stacks and stacks of papers in front of them to fix me with a cold stare.

"Well well, look who it is," said Gill. "If it isn't the Boat Tart. And who will you be cheating with tomorrow then?"

I was a little taken aback at this latest line of insult. "Did you just call me a tart?"

"Yep. But don't feel bad; it isn't just me calling you that. Everyone's saying it. I'm just the only one to call you it to your face." Strangely Gill's comments did little to take the sting out of my new nickname. I had been hoping for something a little more manly— Derek The Destroyer, perhaps, or maybe even Big Fella. But "Boat Tart" seemed a little, well, insulting.

"That's a bit harsh isn't it? Calling me a tart."

But Gill and Mary just laughed. "Well you *are* a tart. You just use 'em and lose 'em don't you?"

I couldn't really deny it, but still... "I'm just doing my job. Do you think I enjoy having to hop from boat to boat every day?"

"Yeah yeah yeah. Whatever. So who are you with tomorrow then?"

"*Lionhead*. Should be a blast," I told her. She dug out the relevant paperwork and I signed in the box. I wished them a sarcastic Goodnight and slinked off in search of a taxi to ferry me to a nearby pub within walking distance to my digs, where I tried to ignore the noisy neighbours until I fell into another fitful sleep.

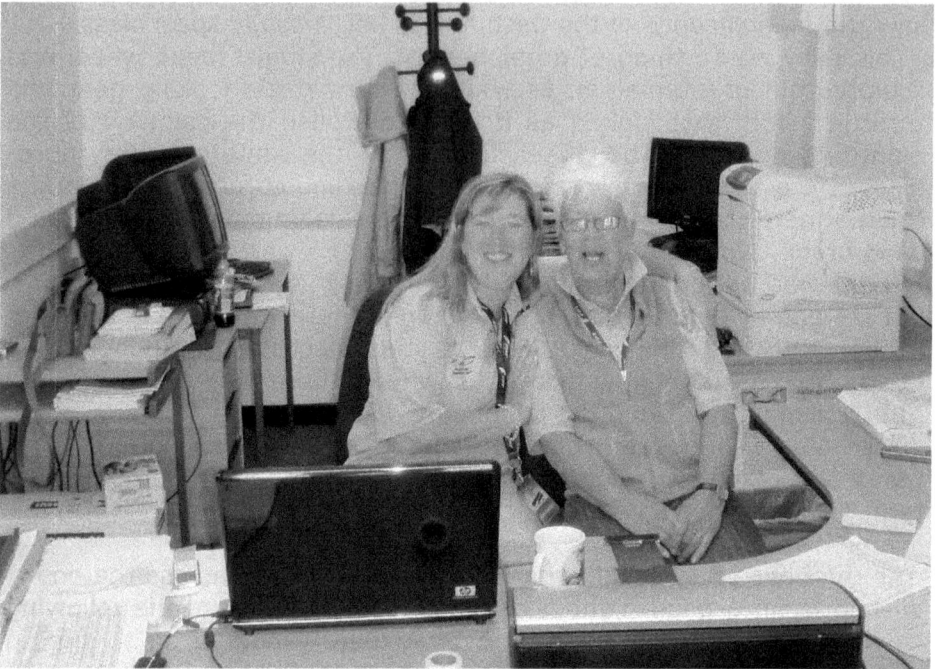

Top– Gill and Mary, evil Race Control goddesses

Below– Waiting for parts, Inverness

Results- Halfway.

Distance to date: 444 nautical miles.

Pos.	Team/ Number	Class	Overall Time	Trailing by:
1st	Lionhead/22	RB3	8:48	-
2nd	Blue FPT/333	MC1	9:01	0:13
3rd	Guttaboyz/33	RB3	9:02	0:13
4th	Hot Lemon/2	RB3	9:21	0:32
5th	Braveheart III/55	MC1	9:26	0:37
6th	Hardleys/4	RB3	9:29	0:40
7th	Vilda/9	RB3	9:52	1:03
8th	Seahound V/80	MC1	9:55	1:07
9th	Birretta/12	MC1	10:10	1:21
10th	Sealbay/77	RB4	10:13	1:24
11th	Going Lean/7	RB3	10:22	1:33
12th	Team Silverline/471	RB2	10:27	1:38
13th	Carbon Neutral/343	RB3	10:53	2:05
14th	Mr Mako/96	RB4	11:01	2:12
15th	Team Bandit/69	RB2	11:11	2:22
16th	Power Products Marine/8	MC2	11:15	2:26
17th	swipewipes.co.uk/43	RB4	11:16	2:27
18th	Venturer/111	RB1	11:25	2:36
19th	Team Scorpion Dubois/16	MC1	11:29	2:41
20th	Seafarer/110	RB3	11:30	2:41

Pos.	Team/ Number	Class	Overall Time	Trailing by:
21st	Northern Spirit/5	MC2	11:34	2:45
22nd	Relentless/47	RB3	11:58	3:09
23rd	Tequila/88	RB3	11:59	3:10
24th	My Pleasure II/3	RB4	12:39	3:51
25th	TFO/17	MC2	12:43	3:54
26th	Fugitive/130	MC2	12:51	4:02
27th	Team Pulsar-Vampire/102	RB4	13:42	4:53
28th	GEE/185	HC1	13:43	4:54
29th	Buro/15	MC1	13:45	4:56
30th	Wettpunkt.com/81	RB1	14:42	5:53
31st	Team Pulsar-Wolf/101	RB4	14:48	5:59
32nd	Mud, Swell & Beers/14	RB4	14:57	6:08
33rd	Team 747/747	HC1	15:03	6:14
34th	Mystic Dragon/6	MC1	19:48	11:00
35th	Team Jersey/45	RB4	24:49	15:59
36th	No Worries/11	RB3	26:02	17:14
37th	Black Gold/10	RB4	26:49	17:59
38th	Ikon/18	RB3	27:29	18:29
39th	Xanthus/1	HC1	30:06	21:18
40th	RIB International/144	RB4	**OTR**	23:23

DNS Denotes Did Not Start
DNF Denotes Did Not Finish
OTR Denotes Out of The Race
* Denotes maximum time allowance exceeded.

Pos.	Team/Number	Class	Overall Time	Trailing by:
41st	Red FPT/177	CC1	**OTR**	23:23
42nd	Racing Garmin/72	RB2	*	23:23
43rd	Team Blastoff/100	RB2	*	23:23
44th	Blue Marlin/99	HC1	**OTR**	23:23
45th	Swordsman/68	HC1	*	23:23
46th	Cinzano/558	RB2	**OTR**	23:23
47th	Ocean Pirate/323	HC1	*	23:23

DNS Denotes Did Not Start
DNF Denotes Did Not Finish
OTR Denotes Out of The Race
* Denotes maximum time allowance exceeded.

Below– Fabio Buzzi's magnificent *Red FPT*. Damage to the gearboxes and drivetrains forced him to retire at Milford Haven

11.
Inverness To Edinburgh.

Friday 27th June.

My taxi driver had little sympathy that morning. I had paid my B&B landlady five quid so that I could take my brimming mug of hot sweet tea away with me, but the cabbie refused to let me into his beaten-up Ford Granada with it. I couldn't see the problem myself; if by some freak occurrence I did accidentally spill some, the beige velour upholstery would never show the stain. Since I was running frantically late as usual I finally relented, and poured the steaming life-juice into the gutter.

The briefing that morning was blissfully short, the Organisers only reminding us of the speed limit out to the muster area ten miles away, and confirming that the weather would be benign, if a little choppy.

It was certainly poles apart from the Inverness leg in the '69 race; back then a heavy fog or "haar" had descended all along the east coast, threatening to cancel the stage. In those halcyon days, radar for small leisure boats was considered a luxury, and some hard-core racers even saw the use of it a cheat. But despite the inherent dangers in setting off into the murky Unknown at 40 or 50 knots, the Organisers decided to run the risk and sent the fleet off into the mist. *Ocean Pirate* was one of the very few boats equipped with radar in the fleet, and John Turvey, her then owner, took full advantage, coming across the line at Dundee in seventh.

Today, most boat were fitted with radar, and even those few that didn't (like *Buzzi Bullet*) had GPS plotters, so there was little chance of running aground should they find themselves in a deep, impenetrable fogbank, like four or five competitors did back in '69. Modern technology might be a hateful and loathsome system to keep the affluent western world locked into an expensive and ultimately futile cycle of desperate consumerism and one-upmanship, raping the planet's finite resources and exploiting the eager-to-please third world high-tech sweat shops, but it occasionally manages to spit out something truly inspiring and life-affirming. Even if it is more often than not created in the bloody crucible of war.

The Muirtown Basin was a hive of activity as sleepy-eyed drivers, navigators and mechanics set about awakening the boats for the mammoth leg down the east coast to Edinburgh. The Goldfish team were already there of course, no sign of tousled hair or barely-contained yawns, even at 5:30 in the morning. Like the Professionals they were they methodically stripped the covers off the two identical RIBs and stowed them neatly in the back of their massive Dodge pick-up truck, then carried out a last check of the engines before firing them up.

I fumbled my way into my drysuit, miserably aware that my hotch-potch of clothing looked embarrassingly scruffy compared to the im-peccably-attired and colour-coordinated Norwegians, and I got a painful mental flashback of being back at school, being mocked by all the cool kids for not wearing the unofficial uniform of Nike trainers and Levis. But my Norwegian crew-mates didn't go so far as to point and laugh, and in fact they seemed as friendly as before, so I shrugged it off as a sleep-deprived hallucination and got on with the job in hand. Which suddenly turned out to be taking a piss.

It took forever to strip back down out of my drysuit, do the business and then strap everything on again, and when I re-emerged the boys were anxiously looking at their watches. I was just about to step on board when I remembered my bag— Could it go in the support truck? I asked.

James pointed towards the main gate to the marina. "You'd better be quick; they're just leaving."

I tried sprinting down the road to catch the pick-up, but sprinting and drysuits are not happy companions, so after a hurried waddle I managed to catch up with the truck and threw my holdall into the back. I got a funny look from the driver, so I yelled that I'd pick it up in Edinburgh. He gave me a dubious thumbs-up then gunned it onto the main road while I shuffled back to the impatient *Lionhead* crew, sweat pouring freely down my back.

As it turned out, there was no need to rush. We dropped our lines and motored down three hundred yards or so to the first of two locks, where it became apparent that Mr Telford never anticipated the notion of forty-odd boats trying to negotiate one lock. We all rafted up as the first group of boats travelled through the first of the locks, teams from different boats all chatting away amongst each other.

We had a pretty full boat— Pål and Henrik Sollie were up front, driving and navigating. Their engineer, Bjorn Erik Eriksen, was a stocky, quiet guy— the kind that would be invaluable if a fight broke out in a pub, but poor company if you were trapped in a lift with him. He sat behind Pål on the port side, with James to starboard. I would be standing behind Bjorn, so that James could keep an eye on me— vital since my lid didn't have an intercom.

I took the opportunity to ask James who else had asked to join the crew. "Actually, the Norwegian Navy wanted to put one of their guys on board." This threw me a little; I was expecting it to be a queue of boating journalists, not government representatives. "The Norwegian Ministry of Defence is looking for a new fast patrol boat, and they seem really keen on the Goldfish, so they asked if one of their top men could join us for a leg or two, but we refused."

"Jesus! That could be a juicy market," I told him. "Just look at what it's done for Buzzi." The Italian had been selling high-speed patrol boats to armed forces around the world for years; in fact the British Marines who were captured by the Iranians in March 2007 had no chance of getting away— their captors were driving FB Design RIBs capable of 80 knots, twice the speed of the British boats.

"Don't get me wrong; we're not knocking the opportunity, we just didn't think that the boats would be ready for that kind of scrutiny. These are still just prototypes remember, which is why they're still a little rough around the edges."

I looked around incredulously. *Christ*, I thought, *If this is rough round the edges, I'd kill to see one of these properly sorted!*

James read my mind— never a tough proposition— and smiled. "I know what you're thinking, but it's true. Take the seats for instance. They look great, and they're pretty comfy too, but we've broken most of them. See?" He pointed to one of the seat bases, which was pointing down towards the deck. Then he pointed out the grab bars, mounted to the back of the seat in front of mine. "We need to get the welding sorted as well. You can see that the aluminium welds have let go. There are several little bits and bobs around the boat that need sorting, but then that's exactly why we're here in the first place."

"So is it just some of the fittings that are showing the strain?"

"We've also been having some trouble with the drives," James told me candidly. "The problem is that we've taken a standard Yanmar engine that puts out 300 horsepower, and we've uprated it to 380. That means that the drive legs have been taking quite a pounding. But then this is one hell of a test drive!"

Goldfish market their boats as "the ultimate tool on water" and it was clear to see that they were living up to their reputation. But at the same time they were also works of art, reminding me of the beautiful, but functional, knives and tools made by Peter Atwood. These RIBs were too good to be wasted on the military, I thought, and looked better suited to the luxury yacht tender market.

It took forever for the fleet of boats to make their way through the first lock, under the swinging railway bridge and through the sea lock until finally we found ourselves in the Moray Firth. But we weren't done yet. We had to crawl our way out to sea at a crippled pace, careful not to frighten the local wildlife. Passing under the Kessock bridge made an impressive sight, as was weaving our way through the dogleg opposite Fort George. Boats with stepped hulls really hate motoring at those speeds, and there was an odd procession of various machines running with their noses pointed high up into the air.

The fleet finally came together about ten miles out, where we were told over the radio to hang fire. Apparently we were missing a couple of boats, and would have to wait for them to catch up. At least Jonathan, Andy and Cormac on board *Miss Daisy* had managed to get the Fairey fixed in time, and I gave the *747* boys a cheery wave as they motored past.

As we drifted idly under the leaden skies the privately-entered Gold-fish *Sealbay* came alongside and rafted up. This RIB was only 29 feet long, with a single 380 hp engine, and so was in the RB4 Class. The two crew, owner Eirik Jaer and Frederik Selvaag, were giving a good account of themselves, currently leading their Class and showing as 10th overall.

Frederik wasn't particularly chatty to me, but I think that had more to do with his limited English than his personality. Eirik, on the other hand, was really friendly and extremely enthusiastic about the race, clearly a novice to the whole scene but loving every minute of it. I took an instant liking to him, and when he lit up a cigarette I liked him even more.

Out of respect for every team I'd been with, I had resisted the over-whelming temptation to light up, often not even bothering to ask if anyone would mind, since the answer would have been a firm No every time. But when I finally saw another man with the good sense to enjoy a smoke, I quickly asked if I could join him.

He looked at me as if I was an idiot. "Of course you can! Step on board. Would you like one of mine?"

I declined and pulled out my battered old tobacco tin and set about rolling a cigarette, almost drooling in anticipation. As I blew out the first, deep lungful I let out an unintentional "*Aahhhh*" in pleasure.

Eirik smiled at me. "Yes, a cigarette always tastes better on a boat, doesn't it?"

He couldn't have been more right. Sitting on the deck, leaning back against a firmly inflated tube, the waves gently rocking the two teth-ered boats and making little wet slapping noises against the hulls, that cigarette was one of the best I'd had in a long while.

Of course the tranquillity didn't last long; it never does. *Guttaboyz* came chugging alongside, and the crew had a heated Norwegian dis-cussion. Pål and Bjorn leapt aboard and the number 33 boat motored clear. Once they were in uncluttered water they opened the throttles, and it was immediately apparent that something was wrong.

The exhausts threw out lots of thick black smoke, and the engines sounded strangled. From a distance we watched as the two engine hatches raised on their electric rams and the powerful figure of Bjorn disappeared inside. A couple of minutes later he emerged, apparently unable to cure the problem. Then he and Pål clambered onto the bow of the boat as the two crew once again opened the throttles.

Eirik explained what they were doing. "It looks like the turbo isn't working. They don't have enough power to get up onto the plane, so Pål and Bjorn are having to keep the bow down with their weight, you see?" I saw. "Once the boat is on the plane, it's no problem to keep it there— but first they have to get there." It was a classic

Catch-22 situation, but there was a further twist that Eirik hadn't considered: what would Pål and Bjorn do if they did manage to get the boat planing? Jump for it? I got my camera ready.

My attention was suddenly drawn to the crackle over the VHF. Mike Barlow on *Ocean Pirate* was asking Race Control if the Historics could leave.

"Negative, nobody's going anywhere. We're just waiting for one more boat. Over."

"That's all good and well, but we slower boats are looking at an eight-hour passage. Why can't we just get going? Over."

The voice on the other end was getting seriously agitated now. "I said Wait! We're still waiting for bloody *Ocean Pirate* to clear the locks. Over."

There was a moment's silence. I filled that moment by looking across at *Ocean Pirate*, less than two hundred feet off our bow in the middle of the Firth.

"Er, Race Control, this is *Ocean Pirate* and we've been buggering about out here with the rest of the fleet for the past bloody hour. So can we please get going? Over."

Gary Manchester, the voice of Race Control, wasn't too happy at being made to look a fool in front of the rest of the fleet, who were all joking either amongst themselves or over the airways. He told everyone sharply to shut up, and five minutes later we saw the Start Boat shouldering its way to the front. And not before time; it was now nearly ten o'clock, and everyone's patience was being stretched to the limit.

Thankfully the boys on board *Guttaboyz* had spotted the Start Boat, and moments later Pål and the mechanic were dropped off onto *Lion-head*. Nick Tollefsen and his son Ivar were left to do the best they could with *Guttaboyz* and we set *Sealbay* loose and settled in for the race start.

I have always been a speed freak, something that had been instilled in me at an extremely early age. While my contemporaries were still fooling with the stabilisers on their bicycles I was learning how to drive. To be more specific, I was learning to drive around Zandvoort, Holland's answer to Silverstone or Monza. And I wasn't crashing through the gears of a dual-control Nissan Micra either; I spent hours and hours on the 2.7 mile track in a race-prepared Renault 5, my teacher a veteran racer and close family friend. I may not have been setting lap records, but even at seven years old I understood completely that Speed and Control were everything, and a life spent stumbling around well within my limits would lead to nothing but misery and humiliation. That is why this race had grabbed me from the very beginning; even though I would not be controlling these machines myself, the knowledge that I would once again be travelling along the very edge of what men and machine were capable of was a powerful and all-conquering concept, and like a junkie invited on a tour of a pharmaceutical factory with the promise of free samples I knew, from the very beginning, that to turn down this opportunity would be like ignoring my own existence.

As I was clipping my kill chord round my right calf James reached over. "Listen, Pål might want you to move across to the starboard seat if the boat needs trimming. We won't know until we're in open water, but just keep an eye on me."

I gave him a big thumbs up, but I wasn't feeling confident about having to change seats halfway through the race. To get to the other seat I would have to bend down, unclip my kill chord, step across a foot-high console that ran the length of the boat, then attach a new chord. I had been struggling with the bugger in nearly flat-calm water; how the hell was I going to manage it at 85 knots across six-foot seas?

Every time I clipped on a kill chord I was intensely paranoid about accidentally pulling the safety switch and stopping the engines mid-race. While stopping the engines dead at high speeds wasn't exactly like stomping on the brakes on a motorway, it was still a potentially dangerous act. As soon as the boat lost the engines, all the weight would move forward, dropping the bow and unsettling the hull. In rough seas, crossing the wake of another boat or half-way through an emergency turn there was a good chance of stuffing the boat, taking on a big lump of water or even causing someone to be thrown overboard. Definitely not something I wanted on my conscience.

"Oh, one more thing," James shouted. "Try to keep as low down as possible. We don't want any wind resistance, OK?"

As Pål hit the throttles, sending a mighty rooster tail spouting up fifteen feet into the air behind the transom I shifted my position. I had been standing, gripping the aluminium grab rail fitted to the back of Bjorn's seat, taking care not to get any flesh caught between the flexing crack where a weld had let go. As the speed picked up, so too did the wind, which tried to rip the open-faced helmet from my head. The strap was slowly strangling me, so I was only too happy to bend through my knees until I was squatting with my arse just a few inches off the deck. Sheltered from the wind by Bjorn's stolid bulk I found that I could once again suck sweet, life-giving air into my lungs. James threw a quick glance in my direction and we swapped thumbs-up signals.

Lionhead was setting a mighty pace, making short work of the five foot seas as we bounded eastwards towards Lossiemouth. After ten minutes or so we had cleared most of the field, and then we found ourselves running right alongside *Buzzi Bullet* of Team *Silverline*.

The gap between us was no more than thirty feet, and the full complement told me that Miles was back on board. I gave them a quick wave, which Jan returned from his seat behind Miles, but I was wary of letting go even for a second.

RIBs, by their very nature, are generally lighter than hard boats.

The difference between *Lionhead* and *Buzzi Bullet* was at least half a ton, and it was blatantly apparent, even to me, as the two boats raced side by side at almost eighty miles per hour. Drew's heavier boat seemed to be handling the chop much better than us, the long, streamlined hull spearing through the water, her weight forcing the sharp prow to slice easily through the smaller waves. But in the lighter boat it felt like we were bouncing across every wave. Our lighter hull lacked the weight to cut through the water as effectively, resulting in a harsher ride as we skimmed from crest to crest.

We ran like this for five minutes or so, the boats evenly matched. It was exhilarating— to my right was the shore, waves breaking on sandy beach just a few hundred yards away; and thirty feet to my left was the magnificent spectacle of *Buzzi Bullet* thundering across the sea as we powered eastwards at eighty-five knots, our rooster tails visible from a mile away.

I was desperate to get a picture of this incredible scene, and fumbled blindly with one hand to try and unzip my jacket pocket. But my lifejacket was in the way, and the boat's motion was too jarring for me to risk using both hands to retrieve my camera. And besides, even if I did manage to whip my Olympus out, the chances were that the pictures would have been blurred into an unrecognisable smudge before dropping the camera over the side with an anguished wail... I heaved a monumental mental sigh and elected to resume my hold onto the grab bar with both hands in a death grip as I tried to keep myself inside the boat.

Losiemouth stands on a low hill, braced by surprisingly pleasant sandy beaches. As we cleared the town Pål turned to starboard, hugging the shore. On *Buzzi Bullet* Miles kept the bow pointing straight ahead, following the direct course Jan had plotted into the chart plotter the previous day. Slowly the gap between the two boats increased, until their rooster tail was lost in the murk.

Pål had chosen to run closer inshore because that was where the sea would be a little calmer. It was a strategy he had followed for the entire race, and even though it made for a greater distance to cover it also meant that in the flatter sea he could keep the speed up. It was a strategy that had worked for him so far, and there was no reason to change it.

Up until now I had been extremely lucky with my lack of injuries. Apart from destroying my feet by walking for miles in ill-fitting shoes I had received none of the sprains, bruises and breaks reported by many other competitors. This definitely wasn't down to any prodigious physical exercise regime; despite my (half-arsed) training programme, by the time I left for Portsmouth I was barely able to complete a dozen push-ups, half a dozen sit-ups, or run for more than two or three minutes at a stretch. By now I was managing to cram at least thirty cigarettes into an average day, and my diet consisted of burgers, crisps and biscuits— when I could find anything to eat at all.

And yet, apart from my poor, shredded feet— which had healed rapidly the moment I swapped my Converse for my battered old trainers— I had managed to escape unscathed from the worst that the British waters could throw at me. Until now.

Hunkering down in the shelter of Bjorn's bulk, my thighs were starting to grumble. Then tremble. Until finally, my leg muscles were burning with a white-hot agony, unable to cope with this new constricted position whilst still having to act as shock absorbers.

I physically hauled myself up to a standing position, silently praying that the already fractured grab bar wouldn't finally give up the ghost completely, sending me sprawling to the violently-jumping deck. James caught my motion from the corner of his eye, and looked at me, his eyes questioning behind his stylish goggles.

I pointed at my trembling legs, and pulled an apologetic face. *Fuck this for a game of soldiers* I thought, massaging my legs with one hand whilst hanging on with the other. The relief was almost instantaneous as my tortured muscles were given a reprieve from my contorted squat.

Standing upright brought with it some new disadvantages however. Firstly, the wind once again set about trying to strangle me by tugging frantically on my lid. I solved this problem by tucking my chin into my breastbone, but that meant that I was forced to stare at nothing more exciting than my own two feet and a bit of grey fibreglass deck.

Secondly, I felt a lot more exposed. The gunwales tapered down from the front of the cockpit, which gave the boat a very pleasing aesthetic profile but by the time the coaming reached me it was below my waist. I suddenly felt very insecure— not in a "everyone's got a bigger willie than me" sort of way, but in a "oh fuck I'm going to be thrown overboard any moment" kind of way. It was a very unsettling feeling, not made any less so by the fact that my grab bar was flexing and springing wildly, it's one remaining weld the only thing keeping me from smacking head-first into the North Sea at 85 knots. Or so it seemed at the time.

We battered on, the shoreline never more than quarter of a mile off our right shoulder. We had to make the occasional quick detour as small orange marker buoys suddenly appeared in front of us, invisible until they were lifted up on the crest of a wave, but apart from that everything was going well. Until I noticed the fire.

I say fire; it was actually more of a smoulder. For a couple of minutes I had thought I had smelled burning plastic, but with the wind whipping up my nostrils at such incredible speed it was hard to be sure. Then I noticed little wisps of smoke streaming out of the centre console between James and Bjorn. I leant forward and urgently tapped James on the arm, pointing down at the console.

Since his helmet was equipped with an intercom he was able to tell Pål and Henrik we had a problem, and Pål quickly brought the boat to a halt. James had already opened the lid on the console, and the problem was immediately plain to see— the two wires that powered the electrical seats had got caught in the console lid, chafing off the insulation and letting the two bare wires touch. James and Bjorn carried out a lightening-quick bodge to keep the two wires well away from each other and anything metallic and within a minute we were back up to speed.

I was feeling very isolated by now. I didn't have an intercom, and I had no-one next to me that I could shout a conversation with. At a pinch I could have tried screaming into the big mechanic's behelmeted ear, but his English wasn't really up to much, and he would have had to shout back, giving the rest of the guys a nasty shock as his voice roared over the intercom. Way back in the stern I couldn't see any of the displays, so I didn't really know how fast we were going, or even where we were, since the plotter's screen was too far away for me to read. I was starting to feel pretty lonely, especially when I thought back to the shouted camaraderie I had shared with Team *747*, or the good-natured joking over the *Silverline* intercom.

I was also struggling to get comfortable. There was no rubber matting on the deck, so my feet were once again taking the full impact of the jarring ride, and the grab bar was slightly too low for me, meaning I took on the posture of a grown man riding a kiddie's bike, and it was causing my shoulders to ache as I tried to hang on for dear life. Every now and then I would resume my squatting position to placate James, but after five or ten minutes my legs would resume their painful burning, forcing me to stand back up again.

During one particularly bumpy section I found myself being attacked by the boat's EPIRB. I had been hunkered down, and the boat came down awkwardly off one particularly large wave. I was thrown backwards and to my left, into the corner where the EPIRB was mounted in its cradle.

An EPIRB, for those who don't know, is an Emergency Position Indicating Radio Beacon. This one looked a bit like a big yellow mushroom, about a foot and a half long, and weighed three or four pounds. They can be activated two different ways; either someone presses the big ON button, or when they get a dunking (i.e. when the boat sinks) the salt water triggers it automatically. They then send a distress signal and their location to the emergency services, who send the Cavalry to fish you out of the briny.

On *Lionhead* the EPIRB wasn't sitting quite as snugly in its cradle as it could have been, and as we smashed down off that awkward crest it decided to make a valiant bid for freedom. It crashed into my arm, then spent the next couple of minutes being rattled around the deck as I scrabbled for it with one hand, hanging on to the base of Bjorn's seat with the other. I finally managed to corner it and somehow twist myself backwards to drop it back into its cradle, but ten minutes later it was free again.

This went on three or four times, but as we rounded the corner at Fife Ness and found the smoother waters of the Firth of Forth the plastic bugger finally settled down, leaving me to enjoy the climax of this uncomfortable leg.

When a boat crosses the finish line its crew rarely, if ever, know what position they've achieved. Once across the line, the boats head straight for the pits, leaving the area clear for the next boat to come hurtling in, so a team crossing the line can't count the boats already there to figure out how well (or badly) they've done. And so it was for us as we raced towards Edinburgh.

Then I noticed the helicopter, the one carrying the film crew. It usually filmed the first boat across the line (to the winner goes the glory and all that), but now it was racing out of Edinburgh to meet us as we neared the line.

A minute or so later it all became clear— or so I thought at the time. Because Pål had taken us much closer inshore, the chopper hadn't seen us, and instead had latched onto *Blue FPT*, an easy target due to its massive length and the awe-inspiring rooster tail its three props threw into the sky.

The further into the shelter of the Forth we got, the calmer the sea got, and we could run with the throttles right up against their stops. The problem was, so could Vassilis Pateras, and he had three engines putting out a combined 1,400 horsepower versus our 760.

As he got closer I could see another rooster tail, which turned out to belong to Team *Silverline*. They were gaining, but *Blue FPT* had the legs on all of us, and overtook us less than quarter of a mile before we crossed the line.

The finish line was another one of those "blink and you'll miss it" affairs, and although it was clearly marked on the map, from the water it was virtually impossible to make it out. We had to rely on Henrik's plotting abilities, and hope he had punched the co-ordinates into the chart plotter carefully. Apparently Drew and the boys had the same concern, and as they came steaming up behind us they suddenly made a big U-turn, clearly concerned that they hadn't passed between the right two buoys that marked the line.

But Pål was confident that we'd got it right, and he eased back on the throttles and motored towards the shore, so as to keep out of the way of following boats while we stretched our weary muscles and figured out how to get to Port Edgar, our berth for the night.

Just then I became aware of a black RIB bedecked in flashing blue lights racing towards us. The marine branch of the local constabulary was coming to say hello, and I managed to warn Pål just seconds before he was about to nail the throttles for the long run under the two bridges that span the Forth.

"Good afternoon gentlemen!" came from one of the three coppers. "I don't suppose you are in any kind of distress are you?"

The question completely flummoxed us, and James shouted back a confused "No, why?"

By now the police RIB was alongside, and normal conversation was once again possible. "Because according to your EPIRB you sank a couple of hours ago."

Oh fuck! This was all my fault. *Bugger, arse, FUCK!*

The policeman went on calmly. "When the coastguard got the signal they checked the co-ordinates, but when they realised that you were still doing 80 miles per hour they kind of figured you weren't really sinking."

Time to confess. "Ah, yes, the EPIRB got loose earlier. It didn't get wet though; see?" I grabbed it out of its cradle to show everyone. And then I spotted the sliding switch was fully in the ON position. "Bugger. It must have smacked into something," I mumbled embarrassed.

"Not to worry Sir. If you could make your way down to Port Edgar Marina, the coastguard there would like to have a quick word just to confirm everything's OK."

I kept my head down so I wouldn't have to make eye contact with anyone. Pål asked if he should follow the police RIB in, but one of the coppers had a better idea.

"I'll tell you what; why don't I come on board and I'll guide you in. Would that be OK?"

Pål agreed, and he transferred across. He took the spare spot just across from me and gave me a smile. "So, what's it like then, this race?"

Good question. "Erm, pretty fucking intense actually," I replied. "Oh, and you might want to hang on to something."

Just then Pål turned to speak to the policeman. "Is there some speed limit here?" he asked, clearly not wanting a speeding ticket.

"Well, there is usually," he smiled, "but if you think you need to give the engines a quick clear-out, then I can't see any problem with that," and he gave the driver a big wink.

"OK then. Hold on to something!"

The copper was standing sideways, facing me. I gave him another warning, but he smiled like I was some sort of a moron. Which I am, but that wasn't the point right then. "It's OK. I spend all day every day on our boat. I'll be fine."

I shrugged and braced myself. Pål threw open the throttles and *Lionhead* dug her stern in and catapulted across the water with phenomenal acceleration. The cocky copper was nearly thrown off his feet and back onto the engine hatches, arms flailing wildly for something to hang on to. I flashed him an unsympathetic look then broke into a big grin as I mentally pictured Plod sliding across the engine hatches and off the stern.

Once he'd managed to find a secure grip and had sucked in a couple of deep lungfuls of air he leaned across to me, his face white and with wide, frightened eyes. "Jesus and Mary, this thing really fucking goes!"

I didn't bother answering him; I nodded my head and kept facing forward as we thundered under the Forth rail bridge, the iconic structure half hidden under scaffolding and sheets of opaque plastic. A few seconds later we had covered half a mile and passed beneath the equally impressive road bridge, which is when the policeman finally told James to get Pål to back off the throttles.

Just to our left we saw Port Edgar Marina, and at a gentle and relaxed pace we motored in and tied up on one of the pontoons. At the same time, *Silverline* were being nudged into the adjoining pontoon, helped in by a couple of small RIBs, not far from where *Blue FPT's* crew were securing their boat. But it seemed like we had all been beaten to the punch, with *Wettpunkt.com* safely tied up, looking like she'd been there for hours.

I stepped onto the pontoon and took great pleasure in stretching all the knots and kinks out of my poor, battered muscles. I had to take hold of the copper's trembling arm to stop him from falling over the side, his face just starting to show some return of colour. I offered him an unsympathetic "You'll be alright" then thanked the boys and made my way along the maze of pontoons and up a long, sloping walkway.

The Port Edgar Marina complex was made up of about a dozen ramshackle wooden buildings, scattered haphazardly over the site. But I was completely unaware of their decrepit appearance, because I suddenly spotted a mechanic emerging from a darkened doorway munching contentedly on what looked— and smelled— suspiciously like a bacon roll.

Like a man emerging out of a desert and stumbling upon an oasis I stopped the mechanic mid-bite. "Is— is that a bacon roll?" I asked incredulously.

"Er, yes. There's a little canteen just in there," the confused man replied, pointing back over his shoulder.

I didn't even bother to thank him; I pushed him to one side and scrabbled up three wooden steps and into the gloom, the smell of warm, fresh food hitting me like a wall.

Just off the main corridor was a small canteen, half a dozen rickety tables taking up most of the space. In the far wall was a wide hatch, with a kindly-looking woman in her forties leaning out, her chubby arms resting on the battered counter.

"Hello there! You look like you're hungry; have a look at the menu and see if there's anything you fancy."

I picked up a laminated menu off one of the tables. *What wondrous surprise was this?* There was so much choice— bacon, eggs, sausages, beans, toast— the list went on and on, and I felt like a kid in a sweetie shop. "Um, I'll have a bacon and egg roll, a sausage roll, and a mug of tea please."

I had just wolfed everything down when Drew, Jan, John and

Bethan strolled in. I greeted them warmly and strongly recommended the food, and we spent half an hour or so eating and catching up.

It turned out that *Buzzi Bullet* had only just made it into Edinburgh by the skin of its teeth. One of the hoses for the bow tank had split, and had sprayed seawater over the engines' alternators, causing the engines to break down just a couple of hundred yards over the finish line, which is why they had to be helped into their berth at the marina.

I wondered where Miles was, and John suppressed a grin as Drew explained all. It seemed that Miles' ribs still hadn't recovered from the pounding sustained during their crossing of the Irish sea, and was suffering so badly during this morning's run that Drew was forced to intercept a fishing boat and ask the bemused crew to put Miles ashore, leaving Drew, Jan and John free to open the taps once again.

I couldn't help but feel sorry for him; not only was he driving an unfamiliar boat, but he was having to do it standing up, a position totally alien to him. Throw in a handful of badly bruised ribs and a vicious swell, and he was bound to be struggling. It was still bloody funny though. (Although we didn't know it at the time, the unscheduled rendezvous probably cost *Silverline* the stage win. The five or six minutes spent transferring Miles to the fishing boat was the difference between first and fourth, their eventual placing for the leg.)

I was still smiling to myself as I stepped outside for a smoke. My grin grew even wider when I spotted one of the Goldfish pick-ups pull into the car park; here was my chance to grab my bag. I flagged down the driver and asked about my holdall, but he told me in broken English that it had been transferred into the back of the support lorry. I managed to track down James Sydenham, who was chatting with an attractive blonde.

"Derek, I'd like you to meet my girlfriend Ellie." We swapped greetings before I asked James if he knew where the Goldfish lorry was, so that I could reclaim my bag.

"Oh, it's just over there," interrupted Ellie, pointing along the access road into the marina. "I've locked it, so I'll walk over with you."

Since I couldn't think of any reason why I shouldn't spend fifteen minutes in the company of a good-looking woman I took her up on her offer, and as we walked towards the anonymous box-lorry we chatted about her involvement in the race.

It turned out she wasn't just along to give James moral support, she was also a vital part of the shore support team. She had been following the fleet round in the 7½ tonner, which was loaded with spare parts for the two Goldfish boats. She told me that driving it wasn't a problem, but trying to park the beast was a bit intimidating it first. My admiration of her only grew when she told me about her little drama in Wales.

She was just about to set off for the ferry across to Ireland when she realised one of the other crew had accidentally locked the keys in the cab. When it became obvious that no-one could break into the cab, they finally smashed the window. Ellie had no choice but to drive the lorry for the next two days with a sodding great hole where the driver's side window should have been, enduring constant cold as she grimly covered three hundred miles until they finally found the time to get the glass replaced.

Reunited with my holdall once again I walked back to the canteen, where I sipped on a Coke as I called in my report for the day to Rob at the magazine. While I was waiting for my taxi to my digs I bumped into Peter Verhauter, who had promised me a seat on board *Buro* the following day. I asked him if he wanted anything by way of payment.

"Oh, just bring something for lunch," he replied. I promised I'd try to surprise him and jumped into my cab, directing the driver to my B&B via a supermarket.

After an inspired visit to the massive Tesco my taxi dropped me off at my digs for the night, an anonymous suburban house set back from the busy main road. My usual residence whenever I'm in Edinburgh is the Lochindaal suite at the Royal Terrace hotel, a grand Georgian affair with cavernous rooms and ceilings so high the echo would be epic if it wasn't for the plush carpets, heavy scarlet curtains and overstuffed furniture. They know me there, mainly for all the wrong reasons, but the Royal Terrace was in the heart of the city, a long way away from the marina in South Queensferry, so with a heavy heart I had chosen convenience over opulent luxury.

While my hosts for the evening were perfectly pleasant, I couldn't help but think I'd rented their spare room for the night, so I shut myself in and spent a couple of hours checking emails before grabbing a quick shower in the only bathroom in the house before vainly trying to ignore the constant traffic noise and ubiquitous orange glow so that I could get some sleep.

Below– the stylish cockpit of the Goldfish RIB *Lionhead*

Top– The fleet crammed into the lock

Below– The 100mph Start Boat

Results-
Inverness to Edinburgh.

Distance: 210 nautical miles.

Pos.	Team/ Number	Class	Time	Overall position (Class)
1st	Venturer/111	RB1	3:06:49	10 (1)
2nd	Blue FPT/333	MC1	3:09:57	2 (1)
3rd	**Lionhead/22**	**RB3**	**3:10:21**	**1 (1)**
4th	Team Silverline/471	RB2	3:11:10	7 (1)
5th	Vilda/9	RB3	3:24:29	6 (4)
6th	Braveheart III/55	MC1	3:36:12	4 (2)
7th	Hot Lemon/2	RB3	3:40:34	3 (2)
8th	Hardleys/4	RB3	3:42:28	5 (3)
9th	Wettpunkt.com/81	RB1	3:54:32	23 (2)
10th	Sealbay/77	RB4	4:04:06	8 (1)
11th	Seafarer/110	RB3	4:08:40	12 (6)
12th	Mystic Dragon/6	MC1	4:19:13	32 (7)
13th	Power Products Marine/8	MC2	4:25:30	13 (1)
14th	Going Lean/7	RB3	4:25:57	11 (5)
15th	Seahound V/80	MC1	4:27:42	9 (3)
16th	Fugitive/130	MC2	4:42:18	21 (3)
17th	TFO/17	MC2	4:43:34	20 (2)
18th	Black Gold/10	RB4	4:46:20	35 (8)
19th	Carbon Neutral/343	RB3	5:01:39	14 (7)
20th	Team Scorpion Dubois/16	MC1	5:01:59	15 (4)

Pos.	Team/ Number	Class	Time	Overall position (Class)
21st	My Pleasure II/3	RB4	5:04:12	22 (4)
22nd	Tequila/88	RB3	5:12:11	18 (8)
23rd	Team Pulsar-Vampire/102	RB4	5:12:13	25 (5)
24th	swipewipes.co.uk/ 43	RB4	5:25:56	16 (2)
25th	Garmin Racing/72	RB2	5:29:39	37 (3)
26th	Team Bandit/69	RB2	5:39:52	17 (2)
27th	Team Pulsar-Wolf/101	RB4	5:44:41	28 (6)
28th	Buro/15	MC1	5:58:36	26 (5)
29th	GEE/185	HC1	6:07:12	27 (1)
30th	Mud, Swell & Beers/14	RB4	6:12:01	29 (7)
31st	Mr Mako/96	RB4	6:18:56	19 (3)
32nd	Team 747/747	HC1	6:38:50	30 (2)
33rd	Team Jersey/45	RB4	7:36:02	36 (9)
34th	Ocean Pirate/323	HC1	7:39:35	42 (5)
35th	Xanthus/1	HC1	7:40:18	38 (3)
36th	Swordsman/68	HC1	8:00:54	40 (4)
37th	Guttaboyz/33	RB3	9:38:13	24 (9)
38th	No Worries/11	RB3	**DNF***	39 (11)
39th	Cinzano/558	RB2	**OTR**	47 (5)
40th	Birretta/12	MC1	**DNF***	31 (6)

DNS Denotes Did Not Start
DNF Denotes Did Not Finish
OTR Denotes Out of The Race
* Denotes maximum time allowance exceeded.

Pos.	Team/ Number	Class	Time	Overall position (Class)
41st	Relentless/47	RB3	**DNF***	33 (10)
42nd	RIB International/ 144	RB4	**OTR**	43 (10)
43rd	Ikon/18	RB3	**DNS***	41 (12)
44th	Blue Marlin/99	HC1	**OTR**	46 (6)
45th	Red FPT/177	CC1	**OTR**	44 (1)
46th	Team Blastoff/100	RB2	**OTR**	45 (4)
47th	Northern Spirit/5	MC2	**OTR**	34 (4)

DNS Denotes Did Not Start
DNF Denotes Did Not Finish
OTR Denotes Out of The Race
* Denotes maximum time allowance exceeded.

Below– *Lionhead* at full throttle

12.
Edinburgh To Newcastle.

Saturday 28th June.

After another night spent wrestling with the covers and only managing to drop off for a few minutes at a time, it seemed only natural that I finally managed to fall into a deep, coma-like sleep half an hour before my phone's alarm clock went off. As I reluctantly got up and dressed I felt like I was up to my neck in treacle, my movements slow and clumsy. Once again my taxi arrived ten minutes early, denying me my essential morning mug of tea, and as I clambered into the car my landlady came running out after me, clutching the carrier bag with the goodies for the crew of *Buro* that she had kindly agreed to store in her fridge.

I hadn't felt this rough since the start of the race, the effects of too little sleep at night and stress, adrenaline and pounding seas during the day slowly wearing me down. I tried to cheer myself up by mentally calculating how many miles stood between me and the finish line, but my brain simply wasn't up to it.

Even if my synapses had been firing on all cylinders, it seemed unlikely that I would have been able to complete such a simple calculation thanks to the torrent of verbal diarrhoea pouring unceasingly from my driver's lips. Short, fat and balding, the man was clearly spending most of his income on vast supplies of amphetamines, the speed flowing freely through his veins, causing his mouth to run non-stop and his body to perform a variety of bizarre and unsettling tics.

"So have ya got a boat then? Aye, 'course ya do. Why else would ya wanna go doon the marina eh?" He jabbered, his left thumb tapping the steering wheel in perfect time to every syllable. "Aye, that's a stupid question right enough. So, what sort-a boat ya got then? Is it a sailing boat? 'Cos my mate Bobby-" he pronounced it "Boabby"—"He's got one o' yon sailing boats, a wee cracker, you'll know it 'cos it's called, er, bugger, I forget the name, but it's a canny name for a boat, it's like "Windchaser" or "Stormwind" or "Stormchaser", I cannae mind now, but you'll see it clear as day." He stopped to spit a piece of gum out the window, then unwrapped another piece and started to annihilate the new stick. He gave me a sidelong glance, one eye twitching uncontrollably. "So you never answered us. Is it a sailing boat or what?"

I sighed and gave up trying to fake sleep. "No, I'm taking part in a powerboat race round Britain," I replied.

"Wow! That's cool! Must be mental, you know, racing round in speedboats. Is there many of youse like?"

He fixed me with a pair of pinprick pupils, blissfully unaware that we were rapidly approaching a red traffic light. My short explanation had completely overwhelmed what little attention span he had left, and it took a shouted warning from me to shift his intense focus back to the road.

One we had squealed to a slippery halt he once again turned to ask me about the race, and tiredly I explained to him the ins and outs. Even in my exhausted state I could see why the idea of such an event would appeal to him; when you're off your tits on speed all you really want to do is get from A to B as quickly as humanly possible, with the absolute minimum of direction changes or stops for traffic lights. I realised then what a fool I'd been— instead of stocking up on powerful and illegal painkillers I should have filled my pockets with every chemical variation on speed I could lay my hands on instead.

He listened enthralled as I told him of the marathon race I had somehow become involved in while he chewed his gum frantically to keep from grinding his molars to dust, one leg spasming wildly. He was so engrossed that I had to tell him twice that the lights had changed, and he got the car moving again with tremendous wheel-spin, all the while babbling excitedly. "Wow, racing speedboats! Too fucking cool! I'd love to do that— hey! D'you think maybe someone would give me a shot?"

I told him it was pretty unlikely, but I doubt he even heard me. In his mind he was already off, blasting across the sea in a gaudy golden power machine, leaving the rest of the world behind in a cloud of spray and exhaust gases, unhindered by mini-roundabouts and cumbersome buses.

When we rolled up at the marina he was practically drooling at the thought of hundreds of fire-breathing powerboats rumbling and throbbing impatiently, straining to thunder towards the horizon, but instead all he saw were a couple of hung-over mechanics and the odd driver trying to make sense of the day's Race Instructions sheet.

He shouted "Good luck!" as he screeched out of the carpark, leaving people to wonder what I was doing in the company of such a reprobate, but I ignored their quizzical stares and made a beeline for the canteen, where a mug of hot, steaming tea did its best to jump-start my body and brain.

I bumped into one of the Scrutineers and asked him to give my gear the once-over. He raised his eyebrows at the new number stuck to the top of my lid— 15, *Buro's* number— but by now they had all learnt that it was easier just to keep quiet. I went through the rigmarole of unloading flares, knives and medical compresses etc onto the floor, then repacking it all again as best I could while a tick was placed next to my name.

The Driver's Briefing was nothing new, the only item of interest being the weather forecast. They lied to us again, promising a gentle sea state, but by now they were fooling no-one. I put my name next to *Buro* on the official sheet, ignoring the "boat tart" jibes, then grabbed another results sheet from the pile on the table.

It looked like *Wettpunkt.com*'s incredible speed wasn't going to be enough. Hannes and his crew had been given a one hour penalty for planing during the long run out of Inverness to the muster area, so despite being the first boat into Edinburgh with a mighty time of 2 hours and 54 minutes their amended time bumped them down to ninth.

I fully expected to see that *Blue FPT* had been awarded the win, but I was puzzled to see that she had come in second. I scoured the columns of random names and numbers until I spotted the name *Venturer*. Somehow Andy Macateer and his crew had trounced everyone bar Hannes, and with the Austrian being penalised it moved *Venturer* into first place.

In second place then was *Blue FPT*, who had crossed the line a paltry 24 seconds ahead of us on *Lionhead*, and we had only beaten Drew and the *Silverline* boys to third by 49 seconds— another astonishing achievement, after racing for three hours and covering the 210 nautical miles out of sight of each other.

The second Goldfish RIB of *Guttaboyz* had not faired as well. They had failed to get the faulty turbo working on the Inverness startline, and had decided to limp into Edinburgh rather than miss the leg, putting them down in 38th place for the stage.

As I scanned the list for Team *747* I felt a hand on my shoulder. It was Jonathan, coming to say Good Morning. "Just the man! How did you get on yesterday?" I asked.

"To be honest Derek, I'm not sure. I was so bloody exhausted, it's all a bit of a blur," he told me candidly. "I do remember that we caught a lobster pot round one of the props though. We'd gotten most of it untangled when *GEE* caught up with us, and John (Guille) very kindly jumped in to clear the rest. Rather him than me!"

As was so often the case, drivers often had no idea where they'd finished, so the two of us scanned the results list until we found Team *747* lying in 32nd place, crossing the line just over half an hour after their rivals *GEE*. The rest of the Historic fleet had trickled in behind, but for the first time in the entire race all five of the aging boats had managed to complete a leg within the allotted time, with *Swordsman* bringing up the rear with a time of eight hours and fifty-four seconds.

There had also been plenty of retirements and non-starters; the Belgians on board *Birretta* had suffered an engine fire and had to be towed by the RNLI into Macduff, just thirty miles past Lossiemouth; other retirees included *Cinzano*, *No Worries* and *Relentless*. But at least they had managed to start the leg; by now the list of permanent retirees ran to six: *Blue Marlin*, *Ikon*, *Red FPT* and *RIB International* had all dropped out by Milford Haven. They were joined by

Team *Blastoff*, who had finally given up on trying to fix their electrical problems, and *Northern Spirit*, who had been plagued by problems with their Mercury outboards. Their first Optimax unit had failed just minutes after the start in Portsmouth, the second had let go 10 miles before they reached Bangor, and engine number 3— their spare— gave up the ghost just outside Oban. Eventually the relentless pressure proved too much for the crew, who had a major falling-out and disbanded in Inverness— a pity, since they were lying 21st overall, and second in their MC2 Class.

My boat for today, *Buro*, had completed the leg in 28th, after a few minutes shy of six hours' racing. With my holdall over my shoulder and my carrier bag of shopping I walked down the gangway to join my ride, ducking to avoid another boat that had just been craned off its trailer and was swinging six feet in the air, prior to being launched for today's leg to Newcastle.

Except by now I was no longer certain that Newcastle really was our destination; in fact I didn't know what day it was, where I was, or even who I was. I had taken to asking passing strangers if they knew the answers, but most of them were as mentally fucked as I was, and my bewildered questions had, on several occasions, resulted in arguments as people tried to figure out what day it was.

Fortunately the crew onboard *Buro* were about the sharpest, well-rested people in the race. Their Botnia Targa 42 had given them absolutely no cause for concern in the last 920 nautical miles, and there was no reason to think that that would change. She may not have been the quickest boat, but she took all weathers in her stride, and at the end of the day her four crew could sit down to a hot, home-cooked meal, grab a shower and then retire for the night, without ever leaving the boat.

Peter welcomed me on board and introduced me to his team-mates. Louis Massant and Lieven Van Hoecke were both tall, muscular guys in their early forties. Despite their friendly demeanour something about the way they carried themselves told me that they were no strangers to the dark art of violence, a feeling that was to be confirmed later on. Their fourth crew-member was a small, slim fellow with an unstoppable sense of fun. This was Frank Willemkens, who usually worked on board a trawler but was asked to come along for his knowledge of the North Sea. It had been Frank who had dazzled me with his seemingly magical ability to open beer bottles in Bangor, which seemed so very long ago now.

I dumped my gear beneath the large table and stepped back outside to help the crew cast off. They exchanged a few friendly words with Thomas Vandamme and Jean Pierre-Neels, the two Belgians on board *Birretta*, who had worked through the night to get their Buzzi RIB repaired after their engine fire the previous day. The two men were obviously shattered, but despite their exhaustion they were upbeat, happy to be back in the running.

We motored gently out into the Forth, the two iconic bridges seemingly holding up a grey, murky sky. The low clouds had the look of dirty lead, and seemed to promise rain at any moment, but I wasn't worried— for the first time since my disastrous outing on board *Ocean Pirate* I was safely ensconced in a warm, dry wheelhouse.

As we rumbled under the road bridge I commented to my crewmates what a pity it was that we couldn't have used the bridges as a start line, or, better still, a finishing line for yesterday's leg. Peter agreed, echoing the complaints I'd heard from other teams about how poorly marked many of the other finishing lines had been so far. At least there was no mistaking the railway bridge.

It loomed over us, the familiar dull red of its mighty steel spans obscured here and there by scaffolding and plastic sheets as workmen continued their seemingly endless maintenance work. I remembered chatting to someone who had once worked on the historic bridge; he had told me with a shudder that despite the constant work going on there, the bridge seemed so flimsy and tired that he refused to take the train across it. The half-remembered conversation came back to me as we passed underneath the right-hand span, and I looked up cautiously, expecting to be bombarded with chunks of rusted metal at any moment. But of course no such thing happened, and we made it under unharmed.

In 1890, the Forth railway bridge was hailed as "an engineering marvel". Now, over a century later, it still manages to take people's breath away. It measures a mighty 1½ miles long and 330 feet high at its highest points, the three towers. And there was no danger of *Buro* scraping her antennae along the bottom of the bridge either; with 150 feet of fresh air between high tide and the underside, commercial vessels could still navigate upstream to the Grangemouth oil refinery.

It was originally meant to be a suspension bridge, designed by Thomas Bouch, but after his previous creation— the Tay bridge— collapsed, taking 75 lives with it into the stormy waters, his plans were ditched in favour of a cantilever design instead. Since one of the major flaws in the Tay bridge design was the extensive use of cast iron, Sir John Fowler and Sir Benjamin Baker opted to use the newfangled steel instead— the first major British construction to do so.

We mustered just to the west of Inchmickery island, about three miles out from the railway bridge. During the Second World War it was heavily fortified and groaned under the weight of heavy guns, but now it was deserted, its derelict concrete buildings home to seabirds. We took our place in the now-familiar swirl of boats, circling a channel marker anti-clockwise. I slid open the wheelhouse door and snapped away with my camera, stopping to give a wave to former crewmates; *Silverline* slid past, then we slowly cruised past the Norwegians on aboard *Lionhead*.

When the Start Boat took up position on the eastern edge of the pack I slid the heavy door shut and got ready for the off. Lieven was at the helm, and next to him stood Louis, casually leaning on the wooden counter that runs beneath the big glass screens. I was on his left, with the every-cheery Frank wedged in between me and the wheelhouse door. Peter had taken a more relaxed approach, leaning casually against the back of Lieven's seat.

When the yellow flag went up Lieven opened the throttles to keep pace with the Start Boat and the rest of the pack. I was surprised at how lively the big Targa felt; she dug her stern in, raised her bows and scurried forward enthusiastically. Weighing in at around eleven tons and powered by two Volvo Pentas putting out a combined 700 horsepower or so, she was never going to rocket to the front of the pack. But still, I was impressed with how quickly she got to 25 knots, the Start Boat's speed. Sadly when the green flag went up we didn't have long to go until we hit our top cruising speed, maxing out at around 38 knots or so.

Despite the tumultuous sea, whipped into an unpredictable frenzy by forty combined wakes, *Buro* behaved impeccably, tracking nicely with only a little input from the helm. Naturally, this was one of the advantages of her weight, those eleven tons refusing to be bullied into wandering off course, but it also illustrated how well her hull had been designed.

But gradually the rest of the fleet started easing away from us, the sloppy swell doing little to slow the other boats down. As we settled in to the boat's easy-going rhythm the adrenaline that accompanied every race start wore off, and my mind turned to other, more mundane matters. I suddenly remembered my plastic bag. "Peter, I nearly forgot— this is for you."

His face lit up as he emptied the bag. Somewhere in the dark recesses of my brain I knew that Belgians are mad for mussels, so I had managed to get hold of two kilos of fresh Scottish mussels, and two bottles of white wine— one for drinking, and one for cooking the mussels in. My bribe seemed to have done the job, since I wasn't thrown overboard, so I decided to push my luck and ask Peter what in God's name he was doing, entering a powerboat race in such an implausible-looking boat.

He smiled at me indulgently. "Why not? We are warm and comfortable— and can you hear me alright? Of course you can; even at-" he craned his neck over Lieven's shoulder to check the GPS readout "—35 knots, we can have a normal conversation without shouting. And we are in 26th place overall, which is not bad out of 41 boats still running eh?"

I had to admit it— his numbers matched up, and the boat was damned civilised. *Buro* carved her way through the five-foot seas without any drama at all, and whenever we hit an awkward wave there was no slamming or creaking whatsoever.

"So have you had any problems so far?" I asked, carefully watching his friendly eyes for any signs of deceit.

"No, not even for a second," he answered proudly. "Even after we went round Land's End in the storm, the engines never missed a beat."

Peter had reminded me of his incredible trip from Plymouth to Milford Haven on the day bad weather had cancelled the leg. After that morning's briefing, when it was announced that the leg had been scrapped, almost every other team scrabbled to get their boats out of the water and onto the back of a lorry or trailer to take them by road to Wales. But not *Buro*. Instead, Peter and his crew waited as long as they dared to let the storm blow out before firing up the twin Volvo Pentas and heading out into the dying storm.

Admittedly, they had little choice in the matter— without the local knowledge of the other crews, Peter and his team-mates would have struggled to find a haulage firm to transport them to their next destination. But they did have tremendous faith in the Norwegian-built boat, which isn't called "The 4X4 Of The Sea" for nothing. Peter's marine Range Rover was well and truly put through its paces over the next 10 hours or so, as they pushed through 6 meter waves and wind speeds of over 60 mph. (The only other boat to run the course that day was *Vampire*, one of two RIBs entered by Team *Pulsar*. At 25 feet long, *Vampire* was one of the smallest boats in the fleet, and I still haven't made up my mind if Greg Marsden was insane, profoundly stupid or serenely confident to take on monstrous seas in an open RIB with only one engine.)

For the crew of *Buro*, their worst moment was once they rounded Land's End. In the pitch-dark they faced a heavy, unpredictable Atlantic swell, which threatened to knock the boat onto its side at any moment. There was only one thing to do in that situation, Peter told me, and that was to slip a Barry White cd into the stereo and crank it all the way up to eleven.

Peter's attitude towards the race was almost childlike in its simplicity— "We wanted to go around Britain and going around Britain is going around Britain!" Which is why he also seriously considered going round the top of Scotland instead of "cheating" and travelling through the Caledonian canal. And he could have done it too; he could have covered the 350 nautical miles and still made it into Inverness in time to race the next leg with the rest of the fleet, but eventually he and his crewmates decided to join the other boats in making the beautiful passage up the Caledonian canal and made the most of their time off in Inverness by adopting the kilt instead.

It was clear to me that after rounding Land's End at night in atrocious conditions, Cape Wrath would have presented no challenge at all to this solid boat and her experienced crew. I had already learned that Frank Willemkens was a trawlerman, but what of Louis Massant and Lieven Van Hoecke?

It turned out that my first impression of two men was well-founded.

They were both military men, serving in the Belgium Armed Forces. What's more, they specialised in amphibious assaults and Louis had been tasked with developing his country's abilities in this field, training elite units in what I guess you'd call "RIB warfare". Naturally, he had taken an interest in the Goldfish RIBs, and we spent some time discussing the pros and cons of the boats. (Eventually, the price of the Norwegian RIB put him off— at over £300,000 each, he considered them a little overpriced.)

So, safe in the knowledge that *Buro* was an outstandingly capable craft and that her crew could deal with any foolhardy pirates that might attempt to board us, I relaxed completely and settled in for the long slog to Newcastle.

As was the norm, we found ourselves virtually alone on the choppy sea, apart from the occasional fishing boat hauling creels. The small buoys that marked the start and end of their fleets of creels were a constant cause for concern for everyone, as their colours were often dull and faded, and tricky to spot in a lumpy sea. There was a very real danger of running over one of the markers and wrapping the rope round a propeller, as Jonathan Napier had discovered on *Miss Daisy* the previous day. If this happened we would be at risk of damaging the prop shaft or the seals, and even if by some fluke the stern gear emerged unscathed it would still be a nightmare to unwrap the rope. For the boats running outboards it would be relatively easy to dislodge the creel rope; an outboard's prop can be lifted clear of the water, and by hanging over the stern of the boat someone with a knife should be able to cut the line loose. In rough conditions and with the boat dead in the water, however, it's far from simple.

On a boat fitted with inboard engines, like *Buro*, clearing a rope that's fouled a prop is damn-near impossible. The props are tucked away under the hull, with the rudders just aft. Then there's the sodding great bathing platform bolted to the stern— great for swimming from, but a massive obstacle for getting to the propellers. If we caught a rope, there would be only one thing for it— someone would have to get wet.

So during the 5 ½ hours I spent on board, I kept a close eye on the sea as we chatted about this and that. The leg was interspersed with the occasional sandwich, and when Frank popped a Queen cd into the stereo we passed the time by torturing Freddie Mercury's finest tunes. There is something oddly liberating about five grown men howling along to "Fat-Bottom Girls" in the middle of the North Sea, unburdened by the constraints of public perceptions and polite social etiquette. I can strongly recommend it as a powerful, but temporary, cure for almost any ailment.

Apart from the impromptu karaoke, there wasn't much else in the way of excitement or drama as we crashed through the waves towards Newcastle. Everything went exactly according to plan, which was precisely how Peter and his crew wanted it. But how then did they get the reputation amongst the rest of the fleet for being "the party boat"?

Peter smiled when I asked him about this. "Ach, they see us always laughing and joking around," he tells me. "Every night we like to relax with a drink and some good food, and sure, we like to invite others to join us. But they do not see the work we do." His smile slipped, and he grew serious. "Every night we check everything on the boat. We make sure that we are completely ready for the next leg, and then— and only then— do we unwind. This is something that the others do not understand, I think. They only see the partying; they do not believe that we are also being very professional."

"And does this annoy you?" I asked. "Don't you get a little pissed off, with people thinking you're just jokers?"

He thought for a second. "No, not really. Let them think what they like— after all, if we're only "jokers", then how are we still racing when people like Buzzi have dropped out? How is it we're 26th, and so many real race boats are behind us? How did we manage to go around Land's End, one of only two boats to do so? No, if they want to laugh at us, that's fine. But in the meantime, we're still racing!"

It was an admirable ethos, but I wasn't entirely convinced. Personally, I would have been mightily pissed off if I had been in Peter's shoes, but then he's older and undoubtedly wiser than me, so I dusted off my diplomatic skills and dropped the subject. At the end of the day, Peter was fully justified in taking the moral high ground— he had taken a bog-standard production boat and, apart from fitting slightly different props, had made no modifications whatsoever, and was still running solidly slap-bang in the middle of the fleet. I could think of several other teams who had spent many thousands of pounds race-preparing their boats, and who still had to carry out vital repairs at the end of every leg.

Despite the friendly chatter and the familiar Queen tracks bellowing from the speakers, I was struggling to keep my eyes open. The fact that the boat made such light work of the steepening chop probably didn't help matters, and I was glad when we finally reached our destination.

The mouth of the River Tyne is protected by two long seawalls that each arc almost half a mile out into the North Sea, one from Tynemouth and the other from South Shields. Once through the quarter-mile gap we were in sheltered waters, the Tyne hissing past our hull as we gently motored two and a half miles upstream, to the Royal Quays marina.

To our right, just off the main river channel, we finally came across some of our fellow competitors. Beneath a square, stone-built tower were two pontoons, a hive of activity as crews tended to their boats after the 115 nautical mile leg. We tied up alongside *GEE* and stepped onto the aft deck for a couple of deep lungfuls of fresh sea air, where we were soon joined by Thomas Vandamme and Jean Pierre-Neels, the two Belgians on *Birretta*. Within five minutes we had made ourselves right at home, with a cold beer, chicken drumsticks and an assortment of crisps and nuts. There was no getting away from it— my hosts for the day certainly knew how to unwind.

But after ten or fifteen minutes of recharging our batteries we all heaved a heavy sigh and set about our various duties. I left Peter and his crew to check over their remarkable boat and wandered off to find somewhere quiet to call in my report to Rob and take some pictures.

I clumped my way up the steep pontoon ramp, emerging at the top of the lock gates that separated the marina proper from the tidal Tyne. On the other side of the lock stood a magnificent modern tower that looked like the control tower at an airport. It served much the same purpose, giving staff the ability to keep a watchful eye over the 350 boats that were berthed within the sheltered complex.

As I wandered around, taking in my surroundings, I came across a stressed-looking Jonathan.

Half a mile before the finish line he had lost steering, and had to limp into port using the trim tabs. Miraculously he still managed to beat *GEE* across the line, although it was a close-run thing. It turned out that *Miss Daisy*'s impact with the rocks on the early-morning run to Fort William had damaged more than the shaft and prop; the steering linkage had apparently also taken a battering, and had finally given up the ghost.

Still, he was in his usual high spirits, confident that his father and Fred Kemp would be able to get the boat sorted for the next day's leg to Lowestoft. Then he asked me who I would be joining.

Up until now I had achieved the impossible— I had raced every leg on a different boat. It was a plan borne out of desperation, but I had decided to use it to my advantage, and with luck, and a huge amount of other people's generosity and pity, I had somehow managed to make it work. But now I was tired, so very tired. Although my feet no longer looked like they'd been shredded by a pair of surface-piercing cleaver props, they still ached. And so did my legs. And my back. My neck muscles complained bitterly at having to support my crash helmet, and my brain had all but shut down under the constant pressure. I was fucked— both physically and mentally.

My resolve faltered, and my ambitions crumbled. "I, eh, I don't suppose I could grab a ride with you guys tomorrow, could I?"

"Yes, of course you can! No problem at all; just make sure you let Race Control know, OK?" And with that I felt a massive load slip from my shoulders. To hell with the plan. I didn't care any more; I just wanted to cross the line at Portsmouth and climb into a warm bed for three or four days.

I thanked him and wished him luck with his repairs, then went off to explore some more.

I smelled the food before I could see it. Roast chicken, burgers, fried onions... I started salivating like a stray dog, and followed my nose to a large white marquee standing in the middle of a car park. The Race Organisers had pulled a whopping great rabbit out of the hat, with a crew of caterers cooking up a storm for the tired drivers and crew. I dumped my bag and scrabbled over, filling my paper plate with a small mountain of hot and cold food. I did this two or three more times before finally deciding to leave a little for the others, and whipped out my old tobacco tin to roll a much-needed cigarette.

I was joined by Mike Barlow, *Ocean Pirate*'s owner. He was in a foul mood, and I let him blow off steam for a while. In a nutshell, Mike was pissed off because the Organisers hadn't lived up to their promise of allowing the Historic Class boats set off before the rest of the fleet. There had been staggered starts at Portsmouth and Milford Haven, but that had been it. I remembered that Mike had brought it up at the initial Driver's Briefing at Southampton, and vaguely recalled Mike Lloyd making some soothing comment or other, but I couldn't remember much else. Although to be perfectly honest, by this point I would have struggled to name my own parents, let alone the details of some half-forgotten discussion in a drafty shed all those months ago.

But Mike was adamant that the Historics had been promised an earlier start for each leg, and he was getting exasperated that this hadn't been happening. So he was going to take matters into his own hands. The following morning, he told me, *Ocean Pirate* would be leaving Newcastle an hour before the rest of the fleet, and to hell with Mike Lloyd's precious race. He and his crew were sick and tired of staggering into port several hours behind everyone else, he said, missing out on all the socializing that he thought went on while they were still miles out to sea.

At this point I was fighting hard to bite my tongue; I desperately wanted to tell him that if he wanted to get into port sooner, he should have bought a faster boat, and that his fantasies of scantily-clad girls welcoming the conquering heroes in to port were nothing more than an old man's pipe dream. But I managed to stifle my natural instinct, and instead nodded along like a simple-minded buffoon.

Eventually he stormed off to spread dissention amongst the other Historic Class ranks, and I set off in the opposite direction so as to avoid any connection with his intended mutiny.

I came across the ever-cheery Ian Brown, leaning against the empty *Silverline* lorry with a beer in his hand. His powers of persuasion were outstanding, and suitably armed with strong French lager we set about discussing the race, the boats, and the woeful lack of Glamour.

The day prior to the start at Portsmouth, there had been a smattering of showbiz glitter in the form of four good-looking girls tastefully dressed in the tightest of lycra catsuits. I remembered them well; their blue and white outfits had been branded with the *Silverline* logo and they'd been a welcome distraction from all the boats, engines and safety gear on show. Miles had organised them to help with publicity, and I remember thinking at the time he was one hell of a self-publicist. I also had a vivid recollection of two of the girls sitting in a boat, chatting about the mysterious ways of Men.

"...and then 'e turned round to me an' sez 'e finks I look tarty! Wot a bloody cheek!"

Just then a keen photographer approached and asked if he could take a few pictures. Instantly they sucked in their stomachs, thrust their chests forward and assumed the most ridiculous pouts I'd ever witnessed as the ecstatic snapper set to work with his camera. After just a few minutes he was spent, and as soon as he thanked the girls and walked off they reverted to their slouching, picking up their conversation as if nothing had happened.

I also remember nudging Jan at one point, and pointing over to where Miles was posing with two other girls for some publicity shots. "By christ," I leered, "he certainly knows where to find them eh?"

Jan smiled indulgently at me. "Just be careful what you say around Miles; one of them is his own daughter."

But that was the last we'd seen of any eye-candy, and it was starting to demoralise us. With nothing to leer over we wound up talking boats, and when Guy the Scrutineer joined us we were deep into a discussion of the merits of Anderson surface drives.

After the usual attack on my lack of team loyalty and general moral negligence I asked him how he thought the race was going.

"To be honest with you, I'm surprised there are still so many boats running. Before the start all us Scrutineers had calculated on a 10% drop out rate per leg, but it's been a hell of a lot less than that."

I was shocked by his initial pessimism. "Jesus Guy! By your figures, there should only be-" I did some quick number-crunching in my head "-around 27 boats by now!"

He nodded sagely. "Yeah, we reckoned that there would be less than 20 boats crossing the line in Portsmouth. But you bastards keep plodding on, and that means we've still got shit-loads to do every day!" He went on to tell me that the Scrutineers and Race Control crew had started a book on the amount of finishers, and that he had put money on only seventeen boats making it to Portsmouth. This was pretty daunting, given that Guy and the other Scrutineers had been deeply involved in racing for many years— they had seen more than their fair share of racing craft sink, break and blow up, and could be considered Oracles in the dark art of reliability.

But so far the teams were consistently proving everyone wrong, since that morning thirty eight boats had crossed the start line, instead of the twenty seven Guy and his colleagues had supposed. This once again illustrated just how vitally important people like Ian were in keeping teams in the race. Their dedication and selfless devotion to their machines was astounding, and if I had to be painfully honest I doubt that I would have been able to find the motivation to spend endless hours fixing a boat, only to have some ham-fisted driver thrash it to within an inch of its life the next day, then expect me to roll up my sleeves and begin the whole process all over again.

But that was just me, and if the truth were told I've always struggled with what Johnny Vegas' character in Ideal referred to as "stickatit-ness". Take this race for example; my lofty ambition to race each leg on a different boat had just been flung out of the window, my noble aspirations dashed to dust in exchange for an easy ride with the laid-back pilots on board *Miss Daisy*. No doubt a real journalist would have tracked down the Greek crew of *Blue FPT* to negotiate a seat on board the winning boat, but then I never claimed to be a real journalist. I was just some half-bright chancer who'd somehow landed a unique assignment that no-one else at the prestigious *MotorBoat & Yachting* office would touch, but despite my initial enthusiasm for the job, eight punishing days of stress, uncertainty and relentless action had brought me close to the brink of total meltdown. With two more days left to go, I had all but given up, and thoughts of world-wide acclaim in the boating media had been replaced by— well, nothing at all. I was a zombie, lurching from port to port, only coming to my senses during brief episodes whenever my exhausted adrenal gland managed to rouse itself and poison my bloodstream with sweet, addictive adrenaline.

Of course Ian's beer didn't help matters, and after a couple I was starting to feel the effects so I bid Ian and Guy farewell and shuffled off to the base of the harbour's modern control tower.

Thankfully I'd had the foresight to note down the phone numbers of local taxi firms before I started on this insane adventure, and after consulting my notebook I called and booked a cab. They told me it would be fifteen minutes or so, so I gave Rob a quick call and began to inundate him with more meaningless gibberish about the race.

I was just getting started when a Renault Espace with a taxi decal screeched to a stop just a few feet away from me. One passenger got out, and shouldered his bag with a weariness I knew only too well. When the driver also got out and headed towards me I felt a sudden jolt of confusion. *That was bloody quick!* I thought, quickly followed by *Why the hell is he grinning at me like that?*

He bounded towards me, a huge familiar smile on his chubby little face. "Alright man, howya doin'? Braw day eh? How'd yer race go? Did youse win? Whit boat wis ya on then?" His insane babbling and unfathomable familiarity totally threw me. *How the fuck could this taxi driver possibly know me?* And then I realised he had been the cabbie who had driven me to the marina earlier on that morning.

But wasn't that Edinburgh? So what the fuck was he doing *here*?

Unless *this* was Edinburgh. No, wait, that didn't make any sense. I distractedly told Rob I had to go, and tried to back away from this horrific figure that wouldn't stop shouting words at me.

Despite his drug-induced ranting, somehow his fried brain figured out that I was badly shaken and deeply confused at his appearance. "D'ya no' mind me? I drove ya down to the marina in Edinburgh. Pretty mental eh? I just had to drive another fella down; he missed his lift or something. Don't think he's racing mind; I think he's just like a mechanic or something." Finally the penny dropped; I was in Newcastle, and this speed-addled freak had just driven all the way down with another competitor. I stopped trying to push myself back-wards through the wall and tried to force a smile onto my face.

"Oh yeah, the taxi-dude. How are you?"

"Aye, grand like, grand. Some fuckin' day though eh? That guy just paid me £600 to drive him down. He never even blinked. Mental." He froze there, suddenly immobile— clearly his brain was shorting out. I wasn't concerned, it had happened to me too on many occasions, and I knew he'd mentally reboot sooner or later.

Sure enough, after a good three or four seconds of staring blankly at a point some three feet above my right shoulder he suddenly re-joined the physical world with a jolt that was almost painful. "Right! Better get goin' eh? Cannae stand around here all day. Where you off tae tomorrow? Mebbe I'll see ya there eh?" And with that horrific thought stalking my imagination he scurried back to his taxi and sped off in a cloud of diesel fumes and tyre smoke.

His sudden appearance and his similarly sudden departure had given me a bad jolt. With shaky hands I rolled a cigarette and lit it as I dialled the magazine's number. I apologised to Rob and explained what had just happened. He found it hilarious, but he was left hang-ing for several minutes until I managed to regroup my jangled thoughts into some sort of order. Eventually I managed to spew some sort of wisdom over the phone, but it wasn't until much later that I finally managed to sit down in front of a computer and read what Rob had managed to salvage from my ravings. I discovered that he'd even included my personal state of mind:

"Apparently it's Saturday. I don't know what day it is. I have no idea what town I'm in. I'm chatting to people and then realising they're not who I thought they were. I'm nodding to strangers and ignoring friends.
Two more legs and then I can sleep."

When another taxi rolled into the carpark I approached it with a great deal of apprehension. But it was definitely for me, and I grate-fully settled back into the comfortable seat and asked him to take me to my digs for the night.

A month or so before the race I had spent many hours in front of my laptop booking accommodation for all the ports I was due to visit. So far they had all been guesthouses, and very nice most of them had been too. But tonight I would be staying in a room above a pub; something I had been excited about when I had first found it, but now the idea of getting paralytic before staggering a few feet to my room had lost some of its charm. All I wanted to do was eat, shower and sleep.

The Redburn pub stood just a few miles from the clean, modern lines of the Royal Quays marina control tower, but the difference was stark. It looked like a hotchpotch of Victorian buildings, with tall, narrow chimneys and, bizarrely, heraldic shields and medieval swords and pikes mounted high up on the outside walls. It stood surrounded by a tarmac moat, isolated from the housing estate that surrounded it.

Never one to judge a book by its ratty cover, I heaved my bag onto my shoulder and stepped into one of the deserted bars. The décor was tired, the wallpaper faded and peeling, and the bare wooden floors bore innumerable scars. I could tell without any hesitation that not too many years ago there would have been a liberal sprinkling of sawdust on the floor, soaking up spilt beer, blood and the occasional vomit.

But I wasn't daunted by my surroundings; I spent many years working in pubs, and despite the cold, unwelcoming atmosphere that pervaded the empty room I felt oddly at home as soon as the musty smell of stale beer hit my nostrils.

I stepped to the battered bar and dropped my bag to the floor, making sure it hit the deck with a loud thud to announce my arrival. As I peered into the darkness of the kitchen behind the bar I heard a distinctly Geordie voice say: "Fuck off!"

I spun round, surprised to hear that I wasn't alone after all. But despite the gloom I still couldn't see anyone. Then I was told to "Fuck off!" again, and this time I spotted my companion.

Wedged into a corner behind a table stood a steel cage, some six foot square. And inside I saw a pale grey blur, hopping from one leg to another. As I stepped closer I realised that the distinctive odour of bird was getting stronger, no longer masked by the familiar smell of hops and stale yeast. By the time I got up to it I realised that I had been insulted by the scruffiest, mangiest African Grey parrot I had ever seen. This bird had clearly had a rough life, and to emphasise the point it fixed me with a cold, unemotional stare before squawking: "Get out my fucking pub!"

I was too tired to argue with a cantankerous parrot, so I stared back and calmly told it to go fuck itself before turning back to my search for human life.

Clearly nobody was expecting customers in this bar, so I retraced my steps out into the hall and tried the door on the right instead. Here the depressing murk was being kept at bay— barely— by a couple of wall lights, which illuminated the figure of a man sitting at a table, the remnants of a pint in front of him.

When he saw me he stood up and reflexively asked what he could get me. "Well, I've got a room booked for the night, but I guess that can wait until I've had a pint of lager."

He stepped behind the bar and reached under the sticky counter for a glass I didn't expect to be clean. The Harp pump coughed and spluttered, eventually producing a pint that looked cloudy and had a head on it that a Belgian barman would be proud of. I handed him a tenner as I choked down my first warm mouthful, but when I only got a five pound note back I raised an eyebrow at him.

Before I could say anything though, a boy of about fourteen emerged from the far side of the bar. "Can I help ya?"

"Yeah, I was just telling your man there that I've got a room booked for the night."

The barman had slipped back to his table and was concentrating hard on ignoring us. "Fuck's sake Davey! You've been fucking told about coming behind the fucking bar! Jesus!" The boy turned to a surprised me and, excitement over, addressed me in a disinterested monotone. "Me Ma does all that. Hang on a second."

He disappeared into the dark void at the far end of the bar, only to re-emerge a moment later with a happy, vibrant woman in her forties. "Hiya, you must be Derek. Follow me, I'll show you to your room." Too tired to argue over the couple of quid the thieving Davey had pocketed in his role of counterfeit barman, I once again lugged my holdall over my shoulder and followed her into the blackness, emerging a moment later into the kitchen. We weaved our way past stainless fat fryers and up a steep set of stairs, at the top of which about half a dozen anonymous rooms branched off from the dingy landing.

"Now then, this is the bathroom," she told me as she pushed open the door nearest us. As it swung open it revealed an old woman sitting on the pan, a little pile of clothes round her ankles as she strained with grim determination. "Oops! Sorry about that," my landlady told me, before casually pulling the door shut again. "And this is your room," she continued, totally unfazed by the surreal sight of a moment before.

I had a momentary panic as she ushered me into my room, expecting to see an Alsatian humping a teenage girl perhaps, or half a dozen South American drug dealers counting piles of tatty tenners. But instead all I saw was a new-looking pine bed, chest of drawers and a wardrobe. I felt simultaneously relieved and a little disappointed at the normalcy of my room after the all-out weirdness of the rest of the place, but I tried to keep the sorrow out of my voice as I thanked my host and dropped onto the bed.

I lay there for a while, but when I felt my eyelids starting to drop I forced myself to stand up before sleep got a good hold on me. Tomorrow morning would be another early start, and there was no guarantee of any breakfast, so I had better fill my stomach now. Also, I wanted to settle my bill in advance, so that I could get away in the morning with a clean conscience.

Back downstairs I noticed that the fraudulent bar man had left, but the boy was still there, idly trying to knock some life into the tv that hung in a corner. Stupidly I asked if he was serving food. "Nah, we don't do food this time of night." I checked my watch; it was a little after six. "I'd have to fire up the fryers, and they take ages."

"OK, well, it doesn't have to be anything fried. I'd settle for a sandwich," I told him hopefully.

"Nah, that needs fryers."

"What? OK, well, got any salad?"

"Sorry, I can't do nothing without the fryers."

Maybe I had misheard. Maybe not. Either way, my life is too damn short to start dealing with these kinds of morons, and I wasn't about to start with this one. "In that case do you think you can point me towards a Pizza Hut or a chippy or something?" If in doubt, get the fuck out.

Armed with his simple directions I set off in search of my dinner— and possibly my breakfast too. After a couple of minutes walking through some of the crappiest council accommodation this country has to offer its economic drop-outs I finally hit gold— the quintessential cornershop and a traditional chippy right next door. Perfect.

In the shop I grabbed biscuits, crisps and a couple of bottles of juice. As the man handed me a fistful of change I suddenly remembered that I hadn't gotten a receipt— since Rob had told me to keep receipts for everything I had amassed a huge ball of crumpled bits of paper, and it was getting to be a habit.

"I'm really sorry, but is it possible to get a receipt please?"

Without turning a hair he said "No problem. Here you go, and here's the rest of your change." The bastard had short-changed me by three quid, and it was only because I had asked for a receipt that he had decided to give me the rest of my money.

Shocked by his blasé attitude I stepped next door and ordered a fish supper, making an exaggerated show of checking my change. The young girl behind the counter smiled. "Just been next door?" I nodded. "Aye, he's a right thieving git. He tries it on with everyone."

I strolled back to the pub, munching on my flavourless chips and pondering the deviancy that abounded everywhere I looked— first the bogus barman, and now the elderly Asian shopkeeper. What really bothered me wasn't the fact that they had ripped me off, but the casual manner in which they'd done it. When people start stealing indiscriminately and consider it as natural as breathing, that's when you realise that society is slowly but surely starting its inevitable slide down the pan.

With my philosophising over for another day, and the greasy cod and chips lying uneasily in my gut, I stepped back into the bar, expecting it to have filled a little in the time I'd been out. But despite it being almost seven o'clock on a Saturday night, the place was still deserted. I tracked down my landlady and explained why I wanted to pay up front. She took my thirty pounds (conveniently forgetting my five quid change I was due) and told me to let myself out in the morning.

Shaking my head in disbelief I went up to my room and promptly fell asleep fully clothed on top of the covers, secure in the knowledge that my belongings would be safe, since I'd dragged the heavy chest of drawers in front of the door before I hit the bed.

Below– *Team Jersey* leaving Edinburgh

Results—
Edinburgh to Newcastle.

Distance: 115 nautical miles.

Pos.	Team/Number	Class	Time	Overall position (Class)
1st	Wettpunkt.com/81	RB1	1:29:32	21 (2)
2nd	Venturer/111	RB1	1:38:07	8 (1)
3rd	Blue FPT/333	MC1	1:42:22	1 (1)
4th	Going Lean/7	RB3	1:47:09	11 (5)
5th	Vilda/9	RB3	1:47:20	4 (2)
6th	Relentless/47	RB3	1:53:03	32 (9)
7th	Team Silverline/471	RB2	1:53:10	7 (1)
8th	Braveheart III/55	MC1	1:56:56	3 (2)
9th	Hot Lemon/2	RB3	1:57:20	2 (1)
10th	Mr Mako/96	RB4	1:59:38	17 (3)
11th	Team Jersey/45	RB4	1:59:46	35 (9)
12th	Hardleys/4	RB3	2:00:14	6 (4)
13th	Carbon Neutral/343	RB3	2:00:24	12 (6)
14th	Sealbay/77	RB4	2:10:03	9 (1)
15th	Seahound V/80	MC1	2:11:19	10 (3)
16th	Mystic Dragon/6	MC1	2:11:25	30 (6)
17th	swipewipes.co.uk/43	RB4	2:11:38	15 (2)
18th	Team Scorpion Dubois/16	MC1	2:15:20	14 (4)
19th	Black Gold/10	RB4	2:15:40	34 (8)
20th	Tequila/88	RB3	2:17:07	18 (8)

Pos.	Team/ Number	Class	Time	Overall position (Class)
21st	Power Products Marine/8	MC2	2:24:20	13 (1)
22nd	Fugitive/130	MC2	2:29:56	19 (2)
23rd	Team Pulsar-Vampire/102	RB4	2:36:02	23 (5)
24th	TFO/17	MC2	2:36:47	20 (3)
25th	My Pleasure II/3	RB4	2:44:18	22 (4)
26th	Birretta/12	MC1	2:45:55	31 (7)
27th	Team 747/747	HC1	2:45:58	28 (2)
28th	Mud, Swell & Beers/14	RB4	2:49:36	27 (7)
29th	Team Pulsar-Wolf/101	RB4	2:51:44	26 (6)
30th	GEE/185	HC1	2:55:00	24 (1)
31st	**Buro/15**	**MC1**	**3:05:07**	**25 (5)**
32nd	Lionhead/22	RB3	3:07:43	5 (3)
33rd	Seafarer/110	RB3	3:32:20	16 (7)
34th	Garmin Racing/72	RB2	4:01:12	37 (3)
35th	Xanthus/1	HC1	4:03:10	38 (3)
36th	Ocean Pirate/323	HC1	4:13:57	40 (5)
37th	Swordsman/68	HC1	4:20:58	39 (4)
38th	Guttaboyz/33	RB3	*	33 (10)
39th	Team Bandit/69	RB2	*	29 (2)
40th	No Worries/11	RB3	OTR	39 (4)

DNS Denotes Did Not Start
DNF Denotes Did Not Finish
OTR Denotes Out of The Race
* Denotes maximum time allowance exceeded.

Pos.	Team/ Number	Class	Time	Overall position (Class)
41st	Northern Spirit/5	MC2	**OTR**	36 (4)
42nd	Cinzano/558	RB2	**OTR**	47 (5)
43rd	Team Blastoff/100	RB2	**OTR**	45 (4)
44th	Red FPT/177	CC1	**OTR**	44 (1)
45th	RIB International/ 144	RB4	**OTR**	43 (10)
46th	Blue Marlin/99	HC1	**OTR**	46 (6)
47th	Ikon/18	RB3	**OTR**	42 (12)

DNS Denotes Did Not Start
DNF Denotes Did Not Finish
OTR Denotes Out of The Race
* Denotes maximum time allowance exceeded.

Below– *Buro* smashes her way round the coast

13.
Newcastle To Lowestoft.

Sunday 29th June.

As I sat on the front steps of the Redburn pub soaking up the rays of the early morning sun I drew the attention of a police car, circling like a vulture in search of drunken victims of last night's excesses. The occupants crawled past, giving me the evil eye, so I threw them a cheery wave, which clearly unsettled them because they made a full loop of the roundabout a few yards further on then came back to check me out a second time, this time at walking pace. But before they had a chance to turn round for a second time my taxi drew up, and I jumped in before the Federalés started asking awkward questions.

The driver couldn't have been a local, because he charged me five quid less than the cabbie from the day before, demonstrating that not everybody living along the banks of the Tyne was a thieving bastard. He dropped me off at the marina, which was slowly starting to show signs of life. Mechanics and competitors wandered around in differing states of wakefulness, gravitating towards the big white marquee that housed Race Control for the day.

As the marquee filled I found Jonathan, Cormac and Andy. Jonathan confirmed that Fred had managed to repair the broken rudder component, courtesy of the *Blue FPT* shore team, and that he was just putting the finishing touches to *Miss Daisy*. Our conversation was cut short by Mike Lloyd as he started the briefing for the day.

Today we would be running to Lowestoft, a distance of around 205 nautical miles. This made it one of the longest legs of the race, and would see the fleet crossing the Wash, a bloody great bay that acts as an estuary for four rivers— the Witham, Welland, Nene and Great Ouse. It measures some 11 miles wide at its throat, but because the land curves away so steeply, especially at the southern side, teams hugging the coastline would have to think long and hard about where they planned to cross it.

Of course the forecast of gentle seas should mean that even the smallest of boats could have plotted a straight line straight from Newcastle to Lowestoft, but we had all discovered by now that the descriptions of sea states were aimed more at super tankers than our little fleet. A "gentle sea" promised six foot swells at the very least, requiring the smaller, lighter boats to keep well inshore to benefit from the calmer waters.

But this threw up its own dilemma— sure, by hugging the shoreline a boat could run a lot quicker, but it also meant that it would have to cover a much greater distance. There was a very fine line to be drawn, and many of the navigators in the fleet had spent countless hours trying to plot a course that would, they hoped, be the perfect compromise.

Some, like the crew of *Buro*, had done all this many weeks before. They had carefully studied the exact coordinates of the start and finish lines, and had plotted their course with great care and precision, making sure to take any marker buoys into account. For Peter Verhauter and his crew, each morning they merely made their way to their first waypoint of the day, then followed their plotter's directions to the letter.

This was fine for the heavy, plodding Targa 42. This boat had already demonstrated that a bit of wind and a sloppy sea wasn't going to have much of an impact on her average speed; she could just bully her way through whatever Nature threw at her. For the smaller, lighter boats, however, the state of the sea's surface could have a drastic effect on their performance.

Take the Goldfish boats of *Lionhead* or *Guttaboyz* for instance. They were phenomenally quick; they had already proved that many times over. But the main reason they were so fast was because they were, relatively speaking, as light as a feather. This meant that they lacked the sheer mass required to punch through the larger waves, causing them to slow down or risk being battered into submission by the sea. So they were forced to run close to the shore, in the shelter of the land. Here they would find the calmer, smoother waters that enabled them to run much faster, and if they plotted their course perfectly that extra speed would help them cover the greater distance quicker than the boats taking the straight line approach.

For the navigators of the smaller, lighter boats, they had to somehow walk the fine line between covering too much distance inshore and running too far out at sea, where the bigger waves would slow them down. And this meant that every day they had to tweak and fine-tune their course, taking the current weather conditions into account.

Mike then announced that there would be a two-part start to today's leg. The Historic boats would set off at 8:30, followed by the rest of the fleet an hour later. This came to a great relief to Mike Barlow and the rest of the *Ocean Pirate* crew, who had decided not to set off by themselves after all. But it did mean that we would have to get a move on, since *Miss Daisy* was still tied up behind the massive lock gates that kept the water level in the marina basin more or less constant.

After the briefing came the usual roll call, confirming who was racing in each boat for the upcoming leg. Some teams had alternating crew members, like the Scottish *Braveheart* team. For them, this was a unique once-in-a-lifetime adventure, and they wanted the whole team to experience at least one racing leg. For others, the physical demands of racing day in and day out were starting to take their toll, and they gladly gave up their seat to another team member in order to enjoy a rare day of comfort in the back of a car instead.

For me, it was just another daily humiliation. "And tell me Derek, who will you be racing with today?"

"Morning Annie. I'm with Team *747* today."

She fixed me with a cold stare. "Really. Were Peter and the boys too much for you yesterday?" She didn't wait for an answer, instead moving on to the next team while the rest of the tent sniggered.

By now the acerbic comments of Annie, Gill and Mary no longer stung so much, so I made my mark on the form and swung my bag over my shoulder. Together with the rest of the *747* team I made my way down the walkway onto the pontoon where the Fairey Spearfish was tied up. On the way I bumped into Guy and asked him to give my gear the customary once-over. He walked down with us and as I laid my crap out on the pontoon he checked Fred's repair-work. *Miss Daisy* was given a clean bill of health, and so was my safety equipment so I strapped my Grabner on. But just as I made to throw my bag below Fred kindly offered to take it in the caravan instead.

For some incredibly stupid reason that I can't possibly imagine now I agreed, and I walked back up the pontoon with him and up to where the Support Module sat attached to the back of a 5 Series BMW like a cancerous growth on a model's face. I threw my bag onto one of the bunks (diplomatically ignoring to comment on the thick stench of man-farts) and jogged back to the boat.

Why did I do that? Why did I once again entrust my precious belongings to a relative stranger? Had I learnt nothing from the miseries of Milford Haven, when exactly the same blasé attitude resulted in some of the shittiest hours of my entire life?

Obviously not. This would once again cause me much mental anguish, emotional distress and threaten my chances of sleeping in a warm, dry bed that night. But that would come later...

Back on board *Miss Daisy* I made myself comfortable on the padded bench that ran along the transom and took a look at the results for the previous day's leg.

Hannes Bohinc and his crew on *Wettpunkt.com* had once again set a blistering pace, crossing the line in under one and a half hours. Their average speed for that leg was a mighty 76 knots; clearly the potential of this boat was huge, but after failing to finish the first leg and accruing some hefty time penalties for speeding in the muster area in Inverness their chances of winning were non-existent, with the boat lying in 21st overall.

Venturer was in much the same position. Andy Macateer had lost time on the first leg due to a blocked water intake, and on the second leg a blocked fuel filter meant he could only manage 12th. Since then, however, his Buzzi-designed RIB had shown what she was capable of, finishing consistently in the top three. *Venturer* had been second into Newcastle, but despite being pipped to the post by the only other boat in their Class, Andy Macateer's four hour lead over Hannes Bohinc meant that the RB1 Class championship was his— provided nothing went wrong.

Four minutes behind *Venturer* and thirteen behind *Wettpunkt.com*, *Blue FPT* claimed third place. Vassilis Pateras and his crew had covered the 115 nautical miles at an average speed of 67 knots— a full ten knots slower than Hannes and his crew. But by now the old analogy of the tortoise and the hare had been hammered to death; their lead over the overall second-place boat *Hot Lemon* was over an hour, and their nearest rival for the Class win was— *Braveheart*?!

Stunned, I checked and re-checked the figures, comparing the results to the previous legs. But the numbers confirmed what I could barely comprehend; a team of Scottish trawlermen had somehow managed to blow past some of the fastest boats and drivers ever assembled to put their piss-ugly Scanner RIB third overall!

Nobody had seen this coming, not even Bobby Cowe himself. (When I spoke to him a few months later he freely admitted that he didn't have a clue about what he'd himself in for, and that he and his brother-in-law Hamish Slater had only entered the race for a bit of fun.) What was slightly disturbing was the fact that even now, with *Braveheart* just a few seconds behind *Hot Lemon*, nobody had seemed to pick up on the fact. Everybody had been so focused on the big names— *Blue FPT*, *Wettpunkt.com*, *Lionhead* etc— that Bobby Cowe's incredible achievement had somehow failed to show up on anyone's radar.

But so much for the race for overall victory. That finishing line was still over 430 miles away, and only a fool would predict with utter certainty what the outcome would be. Focussing my attention back to the previous day's results, I noticed that *Going Lean* had come in fourth; another great result for powerboating novice Dean Gibbs in his Sunseeker XRS. Admittedly his other two crewmates were Neil Holmes, a hugely experienced racer with his own powerboat school, and Shelley Jory, one of Britain's top female racers, but still...

My old compañeros of Team *Silverline* had finished in seventh, just three minutes ahead of *Braveheart* whose closest rivals, Dave and Mike Deacon, crossed the line less than thirty seconds later in *Hot Lemon*, their record-breaking Scorpion RIB.

As I scanned further down the sheet nothing caught my eye until I spotted Team *747* lying in 27th, ten minutes ahead of *GEE* in 30th. Apparently I had crossed the line in 31st on board *Buro*, somehow beating *Lionhead* into port by two minutes. Their poor result was because of a blown drive leg, a component that was starting to look like the Goldfish's Achilles heel because their sister boat *Guttaboyz* managed to blow *both* outdrives, resulting in their inability to cross the line within the allotted time.

Another fatality was Team *Bandit*, an ugly, aggressive-looking Hunton RIB crewed by a motley gang of taxi drivers. They too had failed to post a time for the leg after suffering serious engine problems, dropping them down in the overall standings. But I was pleased to see that all three boats had managed to effect repairs overnight, and no doubt they would soon come thundering past us as we pottered along at our maximum forty knots...

Whilst I had been grappling with the numbers on the sheet before me and trying to get some sort of grip on the what they actually meant we had passed through the big lock gates without incident and soon we were gently sliding down the Tyne, through the gap between the massive breakwater walls and once again out into salt water. We were joined by *GEE*, *Ocean Pirate*, *Swordsman* and *Xanthus*— the Historic fleet together again, with the notable exception of Markus Hendricks, whose *Blue Marlin* lay in over a hundred meters of water somewhere in Lyme Bay.

With the sun sparkling and dancing off the water we took the time to get settled down for what would be another long day at sea. At least the weather looked to be holding up, and even the promise of a gentle sea seemed to be right for a change.

The Historics didn't bugger about with the usual anti-clockwise circling nonsense; instead the five boats drifted alongside each other, bows pointing southwards. After a few minutes the Start Boat emerged from behind the breakwater, and with little fuss he cut across our bows and got the penultimate leg underway.

Closest to the shore was *Ocean Pirate*. Then there was us, then *GEE*, then *Swordsman*, and finally *Xanthus* on the outside. As Gary Manchester on the Start Boat raised the green flag Jonathan opened the throttles wide open, and the two mighty Cummins diesels fired us towards the southern horizon.

The only boat keeping up with us now was *GEE* as the rest of the boats fell further and further behind. *GEE* and *Miss Daisy* were closely matched, and it was thrilling to watch the great white hull of *GEE* pound through the water alongside, just a dozen feet or so separating us. Gradually we eased ahead, the calmer water suiting the lighter Fairey, and before long the rest of the pack were nothing more than white flashes of spray on the horizon.

And suddenly it hit me— we were leading the race! As the Sunderland coast whipped past our starboard side, I got great satisfaction of notifying the rest of the boys that there wasn't a single racing boat ahead of us. Admittedly, it was purely an illusion— pretty soon the rest of the fleet would be released and many of the faster boats would haul us in and overtake us somewhere between Flamborough Head and Lowestoft, probably far out to sea where we wouldn't even see their tell-tale rooster tail, but that wasn't the point damnit! At that moment we were Winners, and our hearts filled with pride and a burning joy.

But even Winners have to get their hands dirty from time to time, and we were no exception.

After nearly running out of fuel on the leg from Milford Haven to Bangor, Jonathan had realised that he would need to somehow increase the boat's fuel capacity. To do this he fitted two 50 litre plastic tanks beneath the aft bench and plumbed them in to the main tanks. The Scrutineers had raised an eyebrow at the set-up, but decided to let it go once Jonathan demonstrated that they were securely mounted.

After an hour of running flat out Jonathan decided that the main tanks were now empty enough to take the contents of the two spare tanks. He handed the helm over to Andy and he and I cautiously made our way aft. To transfer the diesel to the main tanks we had to pump the rubber bulb fitted to the fuel line, and we discovered that the easiest and most comfortable way of doing this was to lie on our backs with our legs braced against the rear bench. Naturally, it was while we were lying there like a couple of sunbathing morons that the race helicopter thundered overhead.

We grinned and waved as the chopper kept station just thirty feet above and alongside us, perfectly keeping pace as we raced across the North Sea at nearly 40 knots. In the open doorway we could clearly make out Chris Davies as he snapped away, while next to him someone else was pointing a video camera at us.

They paced us for several minutes, filming and taking photos of the Fairey as she skimmed across the water, before finally banking hard to starboard and racing back up the coast to where the rest of the pack were now undoubtedly hot on our heels.

With the main fuel tanks once again full to the brim we retook our places, but despite the extra fuel load Jonathan was still concerned about running out. To keep our distance to a minimum he had plotted a course that would see us taking a relatively direct line down the East coast. The strategy worked well for a while, but as time went on the sea conditions worsened.

We were somewhere off Skegness when we altered course to port to intercept our next waypoint. As we started crossing the mouth of the Wash the sun disappeared behind a veil of miserable grey clouds and the sea got progressively lumpier. Jonathan was forced to throttle back, but still *Miss Daisy* was spending a lot of time in the air, her props whistling eerily as they spun clear of the muddy water. That old familiar feeling of momentary weightlessness returned, followed by the crashing impact as we returned to the sea.

I had taken up my familiar station on the aft deck, hanging on to the two loops of tubular steel mounted to the deck. I was still convinced that this was the perfect place to ride out the boat's violent movement, and as I watched Andy and Cormac crashed down onto their bench seat again and again it served to prove my instincts correct a little more every time.

This was especially true after one particularly heavy crash. The rule of thumb seemed to be that the longer you were floating weightless in the air, the harder the impact would be when that cruel bitch Gravity reasserted herself. When we took off from one freakishly large wave it seemed that we were hanging in mid-air for uncountable minutes— although no doubt it was no more than two or three seconds. Straight away I knew we would hit hard, and it felt as though I had a lifetime to adjust my grip on the steel rails, plant my feet firmly on the deck and make sure my body was relaxed but ready to absorb the pain I knew was coming.

The impact, when it finally came, was hard. Very hard. In unison we all grunted as the air was expelled from our lungs, and as Cormac and Andy were thrown down onto the bench seat its supporting frame finally relented to the continual abuse and collapsed.

Jonathan pulled back on the sticks as the two men examined the damage. The steelwork was twisted and bent, and way beyond any sort of quick fix they might have planned. They would have to spend the rest of the leg standing up, but this wouldn't be as easy for them as it was for me.

For one thing, there wasn't any room for either of them to join me at my wonderful little spot, so they would have to stand up in the cockpit. The problem with this was that it was never meant for people to stand there in heavy seas; in fact it was nothing more than a narrow passageway to the door leading down below. So as Jonathan spun up the big diesel engines once again, Andy and Cormac found that their knees were being smashed against the bulkhead every time they tried to flex their legs, and the only available grab rail forced their arms up in a deeply uncomfortable position. Soon I could hear their painful cursing, even over the sound of the exhausts.

The wave that crippled our skipper wasn't nearly so dramatic. Instead of flying over the top of the Wash for countless seconds, we were only airborne for a few moments. But the landing was bad, and the hull re-entered the water at an angle, throwing us sideways. Immediately Jonathan hauled the throttles back, and we knew there was a serious problem. His face was twisted in agony, and one hand was behind his back, trying to knead the muscles beneath his Grabner back into shape.

Through gritted teeth he told us that his back had gone into spasm, and we helped him aft before throwing all the bench cushions onto the deck and gently lowering him down onto them. Throughout this little manoeuvre he kept apologising to us, as if he was somehow to blame for costing us precious minutes. Of course we told him not to be so bloody stupid, and it wasn't until we were certain that he was as comfortable and secure as we could make him that Andy took his place at the helm and got us going.

The next half hour or so were undoubtedly miserable for Jonathan as Andy tried to find the right balance between speed and comfort. As we got closer to the northern shore of Norfolk, the sea once again flattened, and bit by bit Andy opened the taps until we were once again running flat out.

From Sheringham onwards we hugged the coast, screaming past deserted sandy beaches and occasionally having to jink left or right to avoid lobster pots. The clouds had once again melted away, and it was a truly fantastic feeling to be skimming along on such a capable boat, in company with a great group of people.

As we steadily approached the finish line we came across a massive wind farm installation. Just over a mile and a half off the town of Caister-on-Sea, thirty massive turbines reach a massive 200 feet up into the sky, their forty-meter blades barely turning in the calm afternoon air. Like some sort of bizarre man-made forest, the smooth white towers stood in regimented ranks, their silhouettes visible from several miles away.

This offshore wind farm— one of the first in the UK— can produce enough electricity to power up to 30,000 homes, showing that developments like this can make a genuine difference in these climate-conscious times. And while some people bitch and moan about the visual impact, I find them oddly elegant and aesthetically pleasing— especially when you compare them to some of the hideous monstrosities we've scarred the landscape with over the years. Where were all the objections when Holyrood was being thrown together by what looks like a petulant toddler? Or Battersea Power station? Or any tower block built in the Sixties and Seventies? No, there is a strange kind of elegance to these turbines; with their crisp white lines and tapering blades each one is as much a work of art as an engineering masterpiece.

We soon passed the strange, modernistic copse of windfarm trees, secure in the knowledge that Lowestoft was only a dozen or so miles down the coast. Which was just as well, as the boat had taken to heeling to one side. Andy quickly dropped us of the plane and a quick look over the transom showed that one of the trim tabs was missing, ripped off somewhere across the Wash no doubt. But in the smoother waters off Great Yarmouth it wasn't a major handicap, and with the smell of chips and candyfloss in our nostrils we hunkered down and sprinted for the finish line.

Twenty minutes later we blasted along the Lowestoft seafront, for once confident that we had crossed the imaginary finish line that lay between a marker buoy and a cabin cruiser flying a huge RYA flag. From his makeshift bed on the aft deck Jonathan managed to raise a weary cry, and we hauled him to his feet as we motored in to the harbour between the two massive stone piers that towered above us.

The marina was a bit of a rat-run; to starboard the harbour opened up to reveal a ratty commercial area known as Waveney Dock, a long single-storey building serving as a fish market running along one side. And beyond that was Hamilton Dock, an area that had only recently been re-invented as a marina, with pontoons for up to 46 boats and little else.

A little further inland and to port was a gap in the forbidding stone wall, which led us into another, cosier little marina. At the far end we spotted the clubhouse for the Royal Norfolk & Suffolk Yacht Club, the temporary home of Race Control. The boys were keen to get Jonathan's back seen to and fuel up the boat for the next leg, as well as checking out the damaged trim tab, so like a fool I offered to jump ashore and sign the team in. As soon as my feet hit the pontoon Andy turned *Miss Daisy* around and made for Hamilton Dock, where they would be berthed for the night. I gave them a quick wave before I turned and scampered up the gangway to sign in, blissfully unaware of just how stupid I really was.

Once again Gill and Mary were sitting behind desks, trying to keep track of the 39 boats that had left Newcastle over five hours before. I signed in on behalf of Team *747* and scanned the list to see who had beaten us in. The answer was pretty much everybody; something I had learnt to accept as part of travelling on board one of the Historics. One surprising omission was Team *Silverline*. We had come in in 29th place, and still no sign of Drew and the boys. I could only assume that they had once again hit mechanical problems, but there was nothing I could do about it so I shrugged it off and wandered off in search of sustenance.

I found a burger stall round the corner, and after loading up on cholesterol and salt I remembered that *Ocean Pirate* was due to make a grand entrance on her return to her home port. I sent Mike Barlow a text asking for his ETA, since I hoped to get some good photos of the team coming home to an adoring public, and when he replied that they'd be a couple of hours yet I asked him to give me a quick call when they were ten minutes out. In the meantime, I decided to grab a beer or two and relax.

Back at the Royal Norfolk & Suffolk Yacht Club I found a good-looking girl serving cool, refreshing drinks, so I settled in for the long wait in relative luxury. After two hours had passed I still hadn't heard from Mike, so I gave him another call. He proudly told me that they'd crossed the line half an hour ago, and they were now safely tied up at Hamilton Dock. *You bloody idiot!* I raged inside. *You bloody asked me for pictures of your big moment, and then you don't tell me when you cross the fucking line!* But of course I didn't say these things; I just muttered my congratulations and hung up.

So, I'd just wasted two hours of my life for nothing. Well, *almost* nothing; I had a nice little beer-buzz going on, and sitting in the sun outside the Yacht Club chatting to the locals wasn't the worst way to spend a little time. I'd phoned in my report to Rob, and even found the time to call my long-suffering wife to remind her I was still sucking air. Duties done, I decided to pop over to Hamilton Dock to see how the Team *747* boys were doing, and to grab my bag out of the back of the caravan— sorry, Support Module— providing Fred and Michael had arrived from Newcastle.

I asked the barmaid how to get to Hamilton Dock, and her directions were deceptively simple— follow the main road to the right, you can't miss it. It seemed easy enough, so I rolled a smoke for the walk and set off.

It turned out that the marina was three quarters of a mile away. It was a warm, humid afternoon and I was already tired from spending five and a half hours on board a wildly-bucking boat, so when I arrived at the marina and found the gates locked I wasn't in the best of moods.

Just then someone walked up behind me and asked if I wanted in. I gratefully said Yes and he punched the code into the panel. I made a mental note of the number and followed him in as the big steel gates swung open, then turned my attention to finding *Miss Daisy*.

Of course she wasn't there; by now I had learnt that that wasn't how things worked— not for me, at any rate. I pulled out my phone to call Jonathan, and wasn't particularly surprised to see that my battery was dead. It was my own stupid fault of course; I still hadn't gotten around to buying a new charger for it, and the "universal" charger required a certain knack to ensure that the badly-fitting jack made a proper contact. So after hanging around for ten minutes or so in case they suddenly materialised I heaved a weary sigh and set off towards the Yacht Club again.

Along the way I discovered *Blue FPT* sitting on her lorry. I went over to try to blag a seat with the number one boat for the final leg, but there wasn't anyone in sight so I shrugged and continued on my way.

Back at Race Control I found an unattended socket, so I plugged in my phone and jiggered with the charger until precious electricity started trickling into the battery. After half an hour of sitting on the floor with the hateful thing on my lap I switched it on and gave Jonathan a call.

Once again I was totally unsurprised to find out that he'd just tied up at Hamilton bloody Dock, and since there still wasn't any sign on Michael and Fred why didn't I come over to wait for them on the boat?

By the time I reached the electric gates my feet were screaming for mercy and I was soaked in sweat. I punched in the number and walked down the pontoon to where *Miss Daisy* lay, secured for the night with her smart canvas covers clipped into place. What? No sign of the guys. Nothing. This was getting tiresome. The alcohol in my bloodstream was starting to turn my buzz into a hangover, and the heat was starting to make me seriously grumpy.

I have never managed to deal well with high temperatures. Whenever I find myself in a hot climate I lose all sense of humour, my reactions slow and I become even quicker to anger than usual. This is because my blood is unusually thin, no doubt a necessary evolutionary response to a lifetime spent in the cold, forbidding climate of Scotland's west coast, so whenever I'm exposed to unnatural heat my blood thins even more, starving my brain of oxygen and rendering my pituitary gland incapable of releasing endorphins, the magical opiate-like compound that makes a person feel good.

As I set off for the Yacht Club one more time I angrily dialled Jonathan's number, ready to verbally tear him a new arsehole. But he managed to explain himself before I could get a word in. "Derek! We've been looking all over for you! Dad and Fred just showed up, and they're ferrying us to the Yacht Club in the car. Where are you?"

"Um, I've just left the marina and I'm walking along the main drag."

"OK, we'll look out for you. See you in a minute!" And with that he hung up.

If there was a chance of a lift I'd be damned if I was going to walk another foot, so I leant against a streetlight and waited for the big BMW to roll into sight. Sure enough, just a few minutes later Fred pulled up and I gratefully jumped in.

Once back at the Yacht Club I was introduced to Mark Jealous, the fourth member of Team *747*. He had injured his ribs on the opening leg, and had elected to sit out the rest of the race until now. Tomorrow would be the final stage, and Mark felt well enough to rejoin his teammates for the last 190 nm.

I calmed down over a beer, disappointed that Jonathan's dad had decided to stay at the caravan site to catch up on some sleep, and finally we decided to set off in search of food. This proved harder than I first imagined. You see, I would have happily walked through the door of the nearest pub, café or restaurant I came across, but for Mark and the others there was a long-standing tradition that demanded that they seek out the finest Indian restaurant in town. Finally, after interrogating half a dozen locals a clear winner emerged, and we set off in search of— surprise surprise— the Taj Mahal.

It meant another fifteen-minute walk, but it was spent in good company and we laughed and joked our way along the street. Once inside we made complete pigs of ourselves, gorging on the smorgasbord of spicy dishes. By the time the coffee and mints arrived I was truly stuffed for the first time since setting off from my home nearly two weeks before, and I finally managed to relax. It seemed that Jonathan also enjoyed the temporary freedom from stress and worry; his head sunk lower and lower until his chin rested on his chest and he started making soft snoring noises. Perhaps it also had something to do with the painkillers he'd taken for his shattered spine; unbeknownst to me he'd been to see the Race doc and he'd passed Jonathan to race the following day.

I felt that I owed the team some sort of repayment for the kindness and generosity they had shown me over the past week or so, so I paid for the meal while Andy and Cormac tried to wake up their skipper.

Back at the car we faced a dilemma— I had to pick up my bag from the caravan, which was at a campsite "a couple of minutes away", but there were six of us and only one car. I offered to follow them in a taxi, pick up my bag and have the taxi take me to my digs for the night, but I was shouted down. (With hindsight I should have stuck to my guns, but we all know that If Only isn't worth shit in the real world...)

Finally we all managed to somehow squeeze into the 5-Series, and with Cormac grinding into my lap we set off for the short drive to the campsite. The "short drive" turned out to be more like twenty minutes as we left the orange glow of streetlights far behind us and travelled south into the heart of the Suffolk countryside. The campsite, when we reached it, was in total darkness, but we could hear the surf pounding the sandy beach just a few yards away. I clambered in to the caravan and grabbed my holdall, and after wishing the boys Goodnight I walked back to the campsite entrance to call a taxi.

With my taxi on its way I decided to call my landlady. I was a little shocked by how late it was, but she kindly offered to wait up for me, so with that taken care of I rolled a smoke and sat under a solitary streetlight to wait for my ride.

After half an hour there still wasn't any sign of the car, so I called them up. I was promised that the driver was on his way, but I was in no mood for their bullshit and warned them that if I was locked out of my B&B because they fucked up they would have an extremely dissatisfied customer on their hands. I then switched to grovelling mode as I called my landlady to keep her up to date. She was sympathetic but reluctant to hang around all night for some babbling Scotsman to turn up whenever he felt like it.

When the taxi's headlights finally cut through the darkness I wasted no time in throwing myself into the passenger seat and giving the driver the address, grimly telling him to drive like a crazy person unless he wanted me sleeping on his sofa. The driver picked up on my foul mood instantly and we set off at a blistering speed, racing along the deserted country roads at a respectable lick.

With a heavy Polish accent the driver gave me the usual litany of excuses that we've all heard before, then asked me what I was up to. Wearily I gave him a quick explanation— powerboats, round Britain, forty-odd teams, no prize money etc— but it was clear that he couldn't get his head round what I was trying to tell him. I gave up, finishing with a lame "It's complicated", and in an uncomfortable silence we sped through the town until he pulled up alongside a dark, unlit house.

The lack of lights worried me. If my landlady had decided to give up on me I was buggered, so I told my driver of my situation and asked if there were any hotels nearby that might be able to give me a room at this time of night.

He sucked on a hollow tooth as he thought about it. "I don't know; it is pretty late now." I glanced at the clock on the dash— it was just coming up to 1am. "I tell you what. If she doesn't let you in, you call me on this number." He scribbled his mobile number onto the back of a business card. "I will come and get you and take you to my brother. He has a small business in town; I am sure that he will let you stay in one of the beds for tonight."

One of the beds? What the hell did *that* mean? "And what sort of business is your brother in exactly?" I asked, knowing the answer even as I spoke.

The driver couldn't maintain eye contact. "Uh, you know. It's like a private club. People come, have some drinks, maybe meet a pretty girl..."

"You know what? It's late, I'm exhausted, I don't really want to know. Thanks for this," I said as I took the card, "but let's hope I won't have to call you, OK?" I settled up and got out, and as my new Eastern European buddy sped off into the night I said a mental prayer and walked up the dark path to the front door.

I only had to lean on the doorbell for three or four minutes before a light came on in the hallway and the beautiful sound of deadbolts being slid back greeted my ears. The door swung open and, silhouetted against the warm light that surrounded her like a glowing halo, Penny Forrester invited me into her home.

We whispered greetings, careful not to wake any of her other guests, and she showed me into my room— spacious, gracefully decorated and right by the front door, perfect for my early-morning getaway. I dropped my bag onto the bed and whispered that I'd like to settle up now, since I'd be sneaking off early the next morning.

Penny led me to the kitchen, and as we waited patiently for the credit card machine to do its thing I stared blankly at the wall. Finally she handed me my card and a receipt, and not a minute too soon— I was nearly asleep.

"Now, did you say on the phone that you were something to do with the powerboat race?" she asked.

Like an automaton I started reciting my tale, fighting to keep from yawning. "In that case, maybe you'd be interested in this." She pointed out a picture hanging on the wall, and I forced my eyes to focus in on what she was showing me.

Mounted in a simple frame was a sepia photograph. It showed a man in his mid-thirties kneeling in what looked like some sort of boat, one hand resting easily on a massive wooden steering wheel. The whole craft couldn't have been more than eight feet long, with the name *White Lady* and racing number OB1 painted onto the white deck, reflecting her status of being the very first motorboat to be registered on the Oulton Broads. A small pennant stood on the bow, whilst bolted to the transom was an agricultural-looking piece of machinery that passed for an outboard engine in those days.

"Those days" turned out to be the mid-thirties, when men were made of sterner stuff than they are now. Penny told me that this was her grandfather, Jack Robinson. Old Jack looked to be quite a character as he stared out of the photo in his racing get-up: a white boiler suit, a kapok lifejacket and a knotted handkerchief to keep the wind off were all he needed to protect himself from the elements; I wondered idly what he would have made of my dry suit, lifejacket and helmet. I think he'd have given a snort of derision before turning back to eating burning coals, or whatever these Fen folk did for fun back then.

(After the race I got in touch with Penny's father, John Robinson. He told me how the boat was made of nothing more than a wooden frame wrapped in canvas, and he recalled how he watched as Jack filled the bow and stern compartments with hundreds of ping-pong balls for buoyancy and poured molten beeswax over them to keep them all in place. And that got me thinking— how many of today's drivers would have the balls to race a couple of laps in Jack's *White Lady*?)

Jack might not have won the Harmsworth or the Duke of York Trophy or any of the other prestigious awards linked with powerboat racing, and he probably never raced alongside legends like Gar Wood, Marion "Joe" Carstairs and other greats, but that didn't make him and *White Lady* any less relevant to what we were doing now. Without the unbridled enthusiasm that people like Jack Robinson brought to the sport— and continue to bring-, the 2008 Round Britain Powerboat Race, along with many other powerboat races held on weekends all over the world, simply would not exist.

The inspirational picture of a man with a knotted hanky on his head sitting in a home-made contraption of canvas and wood brought my own (mis)adventures into perspective, and as I fell asleep that night I considered myself lucky to have been given the opportunity to race with like-minded people seventy years after Jack Robinson's death.

Top– Jack Robinson in his canvas powerboat circa 1935

Below– Hannes Bohinc of *Wettpunkt.com*

Results-
Newcastle to Lowestoft.

Distance: 205 nautical miles.

Pos.	Team/ Number	Class	Time	Overall position (Class)
1st	Lionhead/22	RB3	3:04:12	2 (1)
2nd	Wettpunkt.com/81	RB1	3:09:26	28 (2)
3rd	Going Lean/7	RB3	3:26:31	8 (5)
4th	Blue FPT/333	MC1	3:29:27	1 (1)
5th	Venturer/111	RB1	3:32:00	7 (1)
6th	Mr Mako/96	RB4	3:32:37	13 (2)
7th	Vilda/9	RB3	3:39:00	5 (3)
8th	Braveheart III/55	MC1	3:39:53	3 (2)
9th	Hot Lemon/2	RB3	3:42:18	4 (2)
10th	Carbon Neutral/343	RB3	3:49:32	11 (6)
11th	Hardleys/4	RB3	3:50:03	6 (4)
12th	Sealbay/77	RB4	4:01:49	9 (1)
13th	Mystic Dragon/6	MC1	4:09:07	29 (6)
14th	Seahound V/80	MC1	4:09:13	10 (3)
15th	Team Scorpion Dubois/16	MC1	4:09:31	14 (4)
16th	swipewipes.co.uk/ 43	RB4	4:12:04	15 (3)
17th	Power Products Marine/8	MC2	4:16:04	12 (1)
18th	Tequila/8	RB3	4:19:24	18 (8)
19th	Team Jersey/45	RB4	4:19:46	33 (9)
20th	Black Gold/10	RB4	4:25:18	32 (8)

Pos.	Team/ Number	Class	Time	Overall position (Class)
21st	Fugitive/130	MC2	4:31:34	19 (2)
22nd	Relentless/47	RB3	4:31:39	31 (9)
23rd	Seafarer/110	RB3	4:36:11	23 (9)
24th	TFO/17	MC2	4:41:08	20 (3)
25th	Team Pulsar-Vampire/102	RB4	4:44:59	22 (5)
26th	My Pleasure II/3	RB4	5:03:44	21 (4)
27th	Mud, Swell & Beers/14	RB4	5:21:15	27 (7)
28th	Team Pulsar-Wolf/101	RB4	5:22:06	26 (6)
29th	**Team 747/747**	**HC1**	**5:36:38**	**28 (2)**
30th	Buro/15	MC1	5:36:59	23 (5)
31st	GEE/185	HC1	5:44:45	24 (1)
32nd	Team Bandit/69	RB2	6:05:57	30 (2)
33rd	Garmin Racing/72	RB2	6:41:17	36 (3)
34th	Ocean Pirate/323	HC1	7:05:03	40 (5)
35th	Xanthus/1	HC1	7:21:17	37 (3)
36th	Swordsman/68	HC1	7:29:03	39 (4)
37th	Team Silverline/471	RB2	*	25 (1)
38th	Birretta/12	MC1	**OTR**	34 (7)
39th	Guttaboyz/22	RB3	*	35 (10)
40th	No Worries/11	RB3	**OTR**	41 (11)

DNS Denotes Did Not Start
DNF Denotes Did Not Finish
OTR Denotes Out of The Race
* Denotes maximum time allowance exceeded.

Pos.	Team/ Number	Class	Time	Overall position (Class)
41st	Northern Spirit	MC2	**OTR**	38 (4)
42nd	Cinzano/558	RB2	**OTR**	47 (5)
43rd	Blue Marlin/99	HC1	**OTR**	46 (6)
44th	RIB International/ 144	RB4	**OTR**	43 (10)
45th	Ikon/18	RB3	**OTR**	42 (12)
46th	Team Blastoff/100	RB2	**OTR**	45 (4)
47th	Red FPT/177	CC1	**OTR**	44 (1)

DNS Denotes Did Not Start
DNF Denotes Did Not Finish
OTR Denotes Out of The Race
* Denotes maximum time allowance exceeded.

Below– Leading the pack– momentarily!

14.
Lowestoft To Portsmouth.

Monday 30th June.

Well, this was it. The final leg, the grand finale, the home straight. And I didn't have a ride. I had booked an early taxi to the marina with the faint hope of finding a boat with a spare seat for the 190 nautical mile sprint to the finish, but it soon became apparent that I was clutching at straws.

As I made the early-morning rounds of apologetic but unwilling teams my mood sunk ever lower, so to pass the time until others made it down to the pontoons and to take my mind off my predicament I borrowed the latest results sheet to figure out what had happened on the previous day.

Lionhead had covered the 205 nautical miles from Newcastle in three hours and four minutes, taking first place. *Wettpunkt.com* had crossed the line five minutes later, and quarter of an hour behind the Austrian came Dean Gibbs in *Going Lean*. *Blue FPT* continued her slow & steady approach, coming in in fourth place, while Andy Macateer piloted *Venturer* home in fifth. Further down the field I spotted the name *Braveheart* in eighth, putting in another solid time, and beating *Hot Lemon* in by less than three minutes.

My own ride, Team *747*, crossed the line in 29th place, and I was surprised to see that we had barely beaten *Buro* by less than thirty seconds. None of us on board *Miss Daisy* had realised this at the time; so focused were we on looking ahead for the finish line and then getting Jonathan checked out that we hadn't bothered looking over our shoulders, where we would have seen the bulk of the Botnia Targa looming over us like some madly-grinning ogre.

We had also beaten *GEE* into port, which made us the first Historic Class team in. After *GEE* came Team *Bandit*, their time a result of losing one engine early on in the stage, with *Garmin Racing* this time putting in a poor performance not due to mechanical problems for once, but because one of their crew, Tony Robinson, had to be airlifted off the boat somewhere in the middle of the Wash due to crashing into the wheel of the boat and injuring his chest.

Three boats were showing as posted no time: *Silverline*, *Birretta* and *Guttaboyz*. The Belgian duo of Thomas Vandamme and Jean-Pierre Neels had cooked their starboard engine on the leg from Inverness to Edinburgh, but had managed— somehow— to repair it overnight for the next leg. But on the run from Newcastle *Birretta*'s port engine suffered the same fate, and this time they knew they didn't stand a chance of pulling off another miracle, so they were towed into Hartlepool and reluctantly threw in the towel. Their race was over.

The Norwegians on board *Guttaboyz* had managed to destroy not one but both of their fragile drive legs, but thanks to their massive shore support they had managed to replace both the legs, and today would be joining the rest of the fleet for the final sprint to Portsmouth.

Drew, Jan and John would also make the start this morning, despite having suffered more mechanical problems on the previous leg. They were somewhere off the Norfolk coast when they lost one engine. Unfortunately the one remaining engine couldn't get the hull up onto the plane, due to the type of prop they were running, so the decision was made to try and replace it. Thankfully they were reasonably close to the gently-shelving beach at Cromer, and so they carefully beached the boat to try and change the prop, but to no avail. Like *Birretta*, they too suffered the ignominy of having to be towed into port by the local lifeboat. But unlike the Belgians, they had managed to repair the faulty engine, and were today once again in the running.

So despite Drew's woes, at least he had a boat to get him to Portsmouth. I, on the other hand, was looking at a long, undignified day spent battling with the horrors of public transport. This was partially my own fault— if I'd spent a little more time begging and pleading the previous day and less time drinking, eating and being generally merry, perhaps I would have secured a seat by now.

There was also my stupid belief that I could race with one of the teams who had so far avoided the pleasure of my company. Which is why, when Jonathan once again offered to let me join his crew, I declined his very generous offer. This wasn't just because of my flawed faith in riding with a new team; I also knew that Mark Jealous would be rejoining his team-mates. Not that I had anything against Mark you understand, but I knew that the boat would be cramped with five men on board, and I was wary of being squeezed into an uncomfortable corner for what promised to be at least five hours.

So I politely declined Jonathan's offer, but instead lent him my kidney belt to support his damaged back. I also rummaged through my bag to find my stash of high-powered morphine-based painkillers. Jonathan and Mark were still far from fighting fit, and I thought they could use some medical assistance over the next 190-plus miles.

With my good deeds done, I felt that Karma owed me a favour. Karma thought otherwise. After being rejected by several other teams I bumped into Drew. When he told me he'd be starting the race without Miles I asked if I might be allowed to rejoin Team *Silverline*, but he deep-six'ed the idea. "Sorry Derek, I'm afraid you can't. Miles is going to be waiting on a boat just before the finish line, and we're going to stop to pick him up so that we can cross the line together." It was a noble gesture but of no bloody use to me, so I sighed once more and turned to find another boat.

It was hardly surprising that some teams preferred not to drag a useless writer along; on this final leg there was still silverware to race for, both in the overall placings as well as in the individual Classes.

In the battle for <u>overall</u> winner, *Blue FPT* was leading— but only by 47 minutes. If anything went wrong then *Lionhead* in second was in a position to pounce. At the same time, the Norwegians would have to keep one eye over their shoulder as Team *Braveheart* were less than half an hour behind them in third. The drive legs of the Goldfish RIBs were now a well-known weakness, and Pål Sollie and his crew would have to take care not to push the boat too hard.

Bobby Cowe on board *Braveheart III* couldn't afford to relax either. Dave Deacon and his team on *Hot Lemon* were only two minutes behind *Braveheart*, but they in turn were only two minutes ahead of *Vilda*, the Swedish-crewed RIB.

Throughout the field teams were jostling for position in the overall standings, but the battle for Class supremacy was just as important, if not more so.

This was most apparent in the RB3 Class, where the gap between first and fourth place was less than one hour. *Lionhead* led the Class by thirty minutes. In second was *Hot Lemon*, who led third-place *Vilda* by two minutes. Nineteen minutes behind the Swedes was *Hardleys*, and despite the time gap between them and Class leader *Lionhead*, nothing could be ruled out— any of the four boats could take the Class win.

In RB4 however, it looked like *Sealbay* had the win sewn up. They had a massive lead over *Mr Mako* in second, but John Fuller and Nick Gilley on *swipewipes.co.uk* were just three minutes behind them in third so the battle for second place was set to go to the wire.

There was a similar fight taking place in MC2. *Power Products Marine* were leading by over two hours in their twin-outboard powered Phantom, but Stuart Whitely and his son Francis on *Fugitive* only led third-place team *TFO* by a mere ten minutes.

In the other Classes teams would have to place their faith in the reliability of their own boats and the potential for breakdowns of others. *Venturer* led *Wettpunkt.com* by three and a half hours in the RB1 Class; *Silverline* had nearly three hours over Team *Bandit* in RB2. If *Braveheart* was to stand any chance of taking the win in MC1 then *Blue FPT* would need to suffer some sort of mechanical drama— not likely, given the Greek team's reliability so far.

That left the race for first in the Historic Class. *GEE* was leading this pack by over one and a half hours, so if Team *747* wanted to improve on second place they would have to hope that some catastrophe befell the Clayton brothers. On the plus side, Jonathan's lead over third place boat *Xanthus* was over 18 hours. This meant that he could, in theory, retire now and *still* retain second in the Historic Class.

Sadly, I didn't have the same option. I was determined to finish this miserable race no matter what, and my weary legs eventually carried me to where Mike Barlow and the rest of his crew were chatting. For some reason still not entirely clear to me he agreed to take me to Portsmouth, and so I would be completing the race on board the boat I started off on all those miles before. Once again I had found a seat in the nick of time; Annie was asking the gathered racers for quiet just as I shook Mike's hand in gratitude.

For the last leg we were promised smooth seas. This was met with open mockery, the drivers now hardened to cynicism by the previous seven forecasts. Still, I think that even if they had threatened hurricanes and tsunamis many would still have strapped on their helmets one more time, so grimly determined were the faces that surrounded me.

The briefing itself was a white noise hiss to me, except for the now-ubiquitous insults regarding my boat-hopping, and soon I was shambling down the road with the rest of the fleet towards Hamilton Dock. There would be six of us on *Ocean Pirate* for the final leg: Mike Barlow, Bob Pennington, Tom Brissenden and Paul Carter made up her normal complement, and as well as myself they would also be joined by Sue, Paul's wife. She was a friendly, talkative sort, and despite my personal exhaustion and a strong sense of déjà vu I made a determined effort to be sociable.

The 8:30 start saw the entire fleet mustered just off Lowestoft. Conditions were almost perfect— the sky was the faded blue of an alcoholic's eyes, with white wisps of rheumy cloud streaking across it like cataracts. The sea was only a little choppy, but the appeal was spoilt by the dirty brown colour it takes on in the English Channel. We were down to 38 boats now— the relentless pace proving too much for nine boats and crews. But still, this was a remarkable achievement, and I was reminded of Guy Childs' pessimistic prediction of a 10% drop-out rate per leg. The fleet had somehow managed to beat those odds, but the race wasn't over yet.

And then the Start Boat cut across our bows, the yellow flag rippling taught in the wind. En masse the fleet turned southwards to chase it, the air filling with an orchestra of diesel-turbo rumbles and petrol howls. As we streamed line abreast the yellow flag was replaced with its green counterpart and finally throttlemen could lean down hard on the sticks, open the taps and mash the throttles.

On *Ocean Pirate* Tom did much the same, but it didn't have the same awe-inspiring effect somehow. The big Cummins QSB 380's beneath the cockpit sole did their best, their bellow testament to the efforts they were putting in, but the heavy old hull wanted little to do with it, and at 28 knots Tom steadied the throttle levers and engaged the autopilot.

From my vantage point in the wheelhouse I watched enviously as the rest of the fleet thundered towards the hazy line of the horizon, and no doubt I had a sad, wistful look on my face. If any of the others noticed, they chose not to say anything either to me or their crewmates, which was probably just as well. If ever there was a team that suffered from delusions of adequacy it was this one as they somehow managed to muster an air of "Yee-hah!" racing fever, wilfully engaged in self-denial as the rest of the fleet gradually dwindled to scattered specs in the distance.

By way of passing the time I pulled out my hateful mobile phone and stabbed at it until I found the calculator function. I divided 190 miles by 28 knots, our top speed. The answer was not good. 6.785 hours until we crossed the finish line. That meant that we'd be home by around 3:15— provided we maintained our current speed. Still, it wasn't too bad: the prize giving dinner was scheduled for seven o'clock that night, so I would still have plenty of time to get changed into my last clean t-shirt and grab a beer or two before making my way to the Governor's Green, opposite the Royal Naval and Royal Albert Yacht Club. Sorted.

Of course in the back of my mind a small cynical voice was laughing bitterly at my naivety. And sure enough, once we rounded the point at Dungeness conditions worsened and we dropped our speed. And then we dropped it some more. But the aluminium hull designed by Brooke Marine forty years ago was once again struggling badly in the heavy seas, and green water constantly smashed into the wheelhouse windows. After a while the constant onslaught proved to much for the starboard wiper and it finally gave up the ghost, followed a few minutes later by the starboard bench seat, failing under the weight of Bob and Paul.

It all proved too much for Mike, and he told Tom to turn landward in search of a safe haven. While I fought a massive wave of déjà vu Paul dicked about with the plotter until he found a suitable port, and he gave Tom the heading for Newhaven marina.

Paul wasn't too happy about diverting to Newhaven, and innocent of the south coast I asked why. "Because it's a total shit-house," he replied bluntly. I thought this was perhaps a little harsh, but soon we entered the calm waters of the marina and he was proved right.

Newhaven lies ten miles east of Brighton, in the mouth of the river Ouse. Its marina lies on the western bank, just across from the ferry terminal to Dieppe and Le Havre. Directly across from our temporary berth we watched dumper trucks and bulldozers at work in what looked— and sounded like— some god-awful scrap yard, and the smell of festering mud as it dried in the sun filled my nostrils.

To be fair, the marina itself looked like there had been recent investment made in it, with a smart new building overlooking the marina from the heights. But it also offered an undisturbed view of the scrap yard, so I wondered just how desirable such a residence might actually prove to be. I pondered this and other meaningless rubbish as I stretched my legs on the pontoon. After a short stroll and a leisurely cigarette I asked Mike what the Plan was— if indeed there actually was a Plan.

"To tell you the truth, I'm not quite sure," Mike told me. "Right now it's too rough to carry on, especially with our reduced visibility." He was referring to the deceased starboard wiper motor. "I think we'll make a cup of tea, and then I'll give my son a call to see if he could possibly pick us up and take us into Portsmouth by car— that way we'll still make the prize giving. We can come back for the boat tomorrow."

The plan then was to unfurl the white flag. I should have known better than to be disappointed, but I still was. After the standard-issue cure-all and another handful of cigarettes Mike called his son, who told him in no uncertain terms that everything was all my fault. Mike, Paul and Tom took great pleasure in implying all their woes was my doing, and initially I took it in good humour. But ten minutes later they were still making little digs at me and I quickly lost my Happy Thoughts.

"Now hang on. Don't try pinning all your problems on me," I finally snapped. "Was I with you when you got stuck in Ireland? No. Was I with *Miss Daisy* when she pranged her props? No. Or on board with *Silverline* when they burnt out a drive coupling? No. And what about the trouble-free legs I had on board *Lionhead* and *Buro*? If I'm such a Jonah, why is *Lionhead* running in second, and how come Team *747* are beating you?" I paused, the silence deafening. "OK then, now maybe you can stop with the Jonah crap, all right?" That seemed to get through to them, and muttered apologies were offered.

After another angry cigarette on the pontoon my attention was drawn to *Xanthus* as she motored into the narrow harbour. But instead of tying up alongside, John Skuse and his crew merely waved and pottered up-river. I gave Mike a shout and he hailed the other boat over the radio.

It turned out that the previous day *Xanthus* had struggled with a blocked fuel line to one of her tanks, and because they hadn't been able to fix the problem overnight they were forced to top up their other tanks so that they could make the full distance. John told Mike over the radio that he was simply putting in for fuel; he would be back out there just as soon as he could.

This gave Mike food for thought. *Xanthus* was nearly ten feet shorter than *Ocean Pirate* and had 350 horsepower less, and yet John and his crew were determined to get their Fairey Huntsman across the line. I was, and am still, convinced that the sight of *Xanthus* heading back out to open water fifteen minutes later was the only thing that got Mike to make the decision to carry on. But even then he insisted on waiting quarter of an hour before calling John up on the radio to get his assessment of the sea state.

John reported that the sea was beginning to settle, the earlier chop caused by the wind acting against the tide. But now the tide had slackened, and conditions were once again deemed calm enough for

Ocean Pirate to finish the last part of the stage and the race.

By the time we slipped our lines it was almost half past four. Although I couldn't be sure, I felt confident that the fast boys had already finished their celebratory champagne at Gunwharf Quays and were even now enjoying a catnap before showering and changing for the prize giving dinner scheduled for that evening. (In fact the winning boat had crossed the line in three hours and six minutes, meaning that they had been ashore since well before noon. By contrast, we had been at sea for eight hours already, with around 50 nautical miles still to go...)

Cautiously we battered our way across towards Selsey Bill, passing Brighton, Worthing and Bognor Regis to starboard as we crashed onwards. Initially we were crawling along at a leisurely 12 knots or so, but as Mike slipped into an exhausted sleep Tom gradually tapped the throttles forward until we were back up into the low twenties.

Two hours later we were finally within sight of the impressive Spinnaker Tower, from where we had set off so many days before. Somebody shook Mike awake and the crew managed to muster some sense of excitement as they crossed the finish line. But it was hard for me to manage much more than a tired little grimace. Our welcoming committee consisted of four mildly-interested people on board a cabin cruiser showing a massive RYA flag, and with a curt wave they indicated that we were to follow them into Gunwharf Quays.

Our victorious entry into this small harbour was deafeningly quiet. Less than half of the fleet was tied up here, the rest having had plenty of time to make for Port Solent Marina, where they would be lifted out. Only a few curious onlookers witnessed our arrival; everyone else had packed up and gone home long ago.

It was a hugely anticlimactic end to my race, and I was bitterly disappointed by my massively underwhelming welcome. We all shook hands amongst ourselves, no-one else there to congratulate us on our achievement. I checked my watch— ten minutes to seven. It had taken us ten and a half hours to cover the final stage; by now pretty much par for the course for *Ocean Pirate*.

Hang on! Ten to seven? The prize giving awards were due to begin in ten minutes! I grabbed my bag, told Mike and his crew I'd see them later, and clattered up the walkway at full tilt. I jogged my way through the deserted pedestrian streets surrounding Gunwharf Quay and headed towards the Governor's Green, where I had been told there would be a big marquee.

Sure enough, five minutes later I found myself on the edge of the Green, my way blocked by a fence and a couple of Sea Scouts, immaculately dressed in their uniforms and politely barring entry to anyone without a valid invitation. An invitation I didn't have. I gave Jonathan a call, remembering vaguely that he'd offered me a seat at the Team *747* table. Like a modern-day Good Samaritan he came through for me yet again, and told me to sit tight— he'd be with me in ten minutes.

Thoroughly exhausted I dropped to the grass, and with my eyes closed against the rays of the warm evening sun I rolled a cigarette and sucked the air down deeply into my tired lungs. I sat up and watched as two couples, immaculately dressed in formal evening-wear gave me a selection of dirty looks before showing the young Sea Scouts their invitations and passing through the gate. I retaliated by staring blankly, by now totally uncaring about my general appearance, which was pretty far from decent.

My jeans were crusted in salt and dirt, and my t-shirt reeked of stale sweat and seawater. I hadn't shaved for two or three days, but fortunately I had cropped my hair as close to the scalp as I dared before setting off two weeks earlier, so there was at least little chance of sporting an unruly mop-top. I was using my bag as a make-shift pillow, and it too was streaked in dried salt and some undistinguish-able stains that might once have been tomato ketchup. But it was hard to know for sure, and I wasn't about to give it the old taste test.

Striding up the path towards the gate was a ridiculously tall man, doing his best to look dapper in a pale suit despite lugging a heavy hold-all with him. He looked at me once, then twice, and I swear he was within a hairsbreadth of physically rubbing his eyes to check he wasn't dreaming. I fixed him with a cold stare, in no mood for open mockery, but instead he said my name in a faltering tone. "Derek?"

"Yeah. Who the fuck are you?" came my stock response.

"Derek, hi! Good to finally meet you!" He came at me with an out-stretched hand, and from my sitting position I struggled to scrabble out of range. "I'm Hugo. From *MBY*?"

"Christ! Fuck! Hugo! How the hell are you mate? Good to finally meet you!" I jumped up, trying to look vaguely Professional in the face of my occasional boss.

"Good to meet you too. How was the race? Enjoy it?"

"Man, I am fucked. Totally, utterly fucked. That was without doubt the toughest ten days of my entire fucking life man!" I babbled.

Just then I heard someone else call my name. I looked over and saw Jonathan at the gate, waving a piece of card at me.

"Jonathan, hi! Is that my invite? Cheers buddy! I'll catch you inside, OK?" I took the card from him and waved it under the nose of the thirteen year-old in the Donald Duck outfit. Hugo showed him his own invite in a slightly more mature manner, and together we walked up the path towards the massive marquee.

"So what's in the bag Hugo?" I asked.

"This is the *MBY* trophy for first motor cruiser home. I'll be awarding it later on."

"Cool! Looks heavy. Want a hand?"

I was trying to be helpful, but I think by that point he wasn't sure that I wouldn't smack him over the head with it before making a fast getaway, so he politely turned down my offer.

There were dozens of people enjoying the cool evening air, and smartly-dressed men and women chit-chatted and mingled as im-maculately-dressed waitresses weaved in and out with silver platters groaning under the weight of champagne flutes. I stopped gibbering madly at Hugo just long enough to call one of the girls over, and I grabbed a glass off her tray and necked the champagne in one long swallow. The girl smiled uncertainly at me as I grabbed another, then made to offer the tray to Hugo. But she wasn't getting away that easily. I grabbed her elbow as I drained my second glass. Then I put the empty back onto her tray and grabbed another four glasses be-fore finally letting her offer a drink to Hugo, who was watching me with a slightly odd look in his eye. I just shrugged and turned my at-tention back to my four glasses, determined not to go thirsty if I could possibly help it.

"So, yeah, where was I? Oh yeah, Fabio busting *Cesa.* I mean, *Red FPT.* Fucking shame man; I just hope he'll still show up tonight," I gabbled. At that moment, I underwent the closest to a schizophrenic episode I hope I'll ever get. I could see the look in Hugo's eyes, I read his body language perfectly. *Holy shit*, he was thinking, *This guy's a bloody loon!* And it wasn't just him; the waitress was still shooting me wary glances from twenty feet away, as if she expected me to come roaring after her the second my fourth glass was empty. Others had also either witnessed my bizarre behaviour or had picked up on the weird vibe; either way, there was a nice little circle of abandoned lawn surrounding Hugo and I.

I could see all of this, I understood perfectly that my actions had alienated my editor, a man who consistently sent me money in ex-change for Wisdom— or my attempts at it— and at the same time there was nothing I could do. The monstrous Mr Hyde had overcome the sensibilities of my Doctor Jekyll, and even as I cringed at my ranting, babbling, half-mad manner, I still continued to juggle booze, a cigarette and expletives with the manic relish of a speed-addled baboon. It was a horrible, horrible encounter, and I was overwhelm-ingly relieved when Hugo finally managed to make some excuse to walk hurriedly off into the marquee. It wasn't down to alcohol, or even sheer exhaustion for that matter. It was a combination of the two, combined with utter relief and the knowledge that I wouldn't have to worry about finding a seat on another boat. The mix of all those emotions scrambled my brain, and there wasn't a thing I could do to keep them from seriously interfering with my limited people skills.

Rolling a cigarette is one of those things that you either can or can't do. I just so happen to be quite good at it (no doubt a direct result of my Dutch DNA), but even I was surprised when I slowly became aware of the fact that I had somehow managed to roll a perfect smoke— with four champagne flutes in my hands. It was one of those eerie moments, like when a man afraid of heights suddenly finds himself on the top rung of a ladder or an arachnophobia sufferer realises he's holding a red-kneed tarantula. One moment there was only champagne, the next I was smoking a roll-up. That's when I decided to get inside and find some food to counteract the alcohol.

Below– Crossing the finish line at last

Below– *GEE* piling on the power

Results- Lowestoft to Portsmouth.

Distance: 190 nautical miles.

Pos.	Team/ Number	Class	Time	Overall position (Class)
1st	Guttaboyz/33	RB3	3:06:19	34 (10)
2nd	Blue FPT/333	MC1	3:13:06	1 (1)
3rd	Going Lean/7	RB3	3:24:36	7 (5)
4th	Vilda/9	RB3	3:26:56	3 (2)
5th	Relentless/47	RB3	3:30:17	27 (9)
6th	Braveheart III/55	MC1	3:34:52	4 (2)
7th	Hot Lemon/2	RB3	3:35:53	5 (3)
8th	Lionhead/22	RB3	3:45:40	2 (2)
9th	Hardleys/4	RB3	3:46:43	6 (4)
10th	Team Jersey/45	RB4	3:47:06	32 (8)
11th	Team Scorpion Dubois/16	MC1	3:49:40	12 (4)
12th	Carbon Neutral/343	RB3	3:58:14	11 (6)
13th	Tequila/88	RB3	4:04:11	15 (7)
14th	Mystic Dragon/6	MC1	4:05:03	23 (6)
15th	Venturer/111	RB1	4:05:18	8 (1)
16th	swipewipes.co.uk/ 43	RB4	4:09:56	14 (2)
17th	Seahound V/80	MC1	4:15:24	10 (3)
18th	Sealbay/77	RB4	4:21:55	9 (1)
19th	Power Products Marine/8	MC2	4:32:03	13 (1)
20th	TFO/17	MC2	4:32:58	17 (2)

Pos.	Team/ Number	Class	Time	Overall position (Class)
21st	Black Gold/10	RB4	4:34:03	33 (9)
22nd	Fugitive/130	MC2	4:46:40	18 (3)
23rd	My Pleasure II/3	RB4	5:16:40	19 (3)
24th	Seafarer/110	RB3	5:29:09	16 (8)
25th	Team Pulsar-Vampire/102	RB4	5:37:38	20 (4)
26th	Buro/15	MC1	5:46:26	21 (5)
27th	GEE/185	HC1	5:46:58	22 (1)
28th	Mud, Swell & Beers/14	RB4	5:56:03	25 (6)
29th	Team 747/747	HC1	6:07:27	29 (2)
30th	Team Pulsar-Wolf/101	RB4	6:25:02	24 (5)
31st	Team Bandit/69	RB2	6:33:05	30 (1)
32nd	Swordsman/68	HC1	*	40 (5)
33rd	Xanthus/1	HC1	*	37 (3)
34th	**Ocean Pirate/323**	**HC1**	*	**39 (4)**
35th	Garmin Racing/72	RB2	*	36 (3)
36th	Mr Mako/96	RB4	*	26 (7)
37th	Wettpunkt.com/81	RB1	**DNF***	28 (2)
38th	Team Silverline/471	RB2	**DNF***	31 (2)
39th	Northern Spirit/5	MC2	**OTR**	38 (4)
40th	Ikon/18	RB3	**OTR**	42 (12)

DNS Denotes Did Not Start
DNF Denotes Did Not Finish
OTR Denotes Out of The Race
* Denotes maximum time allowance exceeded.

Pos.	Team/ Number	Class	Time	Overall position (Class)
41st	RIB International/ 144	RB4	**OTR**	43 (10)
42nd	Cinzano/558	RB2	**OTR**	45 (4)
43rd	No Worries/11	RB3	**OTR**	41 (11)
44th	Team Blastoff/100	RB2	**OTR**	46 (5)
45th	Birretta/12	MC1	**OTR**	35 (7)
46th	Red FPT/177	CC1	**OTR**	44 (1)
47th	Blue Marlin/99	HC1	**OTR**	47 (6)

DNS Denotes Did Not Start
DNF Denotes Did Not Finish
OTR Denotes Out of The Race
* Denotes maximum time allowance exceeded.

Below– *Ocean Pirate* girding her loins

15.
Prizegiving.

The marquee had a foyer of sorts, and taking centre stage was a Fiat 500, tastefully plastered in Round Britain stickers. This was to be the prize for the boat that showed the most improvement between the legs up the east coast and the second half of the race. It was, unsurprisingly, awarded by Fiat Powertrain Technologies, the company that supplied the engines for *Red FPT* and *Blue FPT*, and they were about as close as the race ever got to having a principal sponsor.

But I had no interest in the cute little Fiat, so I bounced past and into the main marquee. There were tables absolutely everywhere, crowded by people all much better dressed than me. I felt that old familiar burn of self-consciousness, but my alcohol-induced bravado did its bit to keep my insecurities at bay. After a few moments I found my old friends of Team *747*, and I slogged through the crowd to take my seat at their table.

There I was introduced to various wives, whose name I immediately forgot, as well as one of the head men at Swordsman Marine, who played a major part in the sponsorship and preparation of *Miss Daisy*. Again, despite a deep conversation about Bentleys, I forgot the gentleman's name— pretty much around the same time out table number was called over the PA system, telling us to make our way to the rows of hotplates at the back of the marquee.

I thought I was making a fool of myself, the way I piled food onto my plate, but a quick glance at Cormac and Mark Jealous' plates put my mind at ease. If these two "respectable" people could build a small mountain out of beef stroganoff and roast lamb, then so could I.

After a noisy and enjoyable meal our plates were cleared and we were issued with sheets of paper and pens. We were all asked to note down our thoughts of the race, which would later be displayed somewhere for posterity. I declined politely (after all, what sort of a writer would I be if I just gave away my scribblings for free?) but that served to bring to me to the attention of the Belgian team, who were sitting at another table a few feet away.

Peter Verhauten and his band of Belgian brothers called me over to ask for my help. They wanted to write something suitable, but they were afraid that their poor English would hinder them. Would I be willing to write what they wanted to say?

I was happy to oblige, and I settled in with pen and paper at the ready. "OK boys, what do you want to say?" I asked.

It all started off amicably enough, but then things took a darker turn. "Derek, you write this for us: The race was a wonderful event, and we all enjoyed this, uhm, once for a life event. Is that right?" I changed it to "Once *in* a lifetime event", then nodded at Peter to carry on. "But it is a shame that some people have to make objections all the time. The pig-fucker with one eye was all the time being so difficult, it spoiled things for everyone else who-"

"*Whoa!* Hang on a fucking minute! You can't say that!" I objected, stunned by what I was being asked to write.

"What's the problem?" they asked me. "These aren't your words, they are ours."

"That's not the point," I replied. "You can't call Ed a "one-eyed pig-fucker"— it's not very, erm, sporting."

"No, he was not the one being sporting," Peter retorted. "He was always complaining about the rules, trying to change things all the time. Nobody else complained, only him. Now write this down-"

I sighed and shook my head. "OK, what else have you got?"

Peter, helped by Frank and Lieven, carried on, and I did my best to try and keep it as diplomatic as I could. "So, yes— the one-eyed ugly bastard should know that a race is a race, and if he does not like the rules he should not enter. Also-"

Just then we were interrupted by a voice asking if we had finished our notes yet. I looked up and was badly startled to see that it was none other than Ed Williams-Hawkes, standing over me with his hand outstretched.

"Oh, Ed, hi there. I'm not quite done yet. That is, Peter isn't quite done yet. I'm just writing it down for them, you understand. Because they don't speak English. I mean, they do speak English, but they can't write it. So they asked me to help. I'm just writing it you understand; I'm not actually anything to do with them, apart from this," I babbled frantically, my right arm trying to shield the vitriol from Ed's eyes. Or eye. Thankfully he just fixed me with his usual cold stare then dismissed me as just another drunken idiot, turning on his heel to ask another table for their finished notes.

With a greasy sweat sliding down my forehead I finished the rest of the Belgian dictation, toning it down as best I could. But of course they wanted me to read back to them what I had written, and after some more editing the treacherous tale was done to their satisfaction. We shook hands and wished each other luck and I scrambled back to the safety of the Team *747* table, anxiously expecting Ed's hands to slip round my throat from behind once he'd read the vicious ramblings of Team *Buro*.

But nothing happened. Instead the prize giving ceremony swung into action, and soon my hands were starting to hurt from the continual clapping. To be honest, at the time I had no idea who had won what. I had no idea who had won the final leg earlier that day, or who had gained or lost vital places. Added to that was the fact that there were a slew of prizes being handed out, not just for Class wins but for Second and Third places as well, along with other trophies for things like Outstanding Effort and Best Presented Boat. The whole thing was, at the time, incredibly confusing, but that didn't stop me clapping and whistling like a loon whenever one of the teams I'd raced with was awarded something. I felt particularly proud when Jonathan was called to the trophy table not once, but twice to pick up a beautiful silver plate for finishing second in the Historic Class and also the Mermaid Trophy for the first Fairey home, courtesy of Swordsman Marine.

It wasn't until the next day that I finally figured out what had actually happened during that final leg, but in the interests of keeping the timeline flowing smoothly I'll shoehorn it in here. Firstly, the final leg from Lowestoft:
By far the biggest losers of the day (and I mean that sympathetically) were Andy Macateer, Nick Wilner, Andy Sutcliffe, and Mark Wildey. Armed with the devastatingly quick Buzzi RIB *Venturer* they had put in an impressive performance throughout the race, and their final run into Portsmouth had been no exception. They crossed the line in first place, but it wasn't until after they had taken to the podium and hosed everyone down with champagne that it became apparent that they had inadvertently missed a vital marker buoy. They were stripped of their leg win and penalised one hour, knocking them down to 15th place for the stage.
That meant that the new team first to cross the line at Portsmouth were in fact— *Guttaboyz*. Father and son Nick and Ivar Tollefsen spanked the arse off their Goldfish, and for once their Bravo drive legs held together, covering the distance in three hours and six minutes— just seven minutes faster than the ultra-reliable FB55 of *Blue FPT* who took second. While it wasn't exactly a matter of "slow & steady wins the race" for the Greek team and their English navigator— they managed to average nearly 60 knots over the 1164 nautical miles— they did demonstrate perfectly just how incredibly important reliability was in this race. Their three FPT 480 horsepower engines never missed a beat, which raised an interesting notion in the back of my noggin. But more on that later...
So, on the amended results sheet for the Lowestoft to Portsmouth leg, third place was awarded to Dean Gibb on *Going Lean*. This was another outstanding performance, especially when you remember that he entered the race pretty much by accident, and had no previous racing experience.
(In fact it was Jon Fuller and Nick Gilley that had crossed the line in third, but they were found guilty of missing a vital mark and so were given a one hour penalty, knocking them back down to a disappointing 16th.)
Taking fourth place was *Vilda*, the Swedish entry. Mikko Oikari and his team had once again slipped under a lot of peoples' radar, which

was probably down to the fact that the Dahl RIB looked so damn stealthy. The entire boat was one massive matt black beast and looked like it should be ferrying a squad of deadly Ninjas around, not a Swedish DJ with the improbable name of Titti Schultz.

Another unlikely top ten finisher was *Braveheart III*. Bobby Cowe and his fellow Scots had crossed the line in 6th, once again proving that the novices had just as much chance of doing well as the professionals in their race-prepared machines.

Despite only having one functioning drive leg, *Lionhead* managed to finish in eighth place— albeit with the crew draped precariously across the bow so that Pål could get the Goldfish up on the plane and into Portsmouth. They finished just one minute ahead of *Hardleys* and two minutes in front of Toby Clayson on board Team *Jersey*, who later admitted that as he crossed the line in tenth he was in floods of tears, the utter relief of having finally finished the race simply overwhelming.

Other notables (from my admittedly biased perspective) included the team whose ever-present smiles, I now knew, hid vicious and malignant hearts— the Belgians. *Buro* took 26th place with a time of five hours and forty-six minutes. Thirty seconds later *GEE* came galloping up behind; they had carried out a simple bodge repair to their problematic trim tabs just minutes before the start, and it had paid off for them. On board *Miss Daisy* the *747* team had struggled with a similar problem, but they hadn't managed to get their tabs working. The result was a deeply uncomfortable ride, despite my generous donation of illicit drugs. They finally bounced into Portsmouth in 29th, twenty minutes behind *GEE*.

As you might suspect, *Ocean Pirate*'s tardy arrival was well outside the allotted time, but at least we weren't the only ones— *Xanthus* and *Swordsman* also failed to post a time into port.

Hannes, Ed and Max on board *Wettpunkt.com* had little to gain by thrashing the nuts off their Buzzi machine, since they were trailing the only other boat in their Class by over three and a half hours. But that didn't stop them giving it all they had, probably in search of the glory that comes with crossing the line first, and to hell with the Bigger Picture. Unfortunately they couldn't even manage that, and when they damaged a prop and gearbox off Harwich it ended their race.

Others that fell at the last hurdle included Drew and the *Silverline* team, who had blown a head gasket just off the Thames estuary and ended up tied up alongside the stricken *Wettpunkt.com*. Another stricken boat was *Mr Mako*. Jamie Edwards and John Lindsay in their 29 foot Pascoe RIB had been running well up until Lowestoft, second in their RB4 Class and thirteenth overall. But in a freaky repeat of their misfortunes on the Bangor to Oban leg, another dollop of silicone kit mysteriously found its way into their fuel system, cutting off the petrol supply to their engines and they were forced to retire.

The last boat to give up the ghost was *Garmin Racing*, whose most reliable feature was its unreliability. Iain May's entry had been hyped before the race as the "celebrity team", and we were promised the rare spectacle of Nick Knowles and Top Gear presenter James May joining Iain and Jeff Hunton taking part in the event. But sadly Nick Knowles only managed to cope with the first leg before losing his nerve, and James May failed completely to even put in an appearance.

And so much for the final leg. It was merely one piece of an intricate puzzle; the *real* results everyone hankered for where that for the overall standings.

Once the dust had settled and all the calculations had been made, the overall winner of the 2008 Round Britain Powerboat Race was— *Blue FPT*. She had covered the 1100+ nautical miles in the outstanding time of 20 hours, 36 minutes and 47 seconds, without once missing a mark or even hinting at mechanical failure.

Second place overall went to *Lionhead*. Sure, the Goldfish was faster— a lot faster, in fact— but their constant issues with their drive legs eventually cost them the win.

Taking third place were the Swedish team on *Vilda*. All through the race they were pretty much invisible, and I have to admit I don't even remember them picking up their trophy— perhaps they dropped from the ceiling noiselessly on black ropes, snatched their silverware and then sprinted outside, where an unmarked black helicopter stood waiting for them to whisk them off back to obscurity— I really can't say. But the numbers never lie, and since they were only trailing the Norwegians by less than 15 minutes after twenty-two hours of full-on racing, they certainly deserved their trophy.

For the teams who had missed out on a top three placing overall, there was still the Class win to aim for. Naturally *Blue FPT* took this honour in the **MC1** Class, but second place— and fourth overall— went to the boys from Fraserburgh. *Braveheart III*, a widely-ridiculed Scanner RIB that was considered unsuitable for anything other than calm Mediterranean waters, had proved everyone wrong, much to the delight of the Fraserburgh team.

Even more satisfying for them was the fact that they even managed to beat Chris Strickland and *Seahound V* down to third in the MC1 Class, which is no mean feat given that Chris has broken more endurance racing records than I can count.

My nefarious friends on *Buro* managed to take fifth place in the MC1 Class— another impressive achievement for an unlikely boat. Even more impressive was the fact that they had somehow beaten *Mystic Dragon* in the process: her driver, John Puddifoot, is the RYA head of powerboating...

Only three boats in the **MC2** Class had managed to make it all the way around Britain. First place went to *Power Products Marine* in their

28 foot Phantom. Martin McLaughlin and his team were another stealthy outfit, and by keeping their heads down and steering clear of trouble they managed to take the Class win.

Second place went to Tom and Charlie Williams-Hawkes. Their 25 foot *Revenger* had suffered from mechanical problems and poorly-pitched props, but they should consider themselves lucky— just 3½ minutes separated them from *Fugitive*, the third-place team. It was another incredible result, and it still amazes me that after these two boats spent almost thirty hours racing flat-out through almost every sea condition it's possible to experience, they *still* managed to complete the distance only three minutes and thirty-five seconds apart.

Despite a sixty minute penalty for passing a marker buoy incorrectly on the final leg, Andy Macateer on board *Venturer* still managed to comfortably take first place in the **RB1** Class, with *Wettpunkt.com*'s Hannes Bohinc paying the price for poor reliability and a couple of navigational cock-ups.

In the **RB2** Class only three teams were still in the running: *Silverline*, *Bandit* and *Garmin Racing*, since Team *Blastoff* and *Cinzano* had both thrown in the towel at Inverness. When they set off from Lowestoft earlier that morning, Drew and Jan's position was looking promising. They had an overall lead of nearly three hours over the second place team, *Bandit*, and only a catastrophic failure— like, say, a blown head gasket— could take the Class win away from them. One knackered gasket later, and Barry Deakin and his fellow **Bandit** teammates proudly held aloft the trophy for winning the RB2 Class, with Drew and co. having to settle for second place ahead of the *Garmin Racing* team, who had also failed to finish the final leg.

The top three **RB3** boats had been separated by little more than half an hour when they set off from Lowestoft. By the time they crossed the line the running order had been shaken up. Taking the Class win was *Lionhead*, despite crossing the line with one working drive leg. *Vilda* second place, just pipping *Hot Lemon* to the post by a mere seven minutes overall. Another astonishingly short time period after 22 hours at sea.

The— *ahem*— independent Goldfish of *Sealbay* claimed the win in the **RB4** Class, an easy victory over *swipewipes.co.uk*, who trailed the Norwegians by two and a half hours. In turn, they led third-place team *My Pleasure II* by well over three hours.

Bringing up the rear, as always, were the **Historic** Class entries. The Clayton brothers had managed to bring *GEE* home in first place, and there were definitely no hard feelings about their victory from Jonathan and the *747* team who claimed second. Third place was awarded to John Skuse on board *Xanthus*, several hours ahead of *Ocean Pirate*. Naturally their overall times bore no resemblance to the pace set by *Blue FPT*, but the fact that these old chargers had somehow managed to complete the race distance was in itself a remarkable accomplishment, especially when so many other, younger boats (and richer teams) had dropped by the wayside.

Once the top three teams in every Class had been awarded their trophies, I foolishly thought that that was the end of the applauding and paying attention, so I immediately proceeded to get stuck into the complementary wine. Big mistake.

It turned out that there were a great many more trinkets to be handed out. As the race winners, the crew of *Blue* FPT were awarded the Round Britain Trophy, but sadly its previous owner, Fabio Buzzi, had decided not to hand it over personally— probably still smarting from his ignominious retirement. As if that wasn't enough, the Greek team were also presented with the Beaverbrook Trophy, an incredibly prestigious award. And to top it all, my editor Hugo then handed them the *MBY* Trophy for being the first motor-cruiser across the line.

The only other team to be honoured with three trips to the top table were *GEE*. For winning in the Historic Class they received the Classic Offshore Powerboats Owners Club (or COPOC for short) Trophy; they were then called back to collect the Raymarine Trophy for Spirit Of The Event; and finally John Guille and Nathan Ward received the Warbah Trophy for Outstanding Sportsmanship. Despite the fact that the latter trophies had been won, at least partially, at *747*'s expense, Jonathan, Cormac, Andy and Mark were commendably enthusiastic in congratulating their rivals.

It was a dramatic moment when it was announced that Team *Braveheart* had been awarded the Duke of York Trophy for being the first British boat home. As the only Scottish team in the race, Bobby Cowe and his crewmates knew they were honour-bound to put in a decent performance against the English entries, and by Christ did they ever. *Braveheart III* was widely acknowledged to be the ugliest boat in the competition and its crew knew absolutely nothing about powerboat racing. But with no less than twenty-nine English teams (including World Champions and Record holders) in the running, they somehow managed to beat the lot of them to snatch the sought-after prize out from under their noses.

(At the time I didn't really understand just how important this trophy was. It wasn't until later when I was interviewing Bobby for a *MotorBoat & Yachting* article that he confided in me that Miles Jennings had told him that the Duke Of York trophy was the only reason he (Miles) had entered. It was also then that I discovered that Bobby had only held the trophy for a few moments— once the photographers had gotten their shots, it was quickly taken from Bobby and returned to the RYA headquarters, where it now sits under lock and key, encased in an unremarkable wooden box. As Hamish Slater later put it: "It's not so nice to be awarded a trophy and then come home with nothing.")

But their disappointment was lessened a little when a little later on in was announced that they had won the Concourse Cup— the prize for having the best-presented boat, as voted for by the Scrutineers. The humble trawlermen from Fraserburgh had done good.

There was also a pleasant surprise in store for the crew of *Venturer.* The Organisers had decided that Andy Macateer and his crew had made the biggest improvement in the second half of the race, and so they were duly rewarded with the keys to the Fiat 500 sitting just inside the marquee. How the hell they were supposed to get it out of there was anybody's guess...

Of course with all theses trophies and awards flying about, it was inevitable that there would be a screw-up somewhere along the line. When Joe Leckie and Roger and Tom Summerton were awarded the Moore Family Trophy for being the highest-placed smallest boat, they were, as you'd expect, absolutely delighted. It wasn't until a couple of days later that the Organisers realised their mistake, sheepishly telling the *Mud, Swell & Beers* crew that the award *should* have gone to Team *Pulsar*'s *Vampire* instead.

There was another cock-up when Mike Barlow and his *Ocean Pirate* crew were awarded the Brand-Crombie Perpetual Trophy for Outstanding Effort. Again, it wasn't until much later that the mistake was spotted, and the Organisers realised it should have gone to Tom and Charlie Williams-Hawkes in *TFO* instead. Still, these things happen in the heat of the moment.

One thing that only really dawned on me until a couple of days later was the fact that many of the boats who had done better than expected were totally standard production boats. *Braveheart III, Buro, Sealbay—* even *Blue FPT—* they were all running completely unmodified engines. This made them extremely reliable, and that's why they did so well in the overall results. Being capable of 90 knots is all good and well, but if the bugger keeps breaking down after ten minutes you might as well race in a canoe. Reliability is the key to winning these kinds of events.

When it became apparent that there would be no trophy for the writer who'd ridden on the most boats I finally caved in to my body's demand for sleep. I bid farewell to my friends and staggered my way out into the cool night, searching for a taxi to take me to my digs.

Overall Results.

Total distance raced: 1,164 nautical miles.

Pos.	Team/ Number	Class	Overall Time Hr:min	Overall Class Position
1st	Blue FPT/333	MC1	20:36	1st
2nd	**Lionhead/22**	**RB3**	**21:56**	**1st**
3rd	Vilda/9	RB3	22:10	2nd
4th	Braveheart III/55	MC1	22:14	2nd
5th	Hot Lemon/2	RB3	22:17	3rd
6th	Hardleys/4	RB3	22:48	4th
7th	Going Lean/7	RB3	23:26	5th
8th	Venturer/111	RB1	23:47	1st
9th	Sealbay/77	RB4	24:51	1st
10th	Seahound V/80	MC1	24:59	3rd
11th	Carbon Neutral/343	RB3	25:43	6th
12th	Team Scorpion Dubois/16	MC1	26:46	4th
13th	Power Products Marine/8	MC2	26:53	1st
14th	swipewipes.co.uk/ 43	RB4	27:16	2nd
15th	Tequila/88	RB3	27:52	7th
16th	Seafarer/110	RB3	29:16	8th
17th	TFO/17	MC2	29:18	2nd
18th	Fugitive/130	MC2	29:21	3rd
19th	My Pleasure II/3	RB4	30:48	3rd
20th	Team Pulsar-Vampire/102	RB4	31:54	4th

Pos.	Team/ Number	Class	Time	Overall Class Position
21st	**Buro/15**	**MC1**	**34:12**	**5th**
22nd	GEE/185	HC1	34:17	1st
23rd	Mystic Dragon/6	MC1	34:33	6th
24th	Team Pulsar-Wolf/101	RB4	35:11	5th
25th	Mud, Swell & Beers/14	RB4	35:16	6th
26th	Mr Mako/96	RB4	35:22	7th
27th	Relentless/47	RB3	35:23	9th
28th	Wettpunkt.com/81	RB1	35:45	2nd
29th	**Team 747/747**	**HC1**	**36:12**	**2nd**
30th	Team Bandit/69	RB2	38:15	1st
31st	**Team Silverline/ 471**	**RB2**	**41:16**	**2nd**
32nd	Team Jersey/45	RB4	42:31	8th
33rd	Black Gold/10	RB4	42:49	9th
34th	Guttaboyz/33	RB3	43:46	10th
35th	Birretta/12 **OTR**	MC1	53:10	7th
36th	Garmin Racing/72	RB2	60:54	3rd
37th	Xanthus/1	HC1	62:41	3rd
38th	Northern Spirit/5 **OTR**	MC2	63:34	4th
39th	**Ocean Pirate/323**	**HC1**	**65:40**	**4th**
40th	Swordsman/68	HC1	66:32	5th

Pos.	Team/Number	Class	Time	Overall Class Position
41st	No Worries	RB3	77:03:31	11th
42nd	Ikon/18 **OTR**	RB3	79:18:10	12th
43rd	RIB International/144 **OTR**	RB4	*	10th
44th	Red FPT/177 **OTR**	CC1	*	1st
45th	Cinzano/558 **OTR**	RB2	*	4th
46th	Team Blastoff/100 **OTR**	RB2	*	5th
47th	Blue Marlin/99 **OTR**	HC1	*	6th

OTR Denotes Out of The Race
* Denotes maximum time allowance exceeded.

Below- Vassilis Pateras, Panos Tsikopoulos, Lefteris Vasilou and Dag Pike pick up their trophies for Overall Winner and First Motorcruiser home

Top– The *Lionhead* Team came second overall and first in the RB3 Class

Below– Mark Jealous, Jonathan Napier, Lady Violet Aitken, Andy Fielding and Cormac Lundy with *747*'s trophy for second in the HC1 Class

Epilogue.

They say that the percentage of salt in our blood is identical to the levels of salt in the sea. A smarter man might go and look it up, but not me. I am, at heart, a romantic, and curious little factoids like that appeal to me on the most fundamental level. Is that why we're drawn to the ocean like moths to a bonfire? Or is it an ancient yearning to return to the place all of Life originally came from? Who knows? And, more to the point, who the hell cares? The sea is a cold, fickle thing with all the nurturing qualities of a dead rock, and yet we have an overwhelming urge to bestow it with living, sentient qualities; perhaps so that we can claim to "do battle" with a worthy opponent.

And that's good enough for me. The competitors of the 2008 Round Britain Powerboat Race did just that– we were Warriors, and we fought well. There was no quarter asked or given, and although there were victims among our ranks, we prevailed.

Is that too dramatic? Some might say so, but so what? Screw Them I say. They weren't there; they didn't experience the constant pounding that comes from running a boat at the very limits of its abilities in an empty sea for hour after exhausting hour. To race at anything less than top possible speed was to admit cowardice in the face of the enemy. And to get up the next day to do it all over again showed the sort of gritty determination that all true Warriors recognise.

That gladiatorial aspect of our psyche is much more prevalent than many would think. The drive to conquer not only our rivals but also Nature itself is a powerful and addictive thing, and it can surprise us with its persistent nagging. After the Round Britain many teams went on to compete in that year's Cowes-Torquay-Cowes race, which had suddenly fallen onto Mike Lloyd's shoulders at the last minute. The world of endurance racing had received a vital injection of fresh blood, and its newest members drove the sport onwards to what will hopefully turn out to be a resurgence in its popularity.

Cynics claim that there is no room for powerboat racing in the midst of a worldwide economic collapse; men like Jonathan Napier and Markus Hendricks and many others are enthusiastically proving them wrong. Riding on the wave of the sport's new-found popularity, two new endurance races have been announced: Dean Gibbs (*Going Lean*) has just announced a Round Britain 2011 and Neil McGrigor (who raced in *Hardleys* with Tony Jenvey) is organising the 2012 Round Britain race.

Want to know another fascinating little factoid? More people have stood on the summit of Mount Everest than have taken part in the 2008 Round Britain Powerboat Race. How's that for kudos and bragging rights?

To say I had a blast would be an astounding understatement. Sure, I had moments of abject misery, but so what? Ultimately, I wouldn't have missed this for the world, and I'm sure others who took part would agree. Even the Race Officials who worked so tirelessly would agree with me. They too had their low points: endless paperwork, personality clashes, and of course a massive workload that continued even after everyone else had washed the salt out of their hair and gone back to their regular lives. But then they had their own memorable moments that made the whole thing worthwhile; whether it was skimming just above the fleet in their charter plane, holding the start flag aloft at every race, or just seeing their dream come to fruition before their very eyes. Everybody suffered hardships, but when it all came together— damn! There's nothing on the planet like it.

To anyone who's never competed in an endurance race, I strongly suggest that you remortgage the house, rent out the wife and pawn the kids. Fly out to Lake Como and speak to Fabio Buzzi, or if your budget doesn't quite stretch that far, scour the classifieds instead. *TFO* was raced on a shoestring; *Miss Daisy* doubles as the family runabout. If you don't fancy racing day in, day out for a week or two at a time, enter the annual Cowes-Torquay-Cowes. And if the physical pounding sounds too hairy for you, consider helping out the Officials— it's a great way to be part of a unique event that couldn't happen without the men and women who dot the t's and cross the i's. Or something. Stop dreaming; just get on and do it. Be a part of History.

Oh, and if you happen to see a Dutch Scotsman with a scruffy holdall over his shoulder and a hungry, desperate look in his eyes, for the love of god offer him a seat...

...but remember Doctor Thompson's words of warning: *Buy the Ticket, Take the Ride.*

Image Credits

The following images are copyright Chris Davies (www.powerboatpix.co.uk) and are included with his kind permission: page 37 (top), page 55, page 77 (bottom), page 80, page 133 (both), page 136, page 143, page 160, page 179, page 200, page 215 (bottom), page 218, page 243, and page 244 (both).

Image of Jack Robinson (page 215, top) by kind permission of the Robinson family.

All other images remain the property of the Author.

www.ingramcontent.com/pod-product-compliance
Lightning Source LLC
Chambersburg PA
CBHW060015100426
42740CB00010B/1491